1606

 EVAN MCHUGH is the author of *Outback
Heroes*, *Shipwrecks* and the well-known 'Dry
Rot' column published in the *Sunday
Telegraph* and *Sunday Mail*. He lives in
Sydney and is a keen sailor.

1606

An epic adventure

Evan McHugh

NEW
SOUTH

A New South book

Published by
University of New South Wales Press Ltd
University of New South Wales
Sydney NSW 2052
AUSTRALIA
www.unswpress.com.au

National Library of Australia
Cataloguing-in-Publication entry

McHugh, Evan.
1606: an epic adventure.
Includes index.
ISBN 0 86840 866 2.
1. Australia - Discovery and exploration. I. Title.

994.01

Design Di Quick
Back cover photograph Richard Woldendorp, 'Where the Great Australian Bight and the Nullarbor
    Plain meet', Western Australia, 1985; nla.pic-vn3102362, National Library of Australia. It was
    along this forbidding coast that the Dutch first sailed in 1627. Later explorers regarded the lack
    of any description as understandable since 'the most fruitful imagination could find nothing to
    say of it'.
Print Griffin Press, Adelaide

CONTENTS

SHIP GLOSSARY

1 Flying jib	6 Fore topsail	11 Mizzen topgallant sail
2 Jib	7 Main topsail	12 Fore royal
3 Fore topmast staysail	8 Mizzen topsail	13 Main royal
4 Fore course	9 Fore topgallant sail	14 Mizzen royal
5 Main course	10 Main topgallant sail	15 Spanker

ACKNOWLEDGMENTS

Extracts from the following works have been reproduced by kind permission of their authors, their estates or other copyright holders, which is gratefully acknowledged:

Drake-Brockman, Henrietta, *Voyage to Disaster*, University of WA Press, Nedlands WA, 1995.

Gilbert, Kevin, *Living Black: Blacks Talk to Kevin Gilbert*, Penguin, Ringwood, 1978.

Henderson, James, *Phantoms of the Tryall*, St George, Perth, 1993.

Henderson, James, *Sent Forth A Dove: Discovery of the Duyfken*, UWA Press, Perth 1999.

Hercus, Luise, and Sutton, Peter (eds), *This Is What Happened*, Australian Institute of Aboriginal Studies, Canberra, 1986.

Hilder, Brett, *The Voyage of Torres*, UQP, Brisbane, 1980.

Photographs have been credited where they have been reproduced.

Every effort has been made to contact the copyright holders of material reproduced in this book and the publishers would welcome any further information.

NOTES TO READERS

Indigenous people should be warned that the names of their ancestors could be used.

Extracts have been edited for style only. The original spelling has been kept to retain authenticity. Amendments contained in [square brackets] within quotes are clarifications inserted by the author.

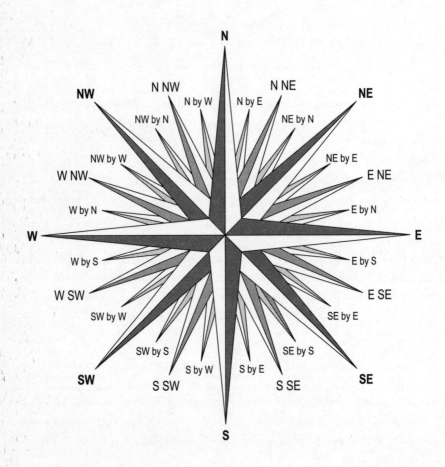

1

THE LITTLE
DOVE

From the deck of a small sailing ship, the curvature of the earth limits the distance you can see to the horizon to as little as seven kilometres. But climb the ratlines up the main shrouds, pause for breath while perched on the massive timber of the main yard, continue up the main topmast shrouds to the lofty spar of the main topsail yard, and it's a different story. If you don't have a head for heights, it's best not to look down, especially if you're on a bigger ship and can continue up the main topgallant shrouds and on to the masthead itself. Now, from a position perhaps 30–50 metres up, pitching and rolling through as much as 45 degrees, your horizon reaches nearly 20–25 kilometres.

From the masthead, it feels like you can see forever. It may also feel like the most terrifying place on earth, where a fall will only be broken by bone-shattering collisions with spars and rigging on the way down. If you're lucky, you'll miss the deck and hit the sea. However, in the time it takes for the ship to turn around or lower a boat to pick you up you'll probably drown anyway.

But at least at the masthead you won't get lonely. Throughout this volume this giddy height will be visited by many famous navigators – Luis Vaéz de Torres, Abel Janszoon Tasman, James Cook, Matthew Flinders and Nicolas Baudin – and the less famous such as Willem Janszoon, Jan Carstenszoon, William Dampier, Willem de Vlamingh and Joseph-Antoine Raymond Bruny d'Entrecasteaux. Many of these explorers clung to this lofty vantage position, spying out the rugged coastline, safe harbours, remote islands and labyrinths of coral reefs of an entire continent that, from the beginning of the 17th century, slowly emerged from the obscurity of ignorance to become a reality on the maps of the known world. From the mere conjecture of Terra Australis Incognita, an unknown south land, it eventually became the more melodious Australia. It may have been inhabited by Aboriginal Australians for thousands of years before then, but only in the last 400 years has it shed the aura of mystery for those beyond its shores.

When the earliest navigators first glimpsed the coastline, they couldn't be sure if they were looking at a collection of islands or part of a much larger whole. They had no concept of its extent; was it a modest landmass or an entire continent? Everything that we take for granted had to be charted, and this took 200 years of perilous adventure, shipwrecks, extraordinary seamanship and considerable hardship and sacrifice. Some who came upon the coast were foolish, and paid dearly for their carelessness. Others were brilliant, and earned enduring recognition for their achievements.

Making maps may seem mundane, but tell that to a navigator whose ship has struck an unseen reef far from any hope of rescue. Tell it, too, to a landing party confronted by the spears of Aboriginal warriors and admonished to get back into their ships and return from whence they came. The European discovery of Australia is a tale of daring; it's a story of seafarers and scientists, and the spirit of enquiry that spurred them on; it's also a fascinating mixture of heroes and villains, and even politicians. It begins in March 1606.

'*Landt in zicht!*' The cry came from a crewman perched at the masthead of the Dutch yacht *Duyfken* (*Little Dove*), Willem Janszoon master. The skipper of the tiny vessel knew the sighting was significant. He had been sent on a mission of exploration, but his sea-stained map had long since ceased to be of any help regarding the shallow, shoal-strewn waters through which he was gingerly picking his way. He was now some 3000 kilometres east of his Dutch East India Company base on the island of Java. It was quite a voyage for this vessel, thought to have been no more than 60 tonnes burthen (a measure of her cargo-carrying capacity), which was only a fifth of the size of the largest ships of her time. She wasn't much bigger than many modern cruising yachts, but with a crew of around 90 crammed aboard in conditions about as intimate as economy class on today's airliners, she had already completed two return voyages from Holland to the Spice Islands of today's Indonesia. Now, however, the crew were about to be rewarded for their efforts, as for all they knew the land they were looking at had never been seen by European eyes before.

The *Duyfken's* crew may well have been filled with anticipation at the prospect of what lay before them. When she'd left Bantam, on the north-east coast of Java near the Sunda Strait (between Java and Sumatra), in

November 1605, the skipper of an English vessel, John Saris, had written in his journal: 'The eighteenth here departed a small pinas [pinnace] of the Flemmings, for the discovery of the iland called Nova ginnea, which, as it is said, affordeth great store of gold.'

Gold was a powerful motivator when it came to exploration. After the Spanish plunder of the treasures of South America in the previous century, the mere mention of its possible existence was often enough to inspire rulers to provide funds to many an adventurous seafarer. To the east of New Guinea, for example, the Solomon Islands had been named by Alvaro de Mendaña, voyaging from Peru in 1568. He thought the islands were home to the fabulous mines of King Solomon, not that he'd actually found any such valuables. A Spanish official later remarked that there were 'no specimens of spices, nor of gold and silver, nor of merchandise, nor of any other source of profit, and all the people were naked savages'. It should also be mentioned that New Guinea had been named after the gold-rich Guinea, in Africa, which the Portuguese had settled and plundered.

However, what the crew of the *Duyfken* didn't know as they climbed the rigging to get a better view of the low sweep of land lifting over the eastern horizon was that, gold or no gold, their discovery had just ensured their place in history. They were the first Europeans known to have laid eyes on the mainland of Australia.

Unfortunately, no ship's journal has survived to fill in the details of such an historic occasion, nor is there an original chart. However, there are Dutch copies of the original chart that were made in the 1670s and records that state: 'This sea chart shows the way, both in sailing outward and back, followed by the yacht *Duiffien* when visiting the lands east of Bunda unto Nova Guinea.'

From the chart it is easy to locate the point where *Duyfken* made her first landfall: the Pennefather River, about 150 kilometres south of the tip of present-day Cape York, in Far North Queensland. Here the sea is extremely shallow with hidden reefs scattered all over it. The hazards make navigation, even in modern times, a matter of intense and ceaseless concentration. For a small vessel lacking charts of any kind, every minute she was under way held the threat of the grinding crash of an unseen reef, even though the *Duyfken* probably only drew a little over two metres.

The *Duyfken* had already spent a harrowing couple of months among the vast shoals south of Os Papua (modern day Irian Jaya, Indonesia) gradually being forced south by shallow water until she was out of sight of land. In our modern times, when even small yachts enjoy safe passages using highly accurate global positioning systems (GPS) and generally accurate charts, with rescue services able to be summoned via satellite in emergencies, most mariners would refuse to proceed if they were confronted by uncharted, hazard-strewn waters, with no way of fixing their position. They'd be even more adamant if the waters were as perilous as those south of Os Papua. Yet Janszoon pressed on, using what old mariners describe as 'masthead navigation', a combination of a masthead lookout spying changes in the colour of the sea (tell-tale warning of submerged obstacles) while crew in the bows stood ready to drop anchor at a moment's notice and other crew 'hove the lead' to determine both the depth and makeup (sand, mud, shell, etc) of the sea floor.

For most of us, masthead navigation would be nerve-racking in the extreme. Yet Janszoon was as steady as they come. At the time he was in his 30s and had seen several years service in the Indies, including work with the recently formed United East-Indies Company (more commonly known as the Dutch East India Company, the *Verenigde Oostindische Compagnie* or VOC, established in 1602). The upstart Dutch wrestled with the dominance of the Portuguese in the East Indies, and Janszoon had been involved in several small yet fierce fleet battles, displaying ample courage and making a name for himself. He would later be appointed governor of Banda and the directors of the VOC (known as the Heren 17) were to describe him as 'a very able and straightforward man ... it were wished that the Company had many such servants in India'. The VOC's governor general in the East Indies, Pieter Both, described him as 'of a natural good nature, modest and pious ... and has not had the least of problems with his crews and always observed good order on his ship'.

The impression one gets is that Janszoon was a capable leader, and while the voyage of the *Duyfken* may have been one of those hellish odysseys historians are fond of describing in order to inspire even greater admiration of the feats achieved, Janszoon sounds more like the kind of skipper who looked after his crew and went about his business with efficiency and skill. And it has to be said that, in our times, the crews of racing yachts undergo more hardship than your average historian would ever contemplate simply for the love of adventure, let alone financial reward. Such characters would leap at the chance of a perilous voyage of discovery to unknown and exotic lands, and it seems reasonable to assume a similar spirit existed back in 1606. Indeed, people have been running away to sea since long before then.

It's quite likely, too, that the *Duyfken's* crew had more say in the voyage than one might expect. For while Janszoon was the *Duyfken's* skipper, a curious form of democracy existed aboard Dutch vessels, especially those engaged in trade. For example, when it came to decisions about commercial transactions, such as whether a ship should return to its home port or continue trading, the ship's officer responsible for those transactions (known as the supercargo) could overrule the skipper. However, should a senior officer of the VOC happen to be on board, even if he was just a passenger, he could overrule both the skipper and supercargo. If that sounds like a recipe for disaster, it sometimes was. However, on well-run ships a council of officers was often convened in order to pass resolutions on the course of action to be taken. This had the distinct advantage of presenting a united front to the guilder counters in the VOC hierarchy should a voyage prove unsuccessful, but it also meant that a good commander could keep his finger on the pulse of crew morale. Junior officers could voice concerns about the crew's mood, and in returning to their watches keep the crew informed of the skipper's intentions. In difficult and dangerous voyages, where success depended on teamwork, keeping the people on side could make all the difference.

Meanwhile, back at the Pennefather River, while still more than five kilometres from the shore, Janszoon found himself in less than 15 metres of water. Not knowing how much the tide rose and fell in the area, but aware that elsewhere in the region it was ten metres or more, it was too risky to take the ship in any closer. Dropping anchor well out from shore also gave the ship a measure of security against any attack that might come from hostile natives. And Janszoon certainly knew he wasn't alone. Even well off shore, Janszoon could see that this new land was inhabited. Smoke rose in columns up and down the coast, as well as inland. This could only come from the fires of human inhabitants.

Although there is no surviving copy of Janszoon's instructions, if subsequent missions are anything to go by, the main task on the expedition was to seek opportunities for trade. That, after all, was the business of the VOC. So there's little doubt that he'd have gone ashore at the Pennefather River looking for people and their knowledge of precious metals like gold, and spices such as pepper, nutmeg and cinnamon; all highly prized and profitable commodities back in Europe.

There were also more mundane tasks such as resupplying the ship with fresh water and wood for her galley, and obtaining any fresh food that might be available. At the same time, the coast had to be charted, with positional fixes made as accurately as possible. The surviving copies of the original chart therefore place the Pennefather River, named by the Dutch '*R met het Bosch*' (River with the Bush), at 11 degrees 48 minutes south. This represents an error of less than half a degree or about 50 kilometres, which is quite good considering the rudimentary instruments for determining latitude at sea: the cross-staff or the improved back-staff invented in 1594.

For the *Duyfken*, longitude was even harder to determine. In 1606 mathematician Galileo Galilei was still six years from devising a method for accurately calculating longitude on land. It wouldn't be until the 1760s that a method using chronometers and the stars became available for determining longitude at sea. The reason is that a ship at sea is never, ever still, and a method that works at a fixed point on solid land is rendered utterly impractical on a pitching, rolling, yawing, turning ship that's tracking through the water at a rate of knots.

For the *Duyfken*, coming up with any kind of number for longitude was (by necessity) a matter of conjecture. It was done using dead reckoning, an estimate of the distance travelled based on the vessel's daily courses and speeds from the last charted landfall. You'd also have to assume that the true position of the charted landfall was itself correct. The course was obtained from compasses, which could vary in the direction they gave for magnetic north from day to day. Estimating speed was even more hit and miss. One method actually involved dropping a stick over the bows (literally, heaving the log) and timing how long it took to pass two fixed points on the ship's side. The time it took gave an indication of the ship's speed. Another method dropped the stick off the stern, attached to a line with knots at regular intervals. The number of knots that ran out in a fixed period of time (measured with an hourglass) indicated the ship's speed in knots; as the speed in nautical miles per hour is still known today. As if that wasn't enough, during the voyage unpredictable factors such as currents, tides and leeway (sideways movement) meant that the *Duyfken's* longitude ended up being out by hundreds of kilometres (well east of the true position).

The consequences of getting one's reckoning wrong were dire, as subsequent chapters will show, but for some canny navigators, these methods and the ability to read the signs that they were approaching land were enough to keep them out of trouble.

Even without a journal of the *Duyfken's* voyage, it's still possible to know what the little yacht found at the Pennefather River, simply because the environment has changed little in the 400 years since the boat's visit. No metropolis has sprung up in this remote Cape York Peninsula location, a sandy spit still covers part of the entrance to an inlet half a kilometre wide that broadens to tidal flats stretching a few kilometres inland. The vegetation is a mix of scrub and casuarinas. While not the most inspiring vista, it was certainly very different to the homeland of the Dutch. In March, the heat of the wet season may have abated, but the air was still thick with a humidity that must have made the Dutch feel like they were in an oven.

From the Pennefather River, the *Duyfken* headed south. Some 40 kilometres down the coast she rounded what Matthew Flinders named Duyfken Point in her honour in 1802. She then entered what she called Vliege Bay, meaning Fly Bay; thus suggesting the first European encounter with these great Aussie nuisances.

Vliege Bay has changed noticeably since *Duyfken* was there. It's now known as Albatross Bay, and within it lies the mining town of Weipa (population 2200). Janszoon might have noticed the red, yellow and white sands of the bay, one of the world's largest deposits of bauxite, the ore from which aluminium is made. It would have been a great find, if aluminium had been discovered in the 1600s instead of the 1820s, and if bauxite was as valuable as gold. Alas, it's the kind of lower-value commodity suited to modern bulk carriers that make their money in carrying huge tonnages in holds so large they could contain the *Duyfken* in its entirety.

This is the first instance of an early explorer finding nothing of interest on the shores of Australia while valuable commodities (by modern standards) were staring them in the face. However, for the comparatively small vessels that set out to span the globe, the demand was for trade goods of extremely high value. Gold and silver were ideal, spices that were sometimes worth more than their weight in gold back in Europe were also highly sought after. It was only the profits from these that could cover the immense cost of outfitting fleets of ships and sending them and their crews to the far side of the world, with the ever-present risks of many vessels being lost on the voyage out or the return.

For the *Duyfken* crew, not even the crocodiles they saw would have excited them, unless the fractious reptiles had a snap at them. Yet today, crocodiles are farmed and their skins prized in making shoes, bags and other accessories. Hearing the powerful claws of mud crabs snapping in the mangroves, the *Duyfken's* crew had no way of knowing that one day they'd be exported live to restaurants around the globe.

Oblivious to all this, Janszoon and his men charted Vliege Bay, indenting the coast for some 40 kilometres (it's easily recognisable when compared to modern charts), then continuing south. As they did so, they continued seeking contact with the local inhabitants in order to investigate the possibilities for trade. However, the local Wik people were semi-nomadic and knew nothing of mining the precious metals and/or growing the spices the Dutch sought. In fact, while there had been human habitation in the Australian continent for perhaps 50 000 years, to the Europeans its flora yielded virtually nothing suitable for cultivation. As such, the *Duyfken's* crew were the first Europeans to get an intimation of just how hard this continent could be.

Janszoon and the *Duyfken* continued south, leaving Vliege Bay and heading to another bay ten kilometres down the coast. Here they marked their chart '*Dubbel Rev*' (Double River). This section of coast was characterised by low cliffs comprised largely of colourful bauxite and particularly shallow water that must have kept the *Duyfken* well out to sea (ten kilometres or more in places) while her boats explored inshore. On his chart Janszoon also marked '*R Vis*' (Fish River, now known as the Archer) suggesting they'd enjoyed a good catch, possibly of barramundi, in the bay marked *Dubbel Rev*.

The *Duyfkens* then sailed another 35 kilometres down the coast to a point on their charts marked as 'Cabo Keerweer' (Cape Turn-about). It's more of a small outlet for the Kirke River on an outward curve of the coastline than a cape, but it was certainly a significant point for Janszoon. He charts the coastline south from Keerweer as far as it was possible to see from *Duyfken's* masthead, and then turns north.

While there is no firsthand account of what happened at what is still known as Cape Keerweer, there is nevertheless a surprising amount of information available. It's extraordinary in that it comes from the descendants of some of people who were there; the local Wik people. Since the 1970s researchers have been recording the oral histories of Wik elders, keepers of the stories of the Dutch visit in 1606. The accounts vary in their detail but the gist is clear.

As Gladys Nunkatiapin told Kevin Gilbert for his book *Living Black* in 1978:

> One day the first six white men came to this country. They crossed the river [the Kirke River, at Cape Keerweer] and met our people. They took one

young woman back across the river. Her husband go and say, 'Let her go, give her back.' No one spoke the language; they could only use signs. The husband came back and said to our people, 'Help me get my wife back.' So the husband and tribesmen went back across the river and made signs. The white men wouldn't let her go. The husband pulled the white man into the river and choked him. I think that's when it all started.

Jack Spear Karntin, told Dr Peter Sutton his version in 1986:

If the Dutchmen had behaved properly, [the Aboriginals] would not have killed them. But they detained their wives … He [Grassbird Man] said to them … 'We've come for our women,' he said.

Then those fellows there, those cousins, said, 'The two women are somewhere in there, in the boat, that's where you've beenen keeping them.'

'Yes, yes, they're here' [said the Dutchmen]. Then they [the women] came up [on deck].

'You two can go!' [said the Dutchmen].

'Hey, would you like my gun? To shoot some of the ducks.' [A Dutch sailor encouraged one of the Aboriginal men to shoot black ducks.]

'No he might shoot you, he wants to shoot you!' [They said to the one who received the gun.] So they wrenched the gun from his hand and threw it into the sea.

'Where is it?' [asked the Dutchman].

They grabbed him [the Dutchman] by the neck, and smashed him down. They clubbed his nose, then the back of his neck! They hit another stone dead!

Another was starting to come out from down below, and they hit him next, striking the back of his neck and his nose.

The whole lot of them that were in the boat got finished off. They threw them into the waters.

Next they incinerated the boat. The others who were up on the bank were attacked with stones, those three, with hand stones …

The rest of the boats came from way out to sea, from well out to sea off Thewena [Cape Keerweer].

From there they wrongly blamed [the Aboriginals] on the south side [of the river mouth], they shot them with guns as they lay sleeping, bang bang bang bang bang bang bang! But they were innocent! Yes!

In 1999, Francis Yunkaporta echoed this story when he told it to James Henderson:

The Dutch shot many Aboriginal people along the river and in the bush land. Also, the warriors speared and killed some Dutchmen and made the Dutch go back to their ship. The warriors and the Aboriginal people saw the Dutch return back to where they came from.

It's possible the stories may be embellishments of stories told to the Wik elders by missionaries at various times during the 19th and 20th centuries. However, the Dutch records, from which the missionaries would have got their information, relate far less of the detail of the story. For example, Jan Carstenszoon, on an exploratory expedition aboard the *Pera*, wrote on 15 May 1623 that:

> In our landings between 13° and 11° we have but two times seen black men or savages, who received us much more hostilely than those more to southward, they are also acquainted with muskets, of which they would seem to have experienced the fatal effect when in 1606 the men of the *Duyfken* made a landing here.

Again, in 1644, in the instructions for Abel Tasman's second great voyage of exploration it was explained:

> By order of the president, John Williamsson Verschoor, who at that time directed the Company's trade at Bantam, which was in the year 1606, with the yacht the *Duyfken*, who in their passage sailed by the islands Key and Aroum, and discovered the south and west coast of Nova Guinea [actually New Guinea and Cape York], for about 220 miles [the then Dutch mile or mijlen is about six kilometres, making a distance of 1300 kilometres] from 5° to 13½° south latitude: and found this extensive country, for the greatest part desert, but in some places inhabited by wild, cruel, black savages, by whom some of the crew were murdered; for which reason they could not learn anything of the land or waters, as had been desired of them, and, by want of provisions and other necessaries, they were obliged to leave the discovery unfinished: the furtherest point of the land was called in their map Cape Keer-Weer, situated in 13½° S.

From the evidence provided by all sources it does appear that in a dispute over women, a misunderstanding over a musket, or as other stories suggest a dispute over the digging of wells near Cape Keerweer, a violent reaction was met with an equal or more severe retaliation. The Englishman, John Saris, also noted later that:

'The Flemmings' [Dutch] pinnace [*Duyfken*] which went upon discovery for New Ginny, was returned to Banda [in the Moluccas], having found the island: but in sending their men on shoare to intreate for Trade, there were nine of them killed by the Heathens, which are man-eaters, so they were constrained to return.

Here, too, is another first from the *Duyfken* voyage, although an unfortunate one. Saris refers to 'man-eaters' when the Dutch accounts only refer to the deaths of the crew. As such it's the first of countless claims of Aboriginal cannibalism that cannot be substantiated, and without the act being witnessed by the author of the claim.

Nevertheless, if the number of Janszoon's casualties is correct, he had lost a tenth of his crew. He was now faced with a clearly hostile local population who made procuring water, wood and knowledge of the country difficult, if not impossible. He had also, by this time, coasted Cape York for nearly 200 kilometres, finding nothing of value to his company. Yet he didn't turn and run for home. He headed north, back along the coast, and continued his exploration north of the Pennefather River.

His chart clearly shows the indentation of the coast that is the mouth of what is now the Wenlock River and Port Musgrave. It was here that Janszoon is thought to have again run into difficulties with the locals. Carstenszoon noted in his journal on 11 May 1623:

In the afternoon we sailed past a large river (which the men of the *Duifken* went up with a boat in 1606, and where one of them was killed by the arrows [more likely spears] of the blacks); to this river, which is in 11 degrees 48' lat we have given the name of Revier de Carpentier in the new chart.

Still Janszoon and the *Duyfken* pressed on. The chart shows that they passed the western side of what is now the Endeavour Strait, which extends north-east for just a few kilometres to reach the tip of the Australian continent at Cape York. Janszoon charted 'de Hooghe Eylandt' (the High Island, later named Prince of Wales Island by Cook), at the Strait's entrance but went no further. At that time of year he may have experienced strong headwinds and currents that prevented him from making any further progress to the east. Then there are the shoals that make traversing the Strait a serious test of seamanship, even when you know where they are. Janszoon didn't, nor did he know that the Strait existed. All he could be sure about was the decreasing depth beneath his keel.

Indeed, James Cook was to write in his journal after charting and naming the Endeavour Strait (after his ship, in 1770) using a route that at one point was just six metres deep:

> It is also very probable that among these Islands are as good if not better passages than the one we have come thro', altho one need hardly wish for a better was the Access to it from the Eastward less dangerous ... the Northern extent of the Main or outer Reef which limits or bounds the Shoals to the Eastward seems to be the only thing wanting to clear up this point, and this was a thing I had neither time nor inclination to go about having been already sufficiently harrass'd with dangers without going to look for more.

Janszoon, having spent months among the shoals between New Guinea and Cape York, would have perfectly understood Cook's sentiment. If he climbed to the summit of the Hooghe Eylandt, he'd have found that the vista of islands and reefs make a daunting prospect. Yet as he gazed at the Strait that lay before him, he had sufficient belief that the land he'd explored to the south was part of New Guinea to the north. He described it as such on his chart, but he didn't go so far as to connect the two. Not having sighted a coastline that did so, he left the space between, and therefore the question of an actual connection, wide open.

Soon the unwittingly famous *Duyfken* was heading west, back to a Dutch base at Banda, where she arrived in April 1606. Her voyage raised more questions than it answered, certainly from a cartographic point of view, but it did answer the question of trade opportunities for the Dutch on the western side of Cape York Peninsula. Desert, it was called; it offered nothing of use to the VOC. Even today, it would still be virtually uninhabited but for the scattered Aboriginal settlements and the mining operation at Weipa. There was certainly nothing to encourage the Dutch to establish a settlement. And yet, the *Duyfken* had clearly been on the coast of a significant landmass. As such, there was plenty of scope for further exploration.

2

TORRES

WAS THE *DUYFKEN* AUSTRALIA'S FIRST
EUROPEAN VISITOR? • THE SPANISH AND
THE GREAT SOUTH LAND • TORRES'
VOYAGE, A MODERN NAVIGATOR TO THE
RESCUE • TRAPPED AND BESET BY STORMS
• DIVINE INSPIRATION • TORRES IN
ENDEAVOUR STRAIT • LARGE ISLANDS OR
THE AUSTRALIAN MAINLAND? • SPANISH
SECRECY • SPANISH MISSIONARIES VERSUS
DUTCH COMMERCE •

With the benefit of more than 400 years of hindsight we now know that
Willem Janszoon and his crew were the first Europeans to accurately chart
any part of mainland Australia. We can even go so far as to say they were
the first Europeans to discover Australia. Dutch historian Jan Ernst Heeres
in *The Part Borne by the Dutch in the Discovery of Australia* wrote in 1899
that: 'All that is asserted regarding a so-called previous discovery of
Australia has no foundation beyond mere surmise and conjecture. Before
the voyage of the ship *Duifken* all is an absolute blank.'

Surmise and conjecture? Possibly. An absolute blank? Not quite. For
example, in Cornelius Wytfliet's *Descriptionis Ptolemaicae Augmentum*,
published in 1598, eight years before the *Duyfken's* voyage, there's this:

The Australis Terra [South Land] is the most southern of all lands, and is
separated from New Guinea by a narrow strait. Its shores are hitherto but
little known, since after one voyage and another that route has been

deserted, and seldom is the country visited unless sailors are driven there by storms. The Australis Terra begins at two or three degrees from the Equator, and is maintained by some to be of so great an extent that if it were thoroughly explored it would be regarded as a fifth part of the world.

Some of this is completely wrong: Australia doesn't begin two or three degrees from the equator and isn't a fifth part of the world. Some is exactly right: it is south of New Guinea and the two lands are separated by a narrow strait. And some of it is a real mystery. What voyages might Wytfliet be referring to? And when did they desert this route?

The finger of suspicion points at the Portuguese. Their voyages of exploration reached the Cape of Good Hope in 1487 and after they entered the Indian Ocean they soon connected with established Arab trade routes and reached spice-rich Java in 1510. It wasn't long before ships were making an incredible profit (400 per cent returns weren't uncommon) on their voyages to the Indies, but they didn't stop there. History records that they reached Timor, just 500 kilometres north-north-west of the Australian mainland, in 1511. In 1512 they discovered the Moluccas, just east of Timor. There, they struck a problem, for although the Portuguese discovered the Moluccas, and had got there first, the archipelago nevertheless belonged to the Spanish.

This curious situation came about due to an agreement brokered by Pope Alexander VI in 1493, the year after the Spanish went into direct competition with the seafaring Portuguese by sponsoring Christopher Columbus' 1492 voyage to America. To keep peace between the two godfearing nations, Pope Alexander simply divided the entire non-Christian world between them. An arbitrary line of demarcation ran down a meridian of longitude initially set 100 leagues (500 kilometres) west of the Cape Verde Islands, roughly down the middle of the Atlantic. It effectively gave everything to the west of the meridian (North and South America) to the Spaniards, and everything east of it (Africa and the Indies) to the Portuguese. In 1494, this was adjusted to 370 leagues, or 46 degrees 37 minutes west of Greenwich in modern longitude.

All was well until the Portuguese reached the limit of their hemisphere on the far side of the world, around 1512, and kept going. The Moluccas, which they discovered soon after, were just on the Spanish side. It didn't matter that no Spanish explorers had ever been near this side of the world; Ferdinand Magellan's ships (engaged in the first circumnavigation of the world), only reached their vicinity in 1521. The Moluccas belonged to Spain.

Still, the Portuguese didn't want to give up the valuable Moluccas. So after considerable wrangling with the Spanish they successfully negotiated the Treaty of Zaragoza in 1529. Both kings married each other's sister, the King of Portugal paid the Spaniard a substantial amount in cash, and they moved the eastern longitude to the east of the Moluccas, at 130 degrees east of Greenwich.

Were the Portuguese ever tempted to explore just a little bit further? If we take the absence of evidence as a sign, we might surmise that they weren't even curious. The riches of 'King Solomon's mines' may have beckoned just a short cruise away, but those honourable Portuguese didn't even make any accidental discoveries after being driven there by storms.

The casual observer might be tempted to come to this conclusion were it not for one tiny scrap of evidence. Thirteen years after the Treaty of Zaragoza, in 1542, a map appeared in Dieppe, France, depicting a continent, Java La Grande, to the south of Java and New Guinea. Not only that, it showed a narrow strait separating the known lands from this unknown south land. At the time, the French lacked the maritime expertise to find such things for themselves. Although their king, Francis I, grumbling about Spain and Portugal's global carve up, reputedly said, 'I should like to see the clause in Adam's will that denies me a share of the new world.'

So where did the French get their information? According to Australian historian Sir Ernest Scott in his *Short History of Australia*:

> It is certain that the French map-maker worked from Portuguese information, not from original observations of his own. Allowing for some defects, the map makes it probable that at least one Portuguese ship had sailed not only along the north-western coast of Australia, but also along the east coast, from Cape York to the south of Tasmania, two centuries and a half before the celebrated voyage of Captain Cook.

It's an extraordinary claim, but if they had actually navigated through this area, the Portuguese certainly weren't telling, with good reason. It would be an admission that they'd been trespassing on Spain's turf. While there is no further evidence to suggest that such a journey took place, the Portuguese were known to have threatened anyone who divulged their navigational secrets with death. However, the only thing that leaks more than an old wooden ship is its crew. The sketchy Dieppe map and its subsequent copies may be dismissed as the product of a fertile imagination, but on the other hand it's possible that someone talked.

So, given that the Pope divided the entire world between the Portuguese and the Spanish, what were the Dutch doing at Cape York in 1606? During the 16th century the Dutch had built a considerable maritime enterprise, but it was limited to distributing goods brought back by the Portuguese throughout the rest of Europe. They soon came to be regarded as some of the best seafarers on the continent. However, towards the end of the 16th century many of the Dutch, who were subjects of Philip II of Spain, broke away from the Catholic church and joined the Protestant religions rapidly gaining popularity in northern Europe. Philip II, devoutly Catholic, vowed to suppress the rebellion, and over the next three decades sacked towns and villages, torturing and executing Protestant heretics.

The Dutch not only defied Philip's might, but they continued to build their seafaring empire and wealth with the help of the Portuguese. The hard-pressed English also supported the Dutch rebellion when they could, in order to split the Spanish forces that threatened them. With these resources the northern states of the Netherlands in particular defied Philip's best troops, until Philip decided to break the Dutch by going after their trade. In 1580 he invaded Portugal, installed himself on that country's vacant throne, and in 1584 closed the vital trading port of Lisbon to Dutch ships (and those of the English for good measure). If he couldn't beat the Dutch on the battlefield, he'd starve them out at sea.

The Dutch, being such good seamen, shrugged-off the loss of the Lisbon trade, bypassed the Portuguese middle men, and instead sailed directly (and more profitably) to the Indies themselves. While the Portuguese had tried to keep their sailing routes to the east secret, the Dutch knew the routes because some of them worked on the Portuguese vessels, even as pilots.

One of those pilots was Jan Huygen Van Linschoten, who smuggled details of Portuguese trading routes back to Holland, and published them in his *Itineraria* in 1596. His information was invaluable to Dutch and English vessels hoping to join the spice trade. The *Itineraria* includes a reference to Java that:

> Of its breadth nothing is known up to now, since it has not yet been
> explored, nor is this known to the inhabitants themselves. Some suppose it
> to be a mainland, [forming part] of the land called Terra Incognita.

In this Linschoten is clearly incorrect. However, his reference to Terra Incognita, south of Java, is intriguing.

Could the Portuguese have kept their discovery of Australia secret, even to the present day? As it happens, supporting evidence for that possibility comes from an unlikely quarter: Spain. For, in 1606, Janszoon and the *Duyfken* weren't the only ones voyaging in the vicinity of Cape York. Indeed, had Janszoon passed the Hooghe Eylandt in the Endeavour Strait around November of that year, he could have exchanged compliments, or more likely cannon fire, with the Spaniard Luis Vaéz de Torres and his two ships, the *San Pedrico* and *Los Tres Reijes* (*The Three Kings*). As the Portuguese may have done, the Spanish subsequently kept details of Torres' voyage secret (they succeeded for over 150 years), and it's only due to luck, war, lax security and dogged research that he has received credit for discovering the strait that bears his name.

In 1606 Torres was part of an expedition sent from Peru under the orders of King Philip III of Spain with a particular goal in mind: to find the much-rumoured, but never officially found, Great South Land. The expedition's leader, the Portuguese-born Captain Pedro Fernández de Quirós (he became a Spanish national at age 15) had long been a strong believer in it, so much so that he'd got a papal blessing (and a piece of the true cross to take with him), then harassed Spanish officials until they sent him on his way, if only to get rid of him.

An artist's impression of Luis Vaéz de Torres on the doors of the Mitchell Library, Sydney. State Library of New South Wales.

Alas, their low opinion of his abilities proved well-founded, and after he'd anchored off the large island of Espiritu Santo, in the New Hebrides, which he was convinced was the much-sought South Land, his crew either mutinied or became so rebellious that he was forced to do their bidding. As Torres stated in a brief account written to the king of Spain that was uncovered sometime around 1762:

> From within this bay, and from the most sheltered part of it, the *Capitana* departed at one hour past midnight, without any notice given to us, and without making any signal. This happened on the 11th of June.

Torres assumed command, and after establishing that Quirós wasn't coming back (and that Espiritu Santo wasn't the South Land) he resolved to complete the expedition's objectives. He consulted with his officers and

> It was determined that we should fulfil [the orders] although contrary to the inclination of many, I may say, of the greater part; but my condition was different from that of Captain Pedro Fernández de Quirós.

In other words, unlike Quirós' crew, Torres' men were still prepared to follow him. It was lucky for him they didn't know what lay ahead.

After tacking about south-west of the Hebrides in search of the South Land, Torres wrote:

> From hence I stood back to the NW to $11\frac{1}{2}°$ S. latitude: there we fell in with the beginning of New Guinea … I could not weather the east point, so I coasted along to the westward on the south side.

From his remarks it appears that he was actually at the eastern extremity of the New Guinea peninsula's chain of islands, possibly Tagula Island, in the Louisiade Archipelago. From there he maintains that he continued 300 leagues (1500 kilometres) along the coast 'and diminished the latitude $2\frac{1}{2}°$, which brought us into 9°'. This would have taken him along the coast past the Gulf of Papua, through Torres Strait, and on to the coast of Irian Jaya. Then he writes:

> From hence we fell in with a bank of from three to nine fathoms, which extends along the coast above 180 leagues. We went over it along the coast to $7\frac{1}{2}°$ S latitude, and the end of it is in 5°. We could not go farther on for the many shoals and great currents, so we were obliged to sail out SW in that depth to 11° S latitude. There is all over it an archipelago of islands

without number, by which we passed, and at the end of the eleventh degree the bank became shoaler. Here were very large islands, and there appeared more to the southward ...

For an armchair navigator armed with anything from an atlas to the latest electronic navigation map, this is rather confusing. It clearly suggests that Torres and his ships went through Torres Strait while hugging the New Guinea coast until he gets to 5 degrees south. However, if you plot his course statement by statement, you get into all kinds of difficulties. He writes that he met a shoal at 9 degrees that extends for 180 leagues along the coast of Irian Jaya. There's no shoal of such dimensions there, and he'd have already met a worse shoal getting through Torres Strait. Then after leaving the Papua New Guinea coast at 5 degrees (or 7½ degrees if he meant that was where he could get no further), if you head out to 11 degrees south on a south-west course, the only islands you're likely to see are those off the Cobourg Peninsula, 350 kilometres east of present-day Darwin. If you allow for a start point of 7½ degrees south, he might have been looking at the Wessel Islands, off the north-eastern tip of Arnhem Land. But both routes are so far off Torres' New Guinea coast-hugging track and so free of shoals that many academics have stated the position of 11 degrees south must simply be wrong.

Fortunately, a modern navigator has come to the rescue. The late Brett Hilder (1911–1981) ran away to sea when he was 15, and spent much of his working life in the waters Torres famously voyaged so many years before. While piloting vessels through Torres Strait, he developed an interest in Torres' voyage and its navigational challenges, and started trying to determine Torres' exact course. After educating himself aboard ship, including studying and learning old Spanish, in the 1970s he applied to do a masters thesis on Torres' voyage. By then, he'd been familiar with the waters in question for nearly 50 years. He actually worked on the thesis, studying copies of the relevant historical documents, while taking ships from Sydney and Brisbane through the Strait and on to the mining towns of Gove, Weipa and Groote Eylandt; the very waters referred to in the documents.

With the benefit of Hilder's considerable local knowledge all becomes clear. First of all, Torres' account is every bit as confused as the waters he was voyaging. Most significantly, his account doubles back on itself at several key points. Second, his accounts of the distances he travelled demonstrate all the problems associated with determining one's position by dead reckoning (as discussed in Chapter 1).

Reconsidering Torres' account from Hilder's perspective, he voyages to 9 degrees south and does indeed meet the extensive shoal. However, Torres' reckoning is out by about 400 kilometres (80 leagues) and the shoal he meets begins not off Irian Jaya, but in the Gulf of Papua, at the eastern side of Torres Strait. Sure enough, there is 'a bank of from three to nine fathoms, which extends along the coast above 180 leagues'. As Torres more correctly approximates 'the end of it is in 5".

Now Torres doubles back to talk some more about navigating the shoal met at 9 degrees, not one met at 5 degrees.

> We could not go farther on for the many shoals and great currents, so we
> were obliged to sail out SW in that depth to 11° S latitude. There is all over
> it an archipelago of islands without number, by which we passed.

That's exactly what's to be found in Torres Strait. Hilder notes that if the sea level dropped 14 metres, one could walk from Cape York to New Guinea, and had James Cook gone searching for the northern extremity of the reefs he'd been battling through (as mentioned in Chapter 1), he'd have found they stopped at the New Guinea shore.

Torres, meanwhile, was in trouble. In September, the month he worked his way through the Strait, the trade winds are blowing from the south-east. So it would have been quite difficult for a Spanish ship of the time to sail on a south-west course, even without having to zigzag around the reefs and shoals that lay across his path. The poor sailing qualities of Spanish ships had been amply demonstrated just a few years before, in 1588, when the Spanish Armada was outsailed and defeated by the English.

As it happens, another account of Torres' voyage has also survived, written by a senior officer on board Torres' ships, Don Diego de Prado. Prado gives an island by island, reef by reef account of the challenges and how they were dealt with. He notes the frustrating efforts to head west, the ships repeatedly blocked by shallow water. Finally, the ships sailed into a promising opening with a favourable wind at their backs. All was well until, to their horror, the passage ended in a cul-de-sac of reefs. The only way out was to the south-east, directly into the prevailing wind. Torres and his men were trapped.

Hilder believes the cul-de-sac is near the aptly named Turnagain Island. There, as Prado relates, the situation went from bad to worse:

> On the 22nd of September there was another eclipse of the moon [it was actually the 16th] ... and on the next night there came such a great wind and tempest while we were anchored that it seemed as if all the elements had conspired against us; so that at midnight we all made confession and prepared to die; of the two cables with which we were anchored one broke, but in commending ourselves very truly to Jesus Maria Joseph, Jesus was pleased to have mercy on us. So great was the water and sand that entered along the bowsprit that the upper deck of the ship was half blocked up. At dawn the storm ceased and the sea became as calm as if there had never been anything.

Lucky to be alive, with their path blocked by ship-wrecking reefs and difficult winds blowing from the only direction of escape, Torres and his men took stock. According to Prado:

> Seeing that we could not get clear of these shoals we took counsel as to what was to be done, and decided not to weigh anchor until ebb water and to go with the foresail only to steer the ship, because the stream would carry the ships through the trough of the water, and to anchor at the flow of the tide. The opinion was as if it had come from heaven, for in this way we secured the ships and our lives.

This translation is Hilder's, and it corrects a 1930s translation in *New Light on the Discovery of Australia: As Revealed by the Journal of Captain Don Diego de Prado y Tovar*, which lacked Hilder's intimate understanding of navigation. The earlier translation confused things by suggesting Torres sailed at low water. In Torres Strait, the flood tide flows to the north-west, which wouldn't have helped Torres, but the ebb flows to the south-east, into the eye of the wind.

Even today, there isn't a sailing ship in the world that can sail directly into the wind. However, by using the strong-flowing tides of the Strait, that's what Torres was able to do. Ships certainly 'sail with the tide', meaning it works with them rather than against them. However, Torres' trick wasn't just to sail with it. He used it as his primary means of propulsion.

Suddenly, Torres was no longer at the mercy of the wind when steering his unwieldy ships through the maze of Torres Strait. Utilising the tidal currents when they were flowing in the right direction, the wind when it was favourable, and (the smartest tactic of all) anchoring virtually anywhere in the shallow waters of the Strait when neither wind nor tide were helpful, Torres had come up with a way of progressing in any direction he chose. Prado called this navigational technique divine inspiration, although sheer desperation was probably closer to the mark. When the ship was underway, the crew couldn't relax for a moment. They had to be ready to trim sails, or drop anchor, the instant the order was given. As an improvement on mast-head navigating through a multitude of reefs, it was still filled with white-knuckled sailing.

According to Hilder, and Prado, from Turnagain Island (at the head of the cul-de-sac) the ships now zigzagged south-east to Long Island (named Isla de Vulcan Quemado by Prado), then south-west to Mt Ernest Island (called Monserrate by Prado) then south to Twin Islands (Prado's Isla de Las Cantarides, so named because of the flies). Here, according to Prado: 'The contrary currents were so great and so strong that it was necessary to have two men at the helm to keep the ship's head against the stream, and this lasted for eight days and nights.'

To the west of the ships lay several channels that in modern times are used by large vessels passing through the islands of the Prince of Wales group. However, they're also used by the waters of the Arafura Sea (the body of water between Australia and New Guinea) to pour through into the Coral Sea (off the north-east coast of Australia), and vice versa, at speeds approaching five knots. The channels are only two to three kilometres wide in places, and for Torres the tactic of using the tide to carry him along would have been more like running rapids, always with the risk that the channel might come to an abrupt end. So as he put it 'we were obliged to sail out SW in that depth to 11° S latitude'.

Referring to a modern atlas or chart, 11 degrees south puts him in the vicinity of Endeavour Strait (10 degrees 49 minutes south), named by Cook after his passage through it in 1770. Support for this position comes from Torres' remark that: 'at the end of the eleventh degree the bank becomes shoaler [or shallower]' which indeed the Strait does at its western end, before deepening into the Arafura Sea that lies beyond it. Prado doesn't give a latitude, but he provides an incident that helps verify the position.

After the said currents ceased we proceeded towards two islands of no great size passing along a very narrow channel which formed some shoals; we did not reach them for we did not need to; and at the end of two days on the eve of St Francis [3 October] we found other islands towards the north and among them one bigger than the rest; and at nightfall we anchored in five fathoms at half a league [2.5 kilometres] from the island; and at midnight the ship began to give bumps on the bottom; which had it not been of clay would have smashed it to pieces, we lightened the deck and loosed the cable and with this it righted.

The smaller islands and narrow channel may have been among the four that guard the eastern entrance to the Endeavour Strait: Entrance, Woody, Meddler and Possession Islands. In the Strait itself, about four kilometres from Prince of Wales Island, there's a small shoal that at dead low tide has less than five metres of water over it. That's shallow enough for the larger of Torres' two ships to touch bottom. Hilder has also calculated what the tides were doing at the time Prado says they were there, using the eclipse of 16 September as a reference point. Low tide would have been around 1 am, Prado's 'at midnight'.

At this point of his account, Torres notes, 'Here were very large islands, and there appeared more to the southward.' In fact, there's only one very large island to the southward: Australia. Ironically, Torres didn't realise he was looking at Cape York, the tip of the Great South Land he'd been seeking. However, looking from the position of the shoal he'd struck in the Endeavour Strait, there's no doubt he could see it. Like Willem Janszoon, he didn't realise what he was looking at, but he and his crew had become the second group of Europeans known for sure to have sighted mainland Australia. As it happened they'd both done so within only months of each other.

Torres nevertheless observed that the islands,

were inhabited by black people, very corpulent, and naked: their arms were lances, arrows, and clubs of stone ill-fashioned. We could not get any of their arms. We caught in all this land twenty persons of different nations, that with them we might be able to give a better account to Your Majesty. They give much notice to other people, although as yet they do not make themselves well understood.

Prado next wrote, 'God was pleased that we should henceforth find more water so that we had not to wait for the tides.' And indeed, not far due west of the shoal in Endeavour Strait, the depth rises to only three fathoms before dropping away again into the relatively deeper waters of the Arafura Sea. Once there, they'd done it; they'd become the first to pass through what was to become known as Torres Strait, an extraordinary feat of navigation and courage.

Beyond the Strait, the ships were again able to steer to the north in open water until they approached New Guinea's False Cape, where they found the waters too shallow to get close. Torres reported:

> We went upon this bank for two months [elsewhere Torres is reported as saying it was 40 days], at the end of which time we found ourselves in twenty-five fathoms, and in 5° S latitude, and ten leagues from the coast. And having gone 480 leagues, here the coast goes to the NE. I did not reach it. We stood to the north, and in 25 fathoms to 4° latitude, where we fell in with a coast.

This last point reinforces the suggestion that Torres hadn't transited Torres Strait by hugging the New Guinea coast. There is an extremely difficult passage along the coast, but in places it's very shallow and the ships would have grounded countless times in heading through it. It's more likely that they'd have been wrecked.

Prado also summarised the voyage, writing that: 'We were among these rocks and shoals for 34 days, they run out into the sea as far as we could judge about fifty leagues [250 kilometres] in a southern direction.' Here Prado appears unaware that they were in a strait, which at its narrowest point is only 150 kilometres wide.

Unlike the Portuguese documents relating to a possible Australian discovery (mentioned at the beginning of this chapter), reports of Torres' voyage survived. However, their fate provides a valuable lesson in the extent of Spanish secrecy in particular and the vulnerability of historical documents in general. Both vessels reached the Spanish base at Manila in the Philippines on 22 May 1607, where Torres learned that Quirós hadn't been dispatched by his crew; he'd survived and eventually returned to Mexico. Torres wrote a full report to Quirós on 15 June 1607, and a brief outline of his discoveries for King Philip III on 12 July.

Quirós got Torres' report in August 1609 and wrote a quick sketch of what was found in a memorial to the King in 1610, calling Torres' report confusing. Torres' report was lost after Quirós' death at Panama in 1615. Torres' letter to the King reached the Spanish court on 22 June 1608, where it was considered by the Council of State, declared too sensitive to be revealed to the world at large, and filed. Spain's maritime star was already on the wane, many of her colonies proving more trouble than they were worth, and Spain didn't want her enemies (such as the Dutch and English) to set up bases that might be used to harass her.

The *Relacion Sumaria de Don Diego de Prada* is dated 1608, but it is thought to have been rewritten by Prado some time later, possibly when he became a monk in the order of Saint Basil in Madrid. The unpublished work received a passing reference from a Spanish historian in 1621, and after that it sank from view. Another memorial, to King Philip IV, written by Dr Luis Arias de Loyola in the early 1630s, also mentioned Torres' voyage with New Guinea on his right hand, though no strait, for at the time it was not known to the writer that the South Land formed it's southern boundary.

The truth remained hidden until 1762, when the English attacked and captured Manila, during the Seven Years' War with France and Spain. According to Australian historian Sir Ernest Scott in *Australian Discovery* a copy of Torres' report to the King was found in the Spanish archive in Manila by English hydrographer Alexander Dalrymple. It was first printed in Captain James Burney's *Chronological History of Discoveries and Voyages in the South Sea*, in 1806. (Burney was also Cook's second lieutenant on Cook's second voyage of 1772–1773.)

Hilder tells a different story. In his version, Dalrymple, an official of the English East India Company who later became the company's hydrographer and the first hydrographer for the British Admiralty, had been searching for details of Torres' voyage for years, until in 1765 he found a copy of Arias de Loyola's memorial in, of all places, a second-hand book-shop in London.

He translated the memorial and eventually published it in *An Historical Collection of the Several Voyages and Discoveries in the South Pacific Ocean* in 1770–1771. However, he also provided Joseph Banks with a copy of the translation before the botanist set sail with Cook in 1768. It was only a decade after Cook's voyage and rediscovery of what Dalrymple called Torres' Strait that a Spanish historian located Torres' letter to the King in the archives of the Spanish government and sent a copy to Dalrymple, who provided it to Burney for his book of 1806.

What of Prado's *Relacion*? It was to be 300 years later, in the 1920s, that it was found among a collection of old documents sold at auction in London. It was bought by a bookseller, Henry N Stevens, who recognised it for what it was and had it translated by George Barwick. The two published it with other relevant documents in 1930 in *New Light on the Discovery of Australia*. It's unfortunate it wasn't found sooner, for Torres' techniques for reef navigation in sailing ships would have been invaluable for those who followed him. As it turned out, most seafarers eventually worked it out for themselves, usually the hard way.

Seeing how tenuous the survival of the Torres documents has been, it's easier to see how documents relating to Portuguese discoveries may have disappeared, especially if there was an effort made to suppress them. Several historians have explored the possibility of a Portuguese discovery, notably Lawrence Fitzgerald in *Java La Grande: The Story of the Portuguese Discovery of Australia, circa 1521* (1984) and the documentary *The Secret Discovery of Australia* (1983). Their investigations include explanations on how the relevant documents may have been lost or destroyed, and the possible fates of voyages of exploration that never returned. Unfortunately, the hard evidence is still missing, and doubts linger.

Whatever may have happened, after 1606 neither the Spanish nor the Portuguese were to play any significant role in the further discovery of Australia. By then, the Dutch were becoming established in the Indies, while Spanish seapower was sapped by opportunistic Dutch and English privateers who loved nothing better than to seize a Spanish galleon laden with valuable goods and money.

For the Spanish, the edicts of the Catholic popes that divided the world between the Catholic nations were no help. They meant nothing to the Protestant Dutch and English. Indeed, the power of Rome stifled the very scientific endeavour that could give Spain and Portugal that technological edge in navigation and other maritime developments. Portugal eventually threw off Spanish control some 60 years after Spain's invasion, however by this time other countries already had too great a head start.

As mentioned, in 1612 Galileo devised his method for calculating longitude on land. It was a major step forward for navigators, but it relied on a model of the solar system devised by Nicolas Copernicus. The church regarded the Copernican model, which placed the sun at the centre of the universe rather than the earth, as heresy, and for his trouble Galileo was to end his days under house arrest. The effect on science in southern Europe was profound. The spirit of enquiry gradually migrated to the universities of northern Europe, and with it the scientific and technological advantage was to shift to the Dutch, English and eventually the French; with superior sailing vessels, weapons, charts and eventually such instruments as the octant, sextant and chronometer.

A memorial by Juan Arias to King Philip III (probably written in 1617) could only bemoan the waning Spanish ascendancy, while arguing a losing case for Spanish voyages of exploration:

> That in consideration of the great advantage which will accrue to the service of Your Majesty, to the extension of the Catholic Church, and to the increase of our holy faith, from the conversion of the Gentiles of the southern land, which is the principal obligation to which Your Majesty and your crown are pledged, he now earnestly begs (great as have been his former importunities) to solicit Your Majesty's consideration to that which is here set forth.
>
> For the English and Dutch heretics, whom the devil unites for this purpose by every means in his power, most diligently continue the exploration, discovery, and colonisation of the principal ports of this large part of the world in the Pacific Ocean, and sow in it the most pernicious poisons of their apostasy, which they put forth with the most pressing anxiety in advance of us, who should put forth the sovereign light of the gospel.

As it turned out, spreading the word of God couldn't motivate the Spanish anywhere near as much as the god of commerce could drive the Dutch. The Spanish could claim to have found Torres Strait, except they guarded their secrets well. The Dutchman Janszoon, probably suspected its presence from the tides and sailors' gossip, but finding it was easier said than done; especially when coming from the west and sailing into the teeth of the wind, which was harder than the one-way ticket Torres got dealt coming from the east with a tailwind. There are hints however, that the Dutch believed in its presence after Janszoon's voyage. One indication comes in a letter from Isack de Brune, governor of Banda, to the governor general, Pieter de Carpentier on 16 May 1623, regarding the return of the yacht *Arnhem*, which had been exploring what would become the Gulf of Carpentaria with the yacht *Pera*: '[They] have not done much worth mentioning, for at the place where the chart they had with them, led them to expect an open passage, they did not find any such ...'

Writing in 1899, Heeres in *The Part Borne by the Dutch in the Discovery of Australia* asserts that the chart referred to was one made by Janszoon. He adds: 'In that case the passage in the text proves that Willem Janszoon already suspected the existence of Torres Strait, since the "open passage" can hardly refer to anything else.'

3

THE BROUWER ROUTE

There's nothing a sailor likes better than the wind at their back. Some modern mariners venturing beyond 50 degrees south may dread the mighty storms and huge seas that threaten to somersault them stern over bow. But when a boat surges forward on a gust and launches itself down the face of a wave, it certainly gets the pulse going. The hull surfs amid a roar of spray and the speed log starts showing numbers not normally associated with sailing (20 knots and more). There's no denying that whatever emotion you're feeling – fear, exhilaration, or a mixture of both – you're going to devour incredible amounts of ocean distance in very short intervals of time.

Dutch merchant vessels of the 1600s couldn't come close to logging such numbers, but one of their commanders, Hendrik Brouwer, realised that the 'roaring forties' of the Southern Ocean could still give the VOC a tremendous speed advantage in reaching the Indies. Prior to 1610, vessels rounding Africa's Cape of Good Hope immediately headed north-east, hugging the

African coast in much the same way as the first Portuguese explorers more than a century earlier. Beyond Madagascar they'd turn onto a more easterly course, towards the Indies, while dealing with contrary winds, reefs and islands along the route. Much of the voyage was in tropical latitudes where the heat and humidity quickly rotted food, spoiled fresh water and spread disease among the crew. The average journey took almost a year.

However, by 1610, Brouwer had noted the prevailing westerlies that blew south of the Cape. A ship that stayed in those cooler southern latitudes for as long as it could before turning north would have the wind at its back, almost a guarantee of a faster, healthier passage. In December 1610, Brouwer was sent to investigate his proposed route aboard the *Roode Leeuw met Pijlen*, along with the ships *Gouda* and *Veere*. They called at the Cape of Good Hope to resupply, then sailed south to latitudes as high as 36 degrees south. It wasn't quite the forties, but the ships still set a cracking pace (relatively speaking). Brouwer and his crews headed east for thousands of kilometres until they calculated they were due south of Java. Then they turned north. To their astonishment, they halved the usual time for the voyage from the Cape; instead of a year, it took six months. The crew arrived healthier, the company's ships and cargos arrived in better condition, and apart from St Peters and St Pauls islands, there wasn't a reef, shoal or rock on the whole journey.

The cautious VOC sent other ships to investigate. Soon a future VOC governor, Pieter de Carpentier, was able to report: 'If we had to sail a hundred times to the Indies we should use no other route than this.'

In 1616, with more and more ships taking Brouwer's Route, the VOC's directors, the Heren 17, resolved that:

> The ships leaving here must follow on their outward voyage the course described by Jan Pieterzoon Coen [governor general in the Indies] in his latest letters and by commandeur Brouwer in his discourse, and by which route many ships have travelled much more quickly; and for better care and attention of the above order, a reward for a voyage to Bantam of less than seven, eight and nine months respectively will be payed.

Increased company profits notwithstanding, the route did have its disadvantages. As ships ventured further and further south in search of the westerlies, they risked encounters with stray icebergs. In the remote wastes of the Southern Ocean a ship that got into trouble was a long way from any kind of land or hope of assistance. And, unknown to the Dutch sailors, there was a major obstacle at the far end of their easterly track. It was only a matter of time before a ship misjudged how far east it had travelled, and found it.

> AD 1616, on the 25th of October there arrived here the ship *de Eendraght*, of Amsterdam; supercargo Gillis Miebais, of Leige; skipper Dirck Hartog, of Amsterdam; she set sail for Bantam on the 27th do; subcargo Jan Steyn, uppersteersman Pieter Ledocker Van Bil.

There's no disputing this first sighting of the Western Australian coast by Europeans. Not only does the above documentation give the date, the name of the ship and the names of her senior crew, but it was inscribed on a pewter

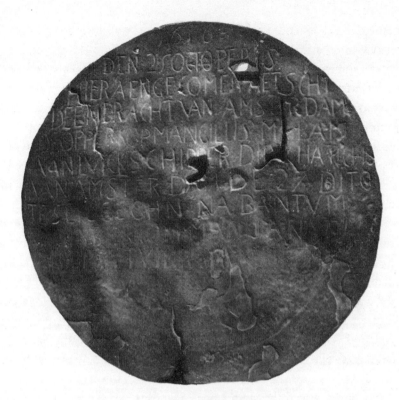

The Dirk Hartog Plate was left by the master of the first European ship to reach the coast of Western Australia in 1616. A translation of the text is to be found on the previous page. Frank Hurley, nla.pic-an23181560
National Library of Australia.

plate and nailed to a post on Dirk Hartog Island, just off the coast in latitude 25 degrees south. It was found 81 years later, returned to Holland, and is now in the Rijksmuseum in Amsterdam, one of the most famous relics in Australia's maritime exploration (see Chapter 8).

The *Eendracht* (*Concord*), was perhaps driven further east by stronger westerlies than usual and thus became the first ship to overshoot the Brouwer Route. She'd already been steering north when she sighted land lying between approximately 27 degrees 35 minutes and 21 degrees 45 minutes south.

Unlike the deliberate exploration of Australia by Willem Janszoon and the *Duyfken*, the *Eendracht's* discovery was the first by the Dutch that was completely accidental. The discovery was something of a mixed blessing.

The new land mass could prove to be a navigational hazard, especially if a ship came upon a low-lying section of coastline at night. However, it could also mean there might be opportunities for trade with the locals, and sources of fresh water and food with which ships could resupply. There might be ports that could serve as bases from which to harass any Portuguese or Spanish merchantmen tempted to try the Brouwer Route as well.

Alas, like the *Duyfken*, no eyewitness account of this encounter with the coast of Australia (other than the inscribed plate) has survived. Indeed, the only direct reference to the *Eendracht's* encounter comes from sketchy maps and a letter sent from Java by supercargo Cornelis Buysero to the VOC: 'The ship *Eendracht*, with which they sailed from the Netherlands, after communicating at the Cabo [Cape of Good Hope] sailed away from them so far southward as to come upon various islands which were, however, found uninhabited.'

As with the *Duyfken*, contemporary visitors can still get an accurate sense of what Hartog and company found at Dirk Hartog Island, for little has changed. The island's barren cliffs still rise sheer from the sea, battered by the huge swells generated in the roaring forties. In many places the vegetation comprises nothing more than low scrub. However, the *Eendracht's* crew may have noticed the abundance of wildlife, for the waters in the area are thronged by fish that are hunted by countless seabirds. They may have seen seals, dolphins, even crocodiles, for despite its initially barren appearance, the area around what would later be named Shark Bay is such a treasure-house of flora and fauna that it has been listed as a World Heritage site. The *Eendracht* may also have found safe anchorages in the lee of Dirk Hartog Island, but that water was scarce, food only available from the sea, and trade opportunities nil.

So as the pewter plate she left behind explains, after a few days the *Eendracht* upped anchor and continued on to the East Indies. There her report may not have created enough excitement to ensure that it survived down to the present day, but many subsequent Dutch maps note Eendrachtsland (the lands charted by the *Eendracht*) alongside later discoveries. For she wasn't to be the last Dutch ship to come upon the Western Australian coast.

In fact, the VOC made that an absolute certainty when, in 1617, they issued detailed instructions for ships sailing the Brouwer Route, possibly before knowledge of the *Eendracht's* discovery had reached the Netherlands.

Article 12 required that 'All ships will, after having taken refreshments at the Cape de Bona Experance or Tafelbay, put their course east in the latitude 34, 36, 40 to 44° South, so that they will find the best westerly winds.' Article 13 said:

> Having found the westerly winds, the ships shall keep an easterly course at least for 1000 mijlen [approximately 6000 kilometres] before they move upwards or make their course northerly, the Javanese coast is no further than $7^1/_2°$ southward, so that because of this precision one should fear nothing; but by crossing before one reaches 1000 mijlen, there is the danger of getting on the coast of Sumatra [west of Java], where because of the SE winds that are there between April and October, one will have to beat against the wind [the south-east trade winds mentioned in Chapter 2] for a long time.

With the benefit of hindsight, these instructions virtually put Dutch ships on a collision course with Australia. As James Henderson notes in his book *Phantoms of the Tryall*:

> According to the VOC sailing instructions, to sail 1000 mijlen [6000 kilometres] east from the Cape in 45°S should put a ship in longitude 112°E. But if the ship sailed north from this position it would in fact be on almost the same longitude as the westernmost point of Australia, about 113°E, and about 500 sea miles [800 kilometres] farther eastward than the Sunda Strait (which is 105°E). If a ship sailed 1000 mijlen in only 35° latitude it would reach longitude 101°E – less distance eastward than if it had sailed in latitude 45°S. The farther south they were, the greater the eastern longitudinal distance they made from their 1000 mijlen.

At the time the instructions were written there was an understanding among cartographers that the length of a degree of longitude shortens the further north or south one moves from the equator. Advising navigators of this would have helped them on the Brouwer Route, but there was a further complication. In the early 17th century there still wasn't an accurate calculation of the earth's overall circumference, so when it came to working out the length of a degree in any particular latitude, it largely depended on who you asked. While scientists pondered the problem, ships set sail and did the best they could. On short distances and routes with plenty of landfalls, they didn't have too much to worry about. However, the new Brouwer Route represented one of the longest open-ocean trade routes on the planet. So it was inevitable that the Brouwer Route would provide important lessons on the need for accurate navigation.

Meanwhile, the encounters with Eendrachtsland continued. On 24 June 1618, the skipper of the *Zeewolf* (*Seawolf*), Hoevick Claeszoon Van Hillegrom, wrote to the VOC:

> On the 5th of May we got into latitude 28°26′S, when we saw numbers of birds many of which seemed to be land-birds, such as a white tropic-bird and a few scissor-tailed ducks, so that I surmised that we were near land. Two or three days afterwards we saw sea-weed floating in long strips. On the 10th do we passed the tropic [of Capricorn, 23 degrees 30 minutes south] in fine weather. On the 11th do we saw land in 21°20′S lat. It was a level, low-lying coast extending to a great length, and bearing mainly south and north, falling off on both sides with high mountains; we could not get near it. Whether it was a mainland coast or islands only, is known to God alone, but from the signs seen at various times I suspect it to be a mainland. The compass has one point north-westerly variation here; we saw a good deal of sea-weed floating about, and observed land-birds up to the 16th degree, both of these being signs of the proximity of the mainland. This land is a fit point to be made by ships coming here with the eastern monsoon, in order to get a fixed course for Java or Sunda Strait; for if you see this land in 21, 22 or 23 degrees, and shape your course north-north-west and north-by-west you will make the western extremity of Java. I write this as a matter of certainty, seeing that we have made the same on a fixed course.

Claeszoon clearly didn't know of the *Eendracht's* discovery, but he was certainly a navigator with his wits about him. Conscious of the difficulties of reckoning longitude on the Brouwer Route, he recognised that while this south land might prove a hazard for ships, it was also an excellent landfall from which to plot a course for Java. His report also provides an excellent insight into the signs that professional seamen of the time could use to determine when they were close to land. In Claeszoon's case, he'd only caught glimpses of it, but his opinion that he was coasting along a mainland was entirely correct.

The same year, the *Duyfken's* former skipper, the resilient Janszoon, unwittingly became the first European to sight Australia twice. As he wrote to the VOC while on board the Bantam-bound cargo vessel *Mauritius*:

> On the 31st July 1618 we discovered an island and landed on the same, where we found the marks of human footsteps; on the west side it extends

north-north-east and south-south-west; it measures 15 mijlen [90 kilometres] in length and its northern extremity is in 22° south latitude.

In fact, the island was the mainland near present-day North West Cape, an extensive peninsula that is easily mistaken for a large island.

Also in 1618, the VOC's managers expressed the hope of 'discovering the southern lands in passing'. They weren't to be disappointed. As the Brouwer Route grew in popularity, more ships came in contact with the vast land that was emerging to the south of Java. In 1619 it was the turn of the ships *Dordrecht* and *Amsterdam*, commanded by another practical Dutch seaman, Frederick de Houtman. While following the Brouwer Route his two vessels had only gone as far south as 36 degrees 30 minutes but they still managed to sail so far east that they found the South Land. When they were in 35 degrees 25 minutes south they'd altered their easterly course to north-east by north. After covering some 60 mijlen (360 kilometres), on the evening of 19 June they suddenly saw land.

Using only the positions and courses given, this works out to be just north of modern day Perth, a section of coast with enough offshore reefs to prevent the ships from safely approaching and investigating the prospects ashore. However, in a letter to Prince Maurice in Holland, Houtman maintained that: 'On the 19th we suddenly came upon the southland of Beach in 32°20'.' That puts him about 50 kilometres south of Perth near present-day Mandurah. From their landfall both ships were then able to head back out to sea. However, they were unaware that more trouble lay ahead. As Houtman wrote:

> On the 29th [June] deeming ourselves to be in an open sea, we shaped our course north-by-east. At noon we were in 29°32'S Lat; at night about three hours before daybreak, we again unexpectedly came upon a low-lying coast, a level broken country with reefs all around it. We saw no high land or mainland, so that this shoal is to be carefully avoided as very dangerous to ships that wish to touch at this coast. It is fully ten mijlen [60 kilometres] in length lying in 28°46'.

The shoal became known as the Houtman Abrolhos, *abrolhos* being a corruption of the Portuguese for *abri vossos olhos* (spiked obstructions). It also has a similarity with the Spanish expression *abre ojos* which means 'open your eyes'. Together, the term was commonly applied to low rocks for which you should keep a sharp lookout. The Houtman Abrolhos are actually a collection of sub-tropical coral reefs and low islands off the coast of Geraldton, where tourism and lobster fishing flourish today. Back in the early 1600s, though, they represented a major obstacle for the Brouwer Route. Houtman took them into account while proposing the use of the South Land as a navigation marker (in a manner similar to that of Claeszoon a year before).

> if you are near this Southland in 23, 24 or 25 degrees S Lat, and shape your course north by west, which deducting the variation [in the compass] is due north-north-west, you will strike the coast of Java [blank] mijlen [he may have meant to write 60 mijlen, 360 kilometres] 'eastward of its south-western extremity. Therefore, in order to have a fixed course from the Cape to Java, it is advisable to set sail from the Caep de Bonne Esperance [Cape of Good Hope] in June or July and to run on an eastern course in 36 and 37 degrees Southern Latitude, until you estimate yourself to have covered a thousand mijlen to eastward, after which you had better shape your course north and north by east, until you get into 26 or 27 degrees, thus shunning the shoal aforesaid which lies off the South-land in 28°46'. When you have reached the 26th or 27th degree, run eastward until you come in sight of the South-land, and then, as before mentioned, from there hold your course north by west and north-north-west, and you are sure to make the western extremity of Java.

However, Houtman's strategy still depended on an accurate reckoning of the thousand mijlen. Ships that overshot, then turned onto a course of 'north and north by east', could come unexpectedly upon land south of the Abrolhos, and unknowingly get themselves onto a collision course with their deadly reefs. However, once having got to a latitude north of the Abrolhos, Houtman was right in suggesting ships could then use the Western Australian coast as a reliable point from which to steer towards Java.

Meanwhile, what of the coast itself? All Houtman wrote of it was that:

> We are all assured that this is the land which the ship *Eendracht* discovered and made in the year [1616] and noways doubt that all the land they saw in 22, 23 and 25° and which we sighted down to 33° is one uninterrupted mainland coast.

That's a reference that encapsulates almost the entire west-facing section of the Western Australian coast – some 1300 kilometres of it – while giving no hint of ports, peoples, flora, fauna, geography or anything else. A similar length of coast, say from Amsterdam in Holland to Bilbao in Spain, would provide plenty of material for an official report. What kind of coast could warrant such sparse description? And what, for that matter, had happened to the South Land's fabled Isles of Gold?

Houtman did refer to the land he saw as Beach, one of the names given to the southern land mass by scholars from the time of Claudius Ptolemy in the first century. These academics felt sure that such a land mass was necessary to balance the land masses of the northern hemisphere. Beach was supposed to be a paradise, referred to on some charts as *provincia aurifera* (gold-bearing land). It had long been sought by fortune hunters and serious explorers alike and now, according to Houtman, it had emerged from the murk of centuries of speculation. Alas, it appears to have left the Dutch completely unmoved.

The Heren 17 continued to press the governors of the Indies to make voyages of exploration, but the reality on the far side of the world was a continuous lack of vessels and crews to carry those instructions out. The Dutch had originally been based at Bantam, on the north coast of Java, just east of the Sunda Strait. However, from 1610 onwards they'd started developing a new base at Jacatra (near present-day Jacarta), 80 kilometres to the east. In 1618, having built warehouses and a hospital within a walled compound, and a small shipyard just outside town, they decided to make the small town their main base.

The local ruler then gave the English permission to build their own warehouse. The Dutch had been allies with the English against the Spanish since before the Armada. As mentioned in Chapter 2, the English had also been shut out of Lisbon, and had formed the English East India Company (EEIC) in 1600. Both the EEIC and the VOC were the predecessors of modern multinational corporations, and were granted monopolies by their respective governments. Gradually they became a law unto themselves (even forming their own armed forces). Yet even in their infancy, long before they grew into two of the richest, most-powerful companies on earth, they'd find that this town wasn't big enough for both of them. The showdown wasn't long in coming.

Not long after the English built their warehouse the Dutch burned it to the ground. The English then blockaded the port with their ships, engaged the Dutch vessels for three hours, and eventually forced the ships and towns-folk to flee. The new Dutch governor general, the young but very capable 32-year-old Jan Pieterzoon Coen, assembled a counterattack with 2000 troops. They took Jacatra, burned every building to the ground and over-threw the local ruler who'd dared play the Dutch off against the English. Coen then founded a new town amid the ruins on 30 May 1619, and built the fortress of Batavia. The Javanese soon rightly nicknamed the place Diamond City.

Under the circumstances it was little wonder the Dutch could spare few resources for the exploration of desolate Australia. At the time, they were also establishing colonies in the Americas and were to establish the fortress of New Amsterdam on Manhattan Island in 1626. Back in Europe the English and Dutch politicians were busily negotiating an amicable arrangement between the two corporate rivals, even as the fracas on the far side of the world was at its worst. However, it took a year for word to reach the Indies, and even then the truce between the two sides was tenuous at best.

Friendlier relations certainly didn't extend to apprising the English of the Brouwer Route and the South Land, let alone providing maps that might assist them. Nevertheless, sailors will gossip, and the English soon had a sketchy idea of the course to follow. They still preferred the old passage through the northern Indian Ocean, however by the 1620s the EEIC had taken the remarkable position of leaving the question of which way to go to the skipper of the vessel making the voyage.

During the year 1622 the English and Dutch became aware of the growing hazards of taking the Brouwer Route to the South Land. Early in the year, two Dutch ships, the 23-year-old 400-tonne *Leeuwin* and 550-tonne *De Gouden Leeuw* were en route to Batavia from Texel in Holland when they became separated on the Brouwer Route. The *Leeuwin* overshot the required 1000 mijlen by so far that in March she ended up on the south-west facing coast of Western Australia. With the prevailing westerlies, it was a dangerous place for a ship with limited upwind sailing ability to find herself. If she failed to weather Cape Leeuwin, subsequently named after her, she'd be trapped on the southern coast of Australia.

As it turns out, there are no first-hand accounts of this voyage, but charts made by Hessel Gerritszoon around 1628 show that she sighted land from what is now known as Hamelin (20 kilometres north of Cape Leeuwin) to what is now called Point D'Entrecasteaux (90 kilometres south-east of the Cape). The charts also explain: 'Dunes with trees and underwood at top – Low land seemingly submerged (by the tide) – land made by the ship *Leeuwin* in March, 1622. – Low land with dunes.'

Jan Ernst Heeres in *The Part Borne by the Dutch in the Discovery of Australia* also notes: 'The ship *Leeuwin* had set sail from the Netherlands on April 20, 1621, and arrived at Batavia May 15, 1622, after a very long voyage, of which the Governor-General and Council did not fail to complain.'

However, it was only ten days later, 100 kilometres north-east of North West Cape, that an English ship, the *Trial*, only the second from that country to attempt the Brouwer Route, got into far more trouble. The *Trial's* skipper, John Brookes, later wrote to his masters at the EEIC:

The 25th day, at 11 o'clock at night, fair weather and smooth the ship struck. I ran to the poop and hove the lead and found but three fathoms [5.5 metres] of water. Sixty men being upon the deck, five of them would not believe that she struck. I cried to them to bear up and tack to the westwards. They did their best, but the rock being sharp the ship was presently full of water.

For the most part these rocks lie two fathoms under water, [so that] it struck my men in amazement when I said the ship struck and they could see neither breach, land, rocks, change of water nor sign of danger. The ship sitting a good while after [that], I hove the lead while I brought my sails a-backstays when she struck [again]. The wind began suddenly to freshen and blow. I struck round my sails and got out my skiff and bid [the crew] to sound about the ship. They found sharp sunken rocks a half a cable length astern. These rocks were steep too, so I made all the way I could to get out my long boat and by two o'clock I had gotten her out and hanged her in the tackles on the side.

Seeing the ship full of water and the wind to increase, [I] made all the means I could to save my life and as many of my company as I could. The boat put off at four in the morning and half an hour after the fore part of the ship fell in pieces! Ten men were saved in the skiff and 36 in the long boat.

From a crew of 139, only 46 escaped in the boats, leaving 93 to perish aboard the disintegrating *Trial* (the number of her crew being all that is known of her size). There was no hope of rescue in this, one of the most remote bodies of water of the time (and the present for that matter). However, there were islands nearby, to which the ship's boat and longboat voyaged to replenish their water supplies. Brookes wrote: 'These rocks and islands with their latitude, longitude, variations, courses and distances I have given two drafts to your worship's president [in the East Indies] which his worship intends to send you by the first conveyance.'

Brookes had struck what are now known as the Trial Rocks, in the Montebello group of islands, on the north-west coast of Western Australia. The *Trial* is the first European ship known to have been wrecked on the Australian coast. We know this now, but at the time Brookes reported that his position was far to the west of where it actually was.

Well before putting his ship on the bricks (as modern mariners often describe going aground, a comparison with abandoned cars being stranded on piles of bricks), Brookes had sighted an island. 'The 1st day of May I saw land being in the latitude of 22 degrees, which land had bene formlie seen by ye flemings … this islande is 18 leagues long and we were all verie joyfull at ye sight thereof'. The island was in fact North West Cape, which Houtman and Claeszoon mentioned as an ideal point from which to steer for Java on a north-west course. However, Brookes maintains that he'd steered from it on a north-east course, first on his ship and, after it had been wrecked, in its surviving boats. Despite this, he writes: 'I fell in with the eastern end of Java the 8th day of June 1622.'

How did he manage that? He explained by saying that 'this island lieth false in his longitude 200 leagues [1000 kilometres]'. By so doing Brookes placed North West Cape and Trial Rocks almost due south of Sunda Strait, right in the path of ships steering north on the final leg of the Brouwer Route. Yet the briefest glance at a modern map reveals that Brookes is completely wrong. Unfortunately, almost no-one seems to have known enough about the true position to argue with him at the time.

One person who did argue with Brookes was his own shipping agent. According to a forthright letter dated 22 August 1622, thought to be written by the *Trial's* supercargo, Thomas Bright:

> I am not one that possesses a mariner's art or any skill therein worth noting yet this much I understand, by relation of journals and plans, that these islands [the Trials] were never discovered by any. [Brookes] would excuse [the loss] to say he followed directly Captain Humphrey Fitzherbert's

journal [the first English captain to follow the Brouwer Route]. Had our journals been compared with his, he should have found Brookes 400 leagues [2000 kilometres] in the latitudes 38 degrees to 34 degrees more to the eastward than he or ever ship was again. We always feared the ship to be beyond [Brookes'] reckoning …

So Brookes must have realised that he was so far out in his navigation that he lied to avoid being blamed for the loss of the ship. He simply moved a large chunk of the Australian coastline 1000 kilometres west to explain how he'd hit it, while following the route taken by Fitzherbert's ships (the *Royal Exchange, Unity* and *Bear*) in 1620.

According to Bright, that wasn't Brookes' only crime:

[Brookes'] crew and fellow and consorts providing provisions and saving his things, bearing Mr Jackson and myself with fair words, promising us faithfully to take us along, but like a Judas, [while I was] turning my back into [the] great cabin [Brookes] lowered himself privately into the skiff only with nine men and his boy. [He] stood for the Straits of Sunda that instant, without care and seeing the lamentable end of ship, the time she split or respect of any man's life …

It did seem strange to me that Brookes so cunningly excused the neglect of the company's letters, spangles and moneys. The moneys he confessed to the president and Mr Brokendon [a company official] to have transferred of me. [Yet] he for nigh two hours [did] nothing but convey from his cabin to his skiff to my knowledge both letters, moneys and spangles in his trunk, whereof many of these things, apparel, and other trifles he has by him now this present … the Black Box, wherein the company's letters were seen, left the ship also and [by] his own confession. Letters I conveyed into the skiff, some for the President, some for Mr Brokendon and others, were heaved overboard. His excuse was they were wet and yet not so wet but he perused the contents thereof, which he well knew would have done him no good if he had honestly delivered them.

Brookes in the skiff and the whistle-blower Bright in the longboat both eventually reached Batavia, a 2000 kilometre voyage across open ocean. There, despite Bright's damning letter, Brookes' story appears to have been believed by both the English and Dutch authorities. However, it's worth speculating that the Dutch, with their more complete knowledge of the Brouwer Route, may have smelled a rat. Coen, governor general in the Indies wrote to the VOC on 6 September 1622:

On the 5th of July there arrived here a skiff with ten men forming part of the crew of an English ship, named the *Trial*, and on the 8th her boat with 36 men. They state they have lost and abandoned their ship with 97 [sic] men and the cargo she had taken in, on certain rocks situated in latitude 20 degrees 10 minutes south, in the longitude of the western end of Java. These rocks are near a number of broken islands, lying very wide and broad ... lying 30 mijlen [180 kilometres] north-north-east of a certain island which in our charts is laid down in 22 degrees south latitude ...

Within this note lies a contradiction. The Dutch knew the 'island' in 22 degrees south latitude was well to the east of the longitude of the Sunda Strait: about 1000 kilometres east. The Trial Rocks are supposedly only 180 kilometres north-north-east of the island. Yet Coen places them due south of the Strait; well to the west. Such garbled and conflicting reports must have been so commonplace that they made it easier for Brookes to escape censure. Pity the poor cartographers back in the Netherlands and England trying to make sense of it all. The VOC cartographer Hessel Gerritszoon appears to have done some selective editing. In his maps dating from 1627 onwards he leaves the 'island' (North West Cape) on the coast of the emerging South Land, and positions the Trial Rocks far from it, close to the longitude of the Sunda Strait.

In England, meanwhile, the cartographer Sir Robert Dudley appears to have had the benefit both of Brookes' chart of the Trial Rocks and nearby islands (since lost) and an ignorance of the true state of affairs when he prepared his sea atlas, the *Arcano Del Mare* of 1646. He places the rocks and the 'island' of North West Cape south of Sunda Strait, just below 20 degrees south latitude. The shape of the Cape is so well plotted that it's instantly recognisable, except for the fact that it's wildly out of position.

Confusion about Trial Rocks was to reign for the next 200 years, and the true fate of the ship wouldn't be illuminated for more than 350 years. The twist was that the phantom Trial Rocks managed to contribute to the further European discovery of Australia by forcing ships to steer towards it in order to avoid their false position.

Those of a suspicious nature might conclude that the Dutch probably saw through Brookes' story, but could think of no reason to disabuse their rivals, the English, of this erroneous belief. They did, however, warn their own commanders, and set out to clarify such important cartographic matters for themselves. Coen wrote to his masters back in Europe:

> Whereas it is necessary that ships, in order to hasten their arrival, should run on an eastward course for about 1000 mijlen [6000 kilometres] from the Cape between 40 and 30 degrees southern latitude, it is equally necessary that great caution should be used and the best measures taken in order to avoid such accidents as befell the English ship *Trial*. They say that they met with this accident through following the course of our ships; that they intend to dissuade their countrymen from imitating their example, and that their masters are sure to take other measures accordingly. For the further discovery of the lands aforeseaid we intend, in conformity with your orders, to send a ship thither as soon as practicable, for which purpose we have selected the yacht *Hazewint*.

By 29 September 1622, Coen had issued instructions for the *Hasewint's* voyage, and added the yacht *Haringh* to the expedition. The instructions demonstrate why Coen was regarded as a meticulous instrument of his company's interests. The following extract published in Heeres' *The Part Borne by the Dutch in the Discovery of Australia*, while lengthy, nevertheless provides ample insight into the man's mind:

> Inasmuch as Our Masters earnestly enjoin us to dispatch hence certain yachts for the purpose of making discovery of the South-land; and since moreover experience has taught, by great perils incurred by sundry of our ships – but especially by the late miscarrying of the English ship *Triall* on the said coast – the urgent necessity of obtaining a full and accurate knowledge of the true bearing and conformation of the said land, that further accidents may henceforth be prevented as much as possible; besides this, seeing that it is highly desirable that an investigation should be made to ascertain whether the regions or any part of the same are inhabited, and whether any trade might with them be established ...
>
> The main object for which you are dispatched on this occasion, is, that from 45 or 50 degrees, of from the farthest point to which the land shall be found to extend southward within these latitudes, up to the northernmost extremity of the South-land, you will have to discover and survey all capes, forelands, bights, lands, islands, rocks, reefs, sandbanks, depths, shallows, roads, winds, currents and all that appertains to the same, so as to be able to map out and duly mark everything in its true latitude,

longitude, bearings and confirmation. You will moreover go ashore in various places and diligently examine the coast in order to ascertain whether or no it is inhabited, the nature of the land and the people, their towns and inhabited villages, the divisions of their kingdoms, their religion and policy, their wars, their rivers, the shape of their vessels, their fisheries, commodities and manufactures, but specially to inform your-selves what minerals, such as gold, silver, tin, iron, lead, and copper, what precious stones, pearls, vegetables, animals and fruits, these lands yield and produce ...

To all the places which you will touch at, you will give appropriate names such as in each instance the case shall seem to require, choosing for the same either the names of the united Provinces or of the towns situated therein, or any other appellations that you may deem fitting and worthy. Of all which places, lands and islands, the commander and officers of these yachts ... will, by solemn declaration signed by the ships' councils, take formal possession, and in sign thereof, besides, erect a stone column in such places as shall be taken possession of; the said column recording in bold, legible characters the year, the month, the day of the week and the date, the persons by whom and the hour of the day when such possession has been taken on behalf of the States-General above mentioned. You will likewise endeavour to enter into friendly relations and make covenants with all such kings and nations as you shall happen to fall in with, and try to prevail upon them to place themselves under the protection of the States of the United Netherlands, of which covenants and alliances you will likewise cause proper documents to be drawn up and signed ...

In virtue of the oath of allegiance which each of you generally and personally has sworn to the Lords States-General, to His Princely Highness and the Lords Managers, none of you shall be allowed to retain for his private use or to abstract any written documents, journals, draw-ings or observations touching this present expedition, but every one of you shall be bound on his return hither faithfully to deliver up the same without exception ...

For the purpose of making a trial we have given order for various articles to be put on board your ships, such as ironmongery, cloths, coast-stuffs [trade items from India] and linens; which you will show and try to dispose of to such natives as you may meet with, always diligently noting what arti-cles are found to be most in demand, what quantities might be disposed of, and what might be obtained in exchange for them; we furthermore hand you samples of gold, silver, copper, tin, iron, lead and pearls, that you may inquire whether these articles are known to the natives, and might be obtained there in any considerable quantity.

In landing anywhere you will use extreme caution, and never go ashore or into the interior unless well-armed, trusting no one, however innocent the natives may be in appearance, and with whatever kindness they may seem to receive you, being always ready to stand on the defensive, in order to prevent sudden traitorous surprises, the like of which, sad to say, have but too often been met with in similar cases. And if any natives should come near your ships, you will likewise take due care that they suffer no molestation from our men.

When you get near the northern extremity and the east coast of the South-land, you will diligently inquire whether it yields anywhere sandal-wood, nutmegs, cloves or other spices; likewise whether it has any good harbours and fertile tracts, where it would be possible to establish settlements, which might be expected to yield satisfactory returns; in a word, you will suffer nothing to escape your notice, but carefully scrutinise whatever you find, and give us a full and proper report on your return ...

In places where you meet with natives, you will either by adroit management or by other means endeavour to get hold of a number of full-grown persons, or better still, of boys and girls, to the end that the latter may be brought up here and be turned to useful purpose in the said quarters when occasion shall serve.

In short he wanted his ships to conduct a maritime survey, trade mission, diplomatic mission, military assessment, territorial expansion and grab a few slaves for good measure. He certainly wanted value for his expeditionary guilder (the extract above covers only his main requirements). Significantly, considerations like scientific research, perhaps a request to collect or describe previously unseen flora and fauna, weren't even considered worthy of mention.

Coen's instructions became the model for numerous subsequent missions. As it turned out, the yachts *Haringh* and *Hasewint* got little further than the Sunda Strait before meeting with an inbound vessel, the *Mauritius*, and were diverted to assist in the search for a missing ship, the *Rotterdam*.

Meanwhile, the thrills and spills on the coast of Western Australia continued. In his letter regarding the loss of the *Trial*, Coen also reported that:

The ship *'t Wapen Van Hoorn* [arrived at Batavia on 22 July 1622] has also been in extreme peril; at night in a hard wind she got so near the land of d'Eendracht or the South-land of Java that she was in six fathom [10 metres] before they saw land, which they could noways put off from, so that they ran on it. But shortly after the storm abating, they got the landwind, and came off safe, for which the Lord be praised.

In 1623 the Dutch ship *Leijden*, Claes Hermanszoon master, touched at the coast south of Dirk Hartog Island and while ashore Australia's first European baby was born. The child, a boy, was named Seebaer Van Nieuwellandt, meaning Seabirth of Newland. Unfortunately, few details of that visit have survived. In 1624 the ship *Tortelduyf* came within sight of an island at the southern extremity of Houtman Abrolhos, naming it Tortelduyf Island. Two years later the *Leijden* (under a different skipper, Daniel Cock) again came within sight of the South Land, again south of Dirk Hartog Island, but this time didn't go ashore.

Within a year of the *Trial* being lost, an expedition to explore the South Land was finally sent out, but the two yachts (both about the size of the *Duyfken*), the *Pera* and the *Aernem* (or *Arnhem*), never got near the Trials. Instead the ships headed south-east from Batavia towards Cape York. Much of the detail of this voyage has survived in the form of the *Pera's* journal (kept by her master Jan Carstenszoon), charts from the voyage and reports from the governors in the East Indies.

Despite Coen's instructions to take care in their encounters with any natives they should meet, on 11 February 1623, disaster struck while the ships were coasting New Guinea. As Carstenszoon wrote:

This same day the skipper of the yacht *Aernem*, Dirck [Meliszoon] without knowledge of myself, of the supercargo or steersman of the said yacht, unadvisedly went ashore to the open beach in the pinnace, taking with him 15 persons both officers and common soldiers, and no more than 4 muskets, for the purpose of fishing with a seine-net; there was a great disorder in landing, the men running off in different directions, until at last a number of black savages came running forth from the wood, who first seized and tore to pieces an assistant, named Jan Willemsz Van Den Briel who happened to be unarmed, after which they slew with arrows, calloways [spears] and with the oars which they had snatched from the pinnace, no less than nine of our men, who were unable to defend themselves, at the same time wounding the remaining seven (among them the skipper, who was the first to take to his heels); these last seven men at last returned on board in a very sorry plight with the pinnace and one oar, the skipper loudly lamenting his great want of prudence, and entreating pardon for the fault he had committed.

Skipper Meliszoon had much to lament, for he died of his wounds within four days. Despite the massacre the voyage continued to the coast of Cape York, where the two tiny vessels turned south. They travelled down the coast beyond Cape Keerweer as far as 17 degrees 8 minutes south by their estimation, but closer to 16 degrees 20 minutes. There Carstenszoon wrote on 25 April:

> In the afternoon I went up a salt river … Since by resolution it has been determined to begin the return voyage at this point, we have, in default of stone caused a wooden tablet to be nailed to a tree, the said tablet having the following words carved into it: 'AD 1623, on the 24th April there arrived here two yachts dispatched by their High Mightinesses the States General'. We have accordingly named the river aforeseaid Staten revier in the new chart.

The location is still known as the Staaten River. From there the ships turned to the north. However, the *Aernem* proved unseaworthy, and not long after parted company with the *Pera*, trying to head directly back to the Indies. Along the way it was to encounter and chart part of what is now known as Arnhem Land.

Meanwhile, the *Pera* continued north. On 13 May the ship approached the mouth of the Jardine River. Less than 20 kilometres away was Prince of Wales Island, sighted by both Janszoon and Luis Vaéz de Torres 17 years earlier. The *Pera*, as the *Duyfken* may have been in 1606, was in the western end of the Endeavour Strait, trying to make its way towards Cape York, 40 kilometres to the north-east. However, Carstenszoon's journal perfectly illustrates the problems the Dutch met when approaching the Strait from the west:

> On the 14th we made sail again before daybreak, with a SE wind and steady weather; from the 9th of this month up to now we have found the land of Nova Guinea to extend N and S. I went ashore here myself with the skipper and 10 musketeers and found a large number of footprints of men and dogs going south; we also came upon a very fine fresh-water river, flowing into

the sea whence fresh water can easily be obtained by means of boats or pinnaces; the river is in 10°50′ and is marked Waterplaets in the chart [possibly Cowal Creek, a short distance east of the Jardine]. The land here is high, hilly, and reefy near the sandy beach; seeing that nothing profitable could be affected here, we returned to the yacht, which was lying by under small sail; towards the evening we were at about 1 mile's distance [six kilometres] from three islets, of which the southernmost was the largest; five miles [30 kilometres] by estimation farther to northward we saw a mountainous country, but the shallows rendered (or render) it impossible for us to get near it; in almost every direction in which our soundings were taken, we found very shallow water, so that we sailed for a very long time in 5, 4, 3, 2½, 1½ fathom and even less, so that at last we were forced to drop anchor in 1½ fathom, without knowing where to look for greater or less depths; after sunset we therefore sent out the pinnace to take soundings, which found deeper water a long way SW of the pinnace, viz 2, 3 and 4½ fathom; we were very glad to sail thither with the yacht, and cast anchor in 8½ fathom, fervently thanking God Almighty for his inexpressible mercy and clemency, shown us in this emergency as in all others.

In the morning of the 15th, the wind being SE with good weather, we set sail on a W course, which took us into shallower water of 2, 2½ and 3 fathom; we therefore went over to SW, when we came into 3½, 4, 5, 6 fathom and upwards; we had lost sight of the land here, and found it impossible to touch at it or follow it any longer, owing to the shallows, reefs, sandbanks and also to the E winds blowing here …

As mentioned in Chapter 2, there was a suspicion among the Dutch that a strait existed between Cape York and New Guinea (the *Duyfken's* Janszoon had left a void between the two on his map), but once again they'd been frustrated in their attempts to find it. Here, as with the *Duyfken*, Carstenszoon's chart left blank the region of Cape York they'd been so close to but hadn't reached. From there, the *Pera* once again turned back to the Indies where, like the *Arnhem*, their voyage was regarded as having achieved little. Nevertheless, Carstenszoon's notes on his discoveries provide one of the earliest detailed European observations of Australia. They were far from encouraging. As he wrote:

The land between 13° and 17°8′ is a barren and arid tract, without any fruit-trees, and producing nothing fit for the use of man; it is low-lying and flat without hills or mountains; in many places overgrown with brushwood and stunted wild trees; it has not much fresh water, and what little there is, has to be collected in pits dug for the purpose; there is an utter absence of bays and inlets, with the exception of a few bights not sheltered from the sea-wind; it extends mainly N by E and S by W, with shallows all along the coast, with a clayey and sandy bottom; it has numerous salt rivers extending into the interior, across which the natives drag their wives and children by means of dry sticks or boughs of trees. The natives are in general utter barbarians, all resembling each other in shape and features, coal-black, and with twisted nets wound round their heads and necks for keeping their food in; so far as we could make out, they chiefly live on certain ill-smelling roots which they dig out of the earth. We infer that during the eastern monsoon they live mainly on the beach, since we have there seen numerous small huts made of dry grass; we also saw great numbers of dogs, herons and curlews, and other wild fowl, together with plenty of excellent fish, easily caught with a seine-net; they are utterly unacquainted with gold, silver, tin, iron, lead and copper, nor do they know anything about nutmegs, cloves and pepper ...

There's a sense that the Dutch were quite shocked by the condition of the Aboriginal people they encountered, which they took to be a strong indication of the quality of the country that sustained them. Life might be hard on the land back in Europe, but it was a picnic compared to this.

Dutch disappointment at the lack of trade opportunities in such a large landmass may be better understood in the context of their activities in the Spice Islands to the north, notably Banda and Ambon. In the Banda Islands they'd established a monopoly in nutmeg and mace, with the local population contracted by the VOC to sell to them exclusively. However, the English went there and managed to buy spices as well. When Governor General Coen learned of the English incursion into his domain he followed the creed: 'Despair not, spare not your enemies, for God is with us.' Unlike the South Land, this was a place worth fighting for. Coen attacked Banda Island with a powerful Dutch force and slaughtered most of the island's inhabitants.

What is now known as the Amboyna Massacre followed in 1623. Although Coen had returned to the Netherlands in February, the new governor general, Pieter de Carpentier continued his policy. Suspicious that the English might be about to attack their fort on Ambon Island, in the Moluccas, the Dutch rounded up the dozen or so English on the island and tortured them. Some accounts suggest they burned their victims' feet, others that they used gunpowder to blow their arms and legs off. In any event, those who survived the torture were executed. The English government was so outraged that it threatened to seize Dutch ships passing through the English Channel. They were eventually compensated (John Milton, author of *Paradise Lost*, outlined the compensation terms in 1650) but in the meantime, the English managed to prevent the Dutch from reappointing the ruthless Coen as governor general. For the record, Carpentier was eventually immortalised in Australia's geography: the Gulf of Carpentaria is named after him.

The Dutch may well have been disappointed by the northern shores of the South Land, but nothing could have prepared them for what they found on its southern coast. It's unfortunate that little detail of the 1626–1627 voyage of *'t Gulden Zeepaart* (*Golden Seahorse*) has survived as it was the first to map 1500 kilometres of Australian coastline, the most substantial coastal voyage to that date. The report on the spectacular though forbidding coastline they found, had it survived, would have made fascinating reading.

From the *Daily Register* of Batavia, it is known that:

> On the 10th [April 1627] there arrived here from the Netherlands the ship *'t Gulden Seepaart* fitted out by the Zealand chamber, having on board the Honourable Pieter Nuyts, extraordinary Councillor of India, having sailed from there on the 22 of May, 1626.

From the charts of Hessel Gerritszoon, notes explain 'This chart has 't land van Pieter Nuijts (discovered Jan 26, 1627).' A reference in the sailing instructions for an exploration by Gerrit Thomaszoon Pool in 1636 suggested that if he got down the east coast of the South Land as far as 32 degrees, he should head west to the eastern extremity 'which in January 1627 was discovered by the ship *'t Zeepaart*'. There was further reference in the instructions given to Abel Janszoon Tasman before his voyage of 1644: 'In the year 1627, the south coast of the Great South Land was accidentally discovered by the ship the *Gulde Zeepard*, outward bound from the Fatherland, for the space of 250 mijlen [1600 kilometres].'

The section of coast shown on the Dutch charts as Nuytsland extends from Cape Leeuwin on the south-western corner of the South Land to the Nuyts Archipelago in what is now South Australia, including the islands of

A modern replica of the yacht Duyfken, *Willem Janszoon master, based on contemporary illustrations of the vessel.* Duyfken 1606 Replica Foundation

't Hooghe Eylandt

noEnt

leyh landt

R. met het Bosch.

Vliege Bay

Wws

ds de Cóst

Gibbel de Ree

R. vis

C. bo Kéérwar,

NOVA GVINEA.

The western side of Cape York from Endeavour Strait to Cape Keerweer, mapped by Willem Janszoon in 1606, reproduced circa 1670. Government Printing Office Collection, State Library of New South Wales *The accuracy can clearly be seen when compared with this modern satellite view of Cape York.* Commonwealth of Australia, Geosciences Australia, ACRES © 2005

Trial

G. F. de Wits landt,
onder A.º 1628.

Willems Revier

't Land van d' Eend.
onder A.º 1616.

Dirck Hartogs Ree

Houtmans Abrolhos

Tortelduyf

I. d' Edels landt,
beseylt A.º 1619.

't Land van de Leeuwin.
A.º 1622. aengedaen

't Landt van P.

Detail from the Dutch cartographer Hessel Gerritszoon's map of the Malay Archipelago in 1618, but showing discoveries on Australia's coasts to 1627 (excepting that of the Duyfken on Cape York), and probably published in 1632. The map includes Trial Rocks, due south of the Sunda Strait.
Mitchell Library, State Library of New South Wales

Tropicus Capricorni

...gedaen met 't Gulden Zeepaerdt van Middelburgh ...uary A°. 1627.

I. S. Francois

I. S. Pieter

18
19
20
21
22
23
24
25
26
27
28
29
30
31
32
33
34
35

The above mosaic in the foyer of the
Mitchell Library in Sydney is a
reproduction of the original chart of
1644, by Abel Janszoon Tasman,
showing the considerable extent of
Dutch discoveries to that time.
State Library of New South Wales.

The treeless islands of the Houtman Abrolhos, off the coast of Western Australia, have changed little since the loss of the Dutch ship Batavia *in 1629. The islands are now home to a lucrative crayfish industry.* Michelle Havenstein

Mount Dromedary, on the far south coast of New South Wales, was named by James Cook. The east coast was markedly more verdant than most of the Australian coastline encountered by previous explorers. Michelle Havenstein

After the atrocities at Batavia's Graveyard, in Houtmans Abrolhos, it was also the scene of Australia's first European trial, with nearby Seal's Island the place where some sentences were carried out. From a facsimile of the 1647 Amsterdam edition *Ongeluckige Voyagie*, published by the Australian National Maritime Museum and Hordern House, Sydney, 1994

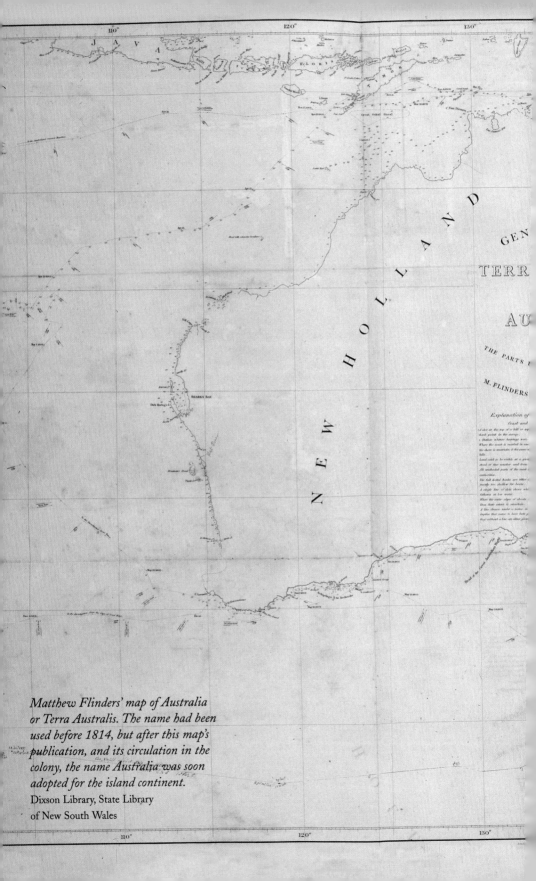

Matthew Flinders' map of Australia or Terra Australis. The name had been used before 1814, but after this map's publication, and its circulation in the colony, the name Australia was soon adopted for the island continent.

Dixson Library, State Library of New South Wales

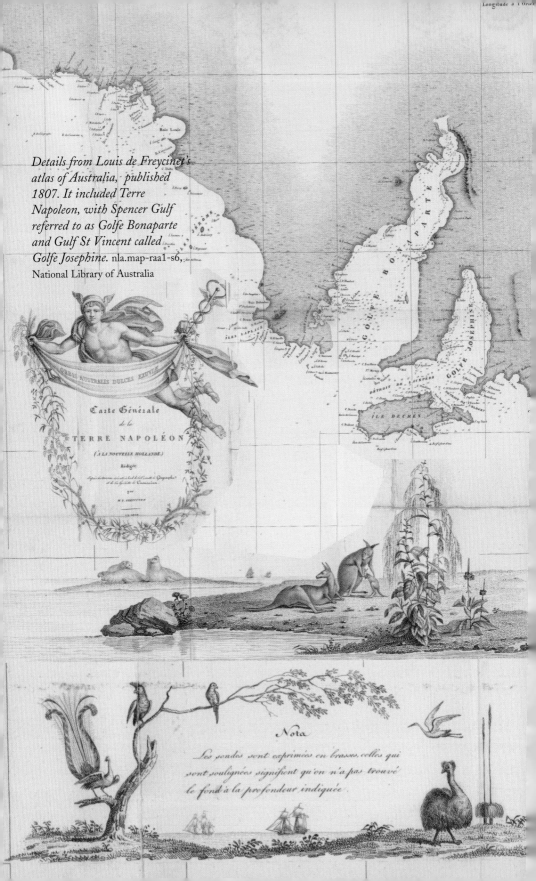

Details from Louis de Freycinet's atlas of Australia, published 1807. It included Terre Napoleon, with Spencer Gulf referred to as Golfe Bonaparte and Gulf St Vincent called Golfe Josephine. nla.map-raa1-s6, National Library of Australia

St Francis and St Pieter. Here, in one vast swoop, an enormous piece in the emerging picture of Australia is suddenly revealed.

Scant information about the voyage has survived. For example, throughout *'t Gulden Zeepaart's* voyage she set an extremely brisk pace. Leaving the Netherlands in late May 1626, she reached Batavia via the Brouwer Route just under 11 months later, despite making a detour that added 3000 kilometres to her trip. She was lucky to have returned at all. Whatever winds drove her beyond the point where she could turn north for Batavia, then pushed her clear cross the Great Australian Bight, must have relented long enough for her to escape back to the west.

The distance the ship sailed to the east suggests that her skipper, Francois Thijssen, may have hoped to reach the eastern extremity of the South Land, then turn north. That or the westerlies gave him little choice in the matter. In either case, he and his crew must have been more than just disappointed by what they saw. They must have been awed. For the Great Australian Bight has one of the longest unbroken lines of sea cliffs on the planet. They extend for nearly 700 kilometres. Day after day the ship must have sailed past ramparts of stone that were 60–100 metres high and extended from horizon to horizon. Even worse, the tops of the cliffs presented no distinguishing features. Where the cliffs marked the abrupt end of the Nullarbor Plain, not even a tree varied its flatness, and across the breadth of the Bight not one river emptied into it.

For the Dutch mariners, such a continuously unapproachable and daunting coast must have transcended their worst nightmares. It's only at the head of the Bight that the cliffs finally relent. Unfortunately, that's where the coastline no longer curves north-east or east. It starts trending to the south-east; both directions away from the desired course to Batavia. Hopes of finding a break in the south land must have been dashed as they finally found some shelter among the islands around present-day Ceduna. They knew they'd have to try to turn back. For all they were aware (and the Dieppe map may have been the basis of their knowledge), the South Land could extend in a continuous coast all the way to the South Pole.

As far as the return journey is concerned, it could only have been harrowing in the extreme. At all times of the year, the Bight is subjected to rough conditions, and much of it is constantly swept by the huge swells rolling in from the south-west. Added to this is a current that flows along the coast to the east. The small ship *'t Gulden Zeepaart* was lucky that she arrived in the Bight during summer, because the conditions in winter are much worse. And further south of the coast, there's a counter current that flows to the west. In summer it's just possible to get an easterly breeze. The combination of wind and current may have helped the ship recross the Bight and finally weather Cape Leeuwin.

There may be little in the records, but *'t Gulden Zeepaart's* discovery must have given the mariners plenty of talk about. However, it says a great deal about the objectives of exploration – finding ports, trading posts, water supplies and useful sea routes – that no Dutch ship ever voyaged there again, accidentally or deliberately. The *Gulden Zeepaart's* voyage didn't even leave any hope of finding something of worth inland; there was no place to go ashore, unless you were more mountaineer than mariner. The best you could expect on the southern coast of the South Land was shipwreck.

Despite this, the significance of what Nuyts and Thijssen found should not be overlooked. The voyage had revealed to European eyes much of the southern extent of the South Land. After their voyage, the outline of the island continent that's so familiar to modern Australian eyes became even more recognisable. By 1627, only 21 years after the Dutch had first set eyes on it, they were in a position to map large sections of coast from Cape York across to Western Australia and down to South Australia.

The Dutch may have sought to keep the details of their discoveries hidden from friend and foe alike, but for their eyes at least the continent of Australia was rapidly emerging from obscurity. There are some things, however, that can't be kept quiet, and it wasn't long before yet another mishap on the Brouwer Route would tear the veil of secrecy to shreds.

4

DESERT
ISLAND

GOVERNOR GENERAL COEN IN PERIL •
AVOIDING THE SOUTH LAND • THE WRECK
OF THE *BATAVIA* • COMMODORE PELSAERT
ON THE AUSTRALIAN COAST • COEN
BESIEGED • PELSAERT TO THE *BATAVIA'S*
RESCUE • MUTINEERS AND MURDERERS
• THE FAUNA OF THE ABROLHOS •
THE DEATH OF COEN •

The voyage of *'t Gulden Zeepaart* may have underlined the importance of turning north at the right point on the Brouwer Route, but it soon got further emphasis from an unlikely source. In 1627 Jan Pieterzoon Coen returned to Batavia with the ships *Galias*, *Utrecht* and *Texel*. The VOC's Heren 17 may have sensed that, protestations aside, the English position had been greatly weakened in the Spice Islands after the Amboyna Massacre. Who better to press home the advantage than Coen? In any case, he was reappointed as governor general of the Indies, although he travelled from the Netherlands under a false name.

First, he had to get there. 'In the afternoon of the 5th of September [1627] in 28½° south latitude came upon the land of d'Eendracht,' he wrote to the VOC on October 30.

We were at less than half a mile's distance from the breakers before perceiving the same, without being able to see land. If we had come upon

this place in the night time, we should have been in a thousand perils with our ship and crew.

Coen explained his ship's overshooting the Brouwer Route in the following terms:

Between Cabo de Bon Esperanca to the Southland in 35° lat gives an over-plus of more than 270 miles [1600 kilometres] of sea, a matter to which most steersmen pay little attention, and which has brought, and is still bringing, many vessels into great perils. It would be highly expedient if in the plane charts most in use, between Cabo de Bon Esperanca and the South-land of Java, so much space were added and passed over in drawing up the reckonings, as is deducible from the correct longitude according to the globosity of earth and sea.

For good measure, he added that in his chart: 'The South-land lies fully 40 miles [240 kilometres] more to eastward than it should be, which should also be rectified.'

Even as Coen was writing to the VOC, they were rewriting their sailing instructions for the Brouwer Route (the English, recognising Coen when he got to Batavia, were prudently evacuating their base to Bantam). The VOC's 1627 instructions tried to address the problems associated with taking such a long open-ocean voyage. They also took note of the supposed position of Trial Rocks.

> The Cape of Good Hope being doubled, it is thought good that you sail in the E direction between 36° and 39° S lat, until you have reached a point eight hundred *mijlen* [4800 kilometres] E of the Cape of Good Hope; that you then direct your course as much N as E, in such a manner that, on reaching 30° S lat, you should find yourself about 950 or 1000 m [5700 or 6000 kilometres] from the Cape of Good Hope.

> These 950 or 1000 m from the Cape being attained, it is advisable – wind and weather permitting – that you bear down upon the land Eendraght at 27° S lat, or more to the N, so as to take thence such a course as will enable you to clear the Tryals Shoals, lying about 20° S lat, without danger, and to touch at the south coast of Java with ease, in order to have the weather gauge of the Straits of Sunda, and thus reach these straits without loss of time.

> It must be understood that this is about the time when the east monsoon blows south of the line, and that the said 900 or 1000 miles E of the Cape may be reached between the beginning of March and the end of September. Observe that the distance between the Cape and the land of Eendracht is, in reality, much shorter than the chart shows; and it may happen, by the aid of currents, that the route may be found to be even shorter than it really is, so that the land might be reached in much less time than we are led to expect. Remember, also, that the land of Eendracht has, south of 27° lat, many perilous sandbanks, and that the soundings are of sharp rocks.

> Consequently extreme caution, and the constant use of the lead at night and in stormy weather, is indispensably necessary, as at seven, six, or five miles from the coast the soundings are found to be one hundred, eighty, or seventy fathoms.

Many skippers must have pondered their employer's competence after reading a line like 'the route may be found to be even shorter than it really is'. As for the Brouwer Route, it had rapidly evolved from a simple 'head east for 1000 mijlen, then turn left' to a set of instructions that warned about the deficiencies of the charts, estimating the distance travelled, the shoals of the Houtman Abrolhos and Trial Rocks.

Understandably, encounters with the South Land continued. In 1627, *'t Wapen Van Hoorn* again came upon the South Land, her skipper taking the opportunity to revise the map of the coast south of Dirk Hartog Island. In 1628 the Dutch ship *Vianen*, Gerrit Frederikszoon de Witt master, sailing from India, also ended up on the coast of the South Land. A letter from Coen to the VOC dated 3 November 1628 (written while he was besieged by 10 000 troops led by the sultan he'd displaced from Jacatra), explained:

> She was by headwinds so far driven to the south-ward that she came upon the South-land beyond Java where she ran aground, so that she was forced to throw overboard 8 or 10 lasts [a unit of measurement of commodities either by weight or volume, but approximately 2 tonnes] of pepper and a quantity of copper, upon which through God's mercy she got off again without further damage.

According to the instructions given to Abel Janszoon Tasman for his voyage of 1644, *Vianen* was 'in the latitude of 21° S ... when they coasted about 50 mijlen [300 kilometres] without gaining any particular knowledge of this great country, only observing a foul and barren shore, green fields, and very wild, black, barbarous inhabitants'. Had they carefully mapped the coast they passed, the mariners might have noticed that part of it bore a striking similarity to the group of islands supposed to comprise Trial Rocks.

Soon, the fate of the *Trial* was to become the least of the VOC's problems. The Dutch had had plenty of close calls off the coast of Western Australia, and despite their best efforts, good luck rather than skillful management saved them from a similar fate. Sooner or later, surely that luck would run out.

Coen had realised the danger of coming upon the South Land's shoals at night. The sailing instructions of 1627 warned that 'extreme caution, and the constant use of the lead at night and in stormy weather, is indispensably necessary'. However, in the darkness of the early hours of 4 June 1629, with a clear, moonlit sky, most of the Dutch ship *Batavia's* 315 passengers and crew were sleeping peacefully, although Francisco Pelsaert, commodore of the fleet from which *Batavia* had been separated in a storm, was fighting a severe fever. On deck, Ariaen Jacobszoon, the skipper of the 300-tonne ship, called to his lookout, 'What's that white ahead?'

The lookout was stationed in the bows, rather than at the masthead. This was, after all, a merchant vessel sailing an established shipping route, not an exploratory voyage with uncharted shoals and jagged rocks to be expected at any moment. There was no need to post a man in such a precarious position, unless you meant to punish him.

'It's the moon shining on the water,' came the reply.

Jacobszoon estimated his position to be 28 degrees south latitude, but still 1000 kilometres west of the South Land. His course was north-east-by-north, he was under full sail before a south-westerly breeze. This course would carry him safely to the north of Houtman Abrolhos which lay due east, but far away by his calculations.

Under full sail, her speed unchecked, the *Batavia* plunged through the dark waters of the Indian Ocean. Then, without warning, she gave a jolt. Her crew felt the ship 'shaking terribly, the rudder touching ground and the keel running against the cliffs'.

Down below, Pelsaert was flung from his bed. Despite being ill, he ran up on deck and saw *Batavia*, as he relates in his journal, 'right in the middle of a thick spray. Round the ship there was only a little surf, but shortly after that heard the sea breaking hard round about.'

'Skipper, what have you done that through your reckless carelessness you have run this noose round our necks?' Pelsaert's question was as good as an accusation to Jacobszoon.

'How could I do better? I did not sleep, but watched out very well, for when I saw the spray in the Distance I asked Hans the gunner, What can that be? Whereupon he said, Skipper, it is the shine of the Moon; upon which I trusted.'

The buck having passed rapidly from commodore to skipper to lowly gunner, the two commanders then considered their position. 'What counsel now?' Pelsaert asked. 'Whereabout do you think we are?'

'God knows,' Jacobszoon replied. 'This is a shallow that must be lying quite a distance from the unknown Land, and I think we are just on the tail of it. We must see now to putting out an anchor astern; perhaps it is low tide, so that it will be possible to wind [the ship] from it.'

It was wishful thinking on two counts. First, sounding with the lead (which might have averted disaster if it had been used earlier) soon revealed that they'd gone aground near the top of the tide. With the tide now falling the ship settled more heavily on the jutting reef. The wind picked up and a rain squall swept in, battering violent breakers against the exposed vessel. Second, daylight revealed some of the islands of the Houtman Abrolhos rising from the sea. Jacobszoon was much closer to the South Land than he had thought.

In an effort to lighten the ship the mainmast was felled, only to land on top of the stricken vessel, pinning it more effectively to the reef. By ten o'clock the strong and newly constructed Dutch ship could withstand the ocean's assault no more; she broke her back. By then many of the ship's passengers and crew were thronging the wave-swept deck, desperate to be saved. The ship's cargo included an immense treasury being sent to support Coen's operations in Batavia, amounting to almost $100 million in today's currency. Pelsaert sought to do his duty by the company and secure the valuables, but the 'yammer' of the people swayed him to save them first.

All that day *Batavia's* longboat and tiny yawl braved rough seas to land people on two small islands nearby. Eventually some 240 people, food and water made it to shore. At least 70 of the crew remained aboard the disintegrating *Batavia*, where discipline was disintegrating as well. On shore the scarce supplies were quickly devoured, with no thought of rationing. On the ship, the crew broke into the liquor supplies, treasure chests and the commodore's cabin. Their drunken rampage had all the abandon of those who are sure they're doomed.

On 5 June *Batavia's* hulk could barely be seen among the high seas that surrounded it, and people ashore had already named the larger of the two islands they'd landed on Batavia's Graveyard. In the longboat and yawl Pelsaert and Jacobszoon tried to reach the ship, but it was too rough to get aboard. A crewman dived into the sea and swam to the boats to beg for rescue. Pelsaert sent him back to suggest the survivors build rafts from the wreckage in order to save themselves.

That night, on the smaller of the two islands, Jacobszoon and the crew of the longboat pressed Pelsaert to set out in search of water. There was none on any of the islands near the wreck, and thirst was starting to afflict the hundreds ashore. Jacobszoon wanted to head to the South Land and search for water, and if necessary continue to Batavia. Pelsaert was reluctant to leave the wreck and its survivors. The reception he could expect from Coen may also have weighed heavily on his mind.

On 6 June Jacobszoon's crewmen physically prevented Pelsaert from taking water to the bulk of the survivors on Batavia's Graveyard. The crew of the yawl were fearful that the crowd that had gathered on the shore would seize them all. Returning to the smaller island, Pelsaert wrote a note explaining that he intended to leave the islands and search for water. He left the note under a bread barrel, and stole away in the longboat. When the note was found, the survivors promptly named the scrap of land on which he'd left it Traitor's Island.

Pelsaert headed to two larger islands that were within sight to the west (today's East and West Wallabi islands), and continued searching for water. All he found were a few brackish pools left by the rain that had fallen on the day of the wreck, barely enough for the 40-odd people who'd accompanied him in the longboat. So they spent 7 June building up the sides of the longboat in preparation for a long sea voyage, joined also by ten people who came across in the yawl and begged to join the expedition.

On 8 June Pelsaert and the others resolved that:

> Since, on all the islands and cliffs round about our foundered ship *Batavia*, there is no freshwater to be found, in order to feed and keep the people who are saved, therefore the Commodore has earnestly requested and proposed that an expedition should be made to the main southland to see whether it is God's gracious will that fresh water shall be found, of which so much may be taken to the people that they shall be certain of having enough provision for a considerable time; that then, meanwhile, someone shall be told off to go to Batavia, in order to let the Lord-General and his councillors know of our disaster and to ask him for early assistance.

Towing the yawl astern, that day the longboat set sail to the north-west, crowded with 48 people, including two women and a babe in arms. By noon they were in sight of the South Land. Rather than land in search of water, with evening approaching they stood out to sea for the night, heading back towards the shore after midnight. In his journal of 9 June, Pelsaert includes a description of the coast that may explain the reluctance to attempt a landing.

> The coast here stretches mostly N by W and S by E. It is a bad Rocky land without trees, [the cliffs] about as high as Dover in England. Here we saw a small Inlet, as well as low dune land, where we intended to land, but approaching, noticed that there was a big surf and many breakers near the

shore; very suddenly the swell out of the West became so heavy and ran so high against the coast that we could not readily keep off it, and the wind increased more and more.

Pelsaert's journal provides the first detailed description of the west coast of the South Land. It didn't get any better during the ensuing days. First they battled a severe storm that threatened to swamp them or wreck them on the shore. They were eventually forced to cast the yawl adrift, and throw most of their supplies overboard while they bailed the flooded and overloaded longboat. After the storm abated the seas remained high, wind and wave pushing the boat north along the coast, still trying to find a place to get ashore. On 12 June:

> Could not find an opportunity to get to land with the boat because of the heavy surf. The Coast very steeply hewn without any foreshore or inlets as have other countries, but it seemed to be a dry cursed earth without foliage or grass.

Clearly, they'd never seen anything quite like this extraordinary continent, and its grim shore was relentless. The stretch of coast they were passing presents a line of cliffs almost like those of the Great Australian Bight. In places they're higher, up to 200 metres, and they extend for over 300 kilometres. On 13 June, in the vicinity of Dirk Hartog Island: 'the land is still entirely red stone hewn off without a foreshore, and generally everywhere at the same level, also it has not been possible to get ashore because of the surf'.

During the afternoon of the following day Pelsaert saw smoke rising from fires on the shore. He and his companions took it as a sign of people being on shore, and that had to mean there was water as well. Wrote Pelsaert:

> I noticed that the ground on shore rose very steeply, full of stones and rocks, and there was also a very big surf, yet 6 men swam ashore, and we remained with the boat at 25 fathoms [46 metres] outside the breakers. Our folk were searching for water everywhere until nightfall but found none. Saw also four men creeping towards them on hands and feet. When our folk, coming out of a hollow upon a height, approached them suddenly, they leapt to their feet and fled full speed, which was clearly seen by us in the boat; they were black savages, entirely naked, without any cover. At night time our folk swam aboard, all very much injured by the Rocks upon which they were thrown by the surf.

The following day, 15 June, the longboat came to an offshore reef with calm water inside it. It was afternoon before they found a break in the reef that would let them reach the calm water. They found, however, that the sheltered water was quite shallow and rocky. Nevertheless, the boat was finally able to get to shore, at a location thought to be just north of Point Cloates.

> This coast had a dune foreland of about one mile width before one comes to the High Land, therefore began to dig in this place, there was salt water, a party of folk therefore went to the High Land where they found by chance some small holes in a rock that were full of fresh water that the rain had left there. It seemed that the blacks had been there a little time before, for there lay bones of Crabs and ashes of fires. We quenched our great thirst a little, for we hardly were able to do more, for since the wrecking of the ship we had been without Wine or other drink except for one or two small mugs of water. Also collected a fair provision, about 80 kannen [approximately 80 litres] of water, and remained there the whole night until ...
>
> The 16 [June] in the morning continued to see whether there were more such holes in the range. But our search was vain, it appeared it had not rained there for a long time, nor was there any sign of running water, for beyond the heights the country was flat again, without trees, foliage or grass, except for high anthills thrown up of earth, which in the distance were not unlike the huts of people. Was also such a host of flies, which came to sit in the mouth and the eyes, that they could not be beaten off. We next saw eight black men, each carrying a stick in his hand, and these approached to the distance of a musket shot, but when we went towards them they ran away and we could not get them to stop where they were so that we might come up to them.

The Dutch, who set sail again later that day, must have been left wondering how the locals survived in such a barren landscape. Where did they find enough water to live? Little did the Dutch know that they were looking at a people who could claim more than 40 000 years' experience at surviving in one of the harshest environments on earth.

Pelsaert had hopes of reaching a river that was marked as being in 'Eendrachtsland', named after Jacop Resmessens and located in about 22 degrees 17 minutes south latitude, but the weather had other ideas. The wind drove them away from the coast, forcing them to choose between searching for water and making a dash for Batavia. With barely enough water for the voyage, on 17 June the longboat turned north, in an attempt to cross 1500 kilometres of open ocean. Ten perilous days later, they made the coast of Java with slightly more than a litre of water left among the 48 of them. Falling in with a Dutch fleet, Pelsaert reached Batavia on 7 July, just over a month after his ship was wrecked.

His epic sea voyage had been full of hardship, and Pelsaert was suffering from a tropical illness (possibly malaria) contracted years before, but both the voyage and tropical illness may have been preferable to the reception given him by Coen. Pelsaert arrived on a Saturday, and Sunday was a day of rest even for the god-fearing yet workaholic Dutch. That meant Pelsaert had a day to learn of the dramas of Batavia before telling the man at the centre of those dramas (Coen) what had happened to one of his ships.

As mentioned earlier, Coen had been besieged by 10 000 troops led by the sultan Coen had ejected from Jacatra back in 1619 (see Chapter 3). Coen had withstood the 1628 siege of the sultan by retreating into fortress Batavia while laying waste to sectors of the surrounding township. Eventually the attackers ran out of supplies and retreated. However, another attack was expected after the Mataramese locals finished the harvest of 1629. To resist them Coen badly needed the treasury Batavia was carrying, not to mention the hundreds of extra Dutch soldiers and sailors who could help defend Batavia.

Just a few weeks before Pelsaert's arrival, while awaiting the assault, Coen shocked his colleagues with an extraordinary display of uncompromising ruthlessness. Sara Specx was the 12-year-old daughter of VOC fleet commander Jacques Specx, left in Coen's care while her father voyaged between Batavia and the Netherlands. Pieter Cortenhoeff was a young cadet, the 15 or 16-year-old son of the town clerk of Amsterdam. The two became romantically involved, but were too young to realise that where a character like Coen is involved, discretion is the better part of lust. When Coen discovered the two together (either in a garden or in his apartments) he ordered Sara drowned and Cortenhoeff beheaded. Amid considerable uproar at such a harsh reaction, Coen could only be persuaded to spare Sara's life. The unfortunate Cortenhoeff was executed. Coen had Sara flogged, in public, in front of Batavia's town hall.

This was the man Pelsaert stood before on Monday 10 July 1629. It's hard to imagine how the CEO of a modern trading company would cope with the news that one of his ships had sunk, leaving 250 people stranded on a remote coral island with very little food and water. This while awaiting the attack of thousands of blood-thirsty locals. Coen may have conceded that even he had been taken unawares by Houtman Abrolhos. He may, however, have realised that Pelsaert's career was at stake and the opportunity for redemption made Pelsaert the ideal candidate to lead the rescue mission.

Coen ordered one of the smaller ships just arrived in Batavia, the yacht *Sardam*, to be rapidly unloaded and prepared for a rescue mission south. Pelsaert was to command the expedition, and Coen demanded that he spare no effort. His instructions for the voyage, included:

> In case through bad weather, storm and hard winds, you are prevented from approaching the reefs where the ship has been wrecked, and do not see any instant means to salvage the money, [you] shall not depart lightly there-from, and turn hither without having fulfilled the purpose, but keep in mind that the sun comes round to the South, that summer is near and that calm and beautiful weather is to be expected day after day, wherefore [you] shall remain there until better opportunity arises, watching for good weather and calm water in order to save, if possible, all the cash (and we have good hope of that) even if it should take three, four or more months.

The *Sardam* set sail the following Sunday. In the interim, two of the *Batavia's* survivors were seized and flung into the dungeons. They were her skipper Ariaen Jacobszoon and her boatswain Jan Evertszoon. Jacobszoon was held responsible for gross neglect in throwing the *Batavia* onto the reefs of Houtman Abrolhos, but also because of a 'gross evil and public assault' that had taken place on the voyage from Cape Town.

Jacobszoon had been much taken by a beautiful passenger, Lucretia Jansdochter, travelling to the Indies to join her husband. When Jansdochter had spurned him, he'd taken up with Lucretia's servant Zwaantie Hendricx who, by some accounts, 'refused him nothing'. On the trip from Cape Town, Jacobszoon appears to have had his revenge. One night Lucretia was grabbed, gagged and stripped naked by several men. She was smeared with faeces, molested and dumped on deck. Lucretia recognised none of her assailants, except perhaps for the voice of Jan Evertszoon.

At the time, Pelsaert was outraged. However, mid-ocean was no place to conduct a witch hunt, especially if it involved senior members of a crew that was responsible for getting his treasure-laden ship to Batavia. Pelsaert, bed-ridden for much of the voyage, may also have been too ill to exert his authority. In Batavia, the situation was entirely different. Torture would ulti-mately reveal who else was involved, and the fate of the two arrested men was certainly grim, especially considering a man of Coen's temperament.

However, despite the attack on Lucretia, she'd been left at Batavia's Graveyard. One could only guess how matters stood down in the Abrolhos, where she may have found herself among several of her persecutors and where the chain of command could only be in disarray after the departure of the two most senior officers. Even *Batavia's* supercargo (the senior officer responsible for all the ship's commercial negotiations), Jeronimus Corneliszoon, had last been seen clinging to the wreckage of the ship, unable to swim.

The *Sardam* made remarkably good time as it headed south, getting into the latitudes of the Abrolhos by 10 August, just two months after *Batavia's* shipwreck. Despite Coen's instructions to take 'good note of lands, shallows, reefs, inlets, bays, and capes, which you may encounter and discover; everything on its correct latitude, longitude, and position' Pelsaert didn't sight the South Land on his voyage south. He did, however, learn a great deal about the contrary winds and currents, countless reefs and outcrops of rock, and low-lying land of the Houtman Abrolhos. Despite being within 100 kilometres of Batavia's Graveyard on 10 August, the *Sardam* searched for weeks for the islands where whoever might have survived was hopefully searching the horizon for a scrap of sail and hope of rescue. Well into September the *Sardam* drifted, sailed, scraped and bumped, the nights often filled with the sound of deadly surf not far from the yacht's anchorage.

At last, on 16 September, according to Pelsaert's journal: 'towards evening saw the rocks of our wrecked ship *Batavia*, and I recognised the High Island [East Wallabi]'. They were forced to anchor for the night, but the next day they were able to run on towards East Wallabi. Wrote Pelsaert:

> Before noon, approaching the island, we saw smoke on a long island 2 mijlen [12 kilometres] West of the Wreck, also on another small island close by the Wreck, about which we were all very glad, hoping to find great numbers, or rather all people, alive. – Therefore, as soon as the anchor was dropped, I sailed with the boat to the highest island, which was nearest, taking with me a barrel of water, ditto bread, and a keg of wine; coming there, I saw no one, at which we wondered. I sprang ashore, and at the same time we saw a very small yawl with four Men rowing round the Northerly point; one of them Wiebbe Hayes, sprang ashore and ran towards me, calling from afar, 'Welcome, but go back aboard immediately, for there is a party of scoundrels on the islands near the wreck, with two sloops, who have

the intention to seize the Yacht.' – Furthermore, told that he was Captain over 47 souls, who had kept themselves so long on one island in order to save their lives, as [the scoundrels] had Murdered more than 125 persons, Men, Women and Children as well, and that 14 days ago he had captured Jeronimus Cornelisz, undermerchant, who had been the chief of the scoundrels, also at the same time they had killed 4 of [Corneliszoon's] principal councillors and Accomplices, namely, Davidt Van Sevanck, assistant, Coenraat Van Huyssen, and Gysbrecht Van Welderen, cadets, and Cornelis Pieterszoon of Wtrecht, soldier, had been killed; because they had been attacked twice by them in a felonious way. But they had bravely repulsed them. – And they next tried treacherous means to overpower and murder them. For they had then come to establish Peace with each other under Oath, and not to remember any more what had passed. Nevertheless, whilst Jeronimus was engaged in pretending to make an agreement through the agency of the Predikant, whom they compelled to go backwards and forwards, at the same time Davidt Van Sevanck, and Coenraat Van Huyssen, were engaged in bribing some of the soldiers to treason by offering them six thousand guilders each if they, the next day when [the scoundrels] came back, would come to their side under cover, as friends, in order to help murder the others. So when the People perceived that their lives were at stake, they have killed the above mentioned, as has been told above. – Moreover, that some one named Wouter Loos, who had been made their Captain after the capture of Jeronimus, had attacked them this same Morning with 2 sloops of men; whom they had also repulsed, and there were in the party of the ditto Wibbe Hayes, four very seriously wounded men.

Pelsaert was the first person from the outside world to learn of the terrible descent into barbarism that had taken place on the islands of the Houtman Abrolhos. However, it wasn't over yet. On the way back to the *Sardam*, he was pursued by a sloop full of the 'scoundrels'. Twice they attempted to fire on Pelsaert's boat, but their muskets failed to discharge. He only just beat them to the safety of the yacht, which rapidly armed itself. Seeing they then had no hope of taking the forewarned *Sardam*, the 'scoundrels' surrendered. Wrote Pelsaert:

When they came over, we immediately took them prisoner, and we forthwith began to examine them, especially a certain Jan Hendricxsz from Bremen, soldier, who immediately confessed that he had murdered and helped to murder 17 to 20 people, under the order of Jeronimus. I asked

A poignant depiction of the horrors that followed the loss of the Dutch ship
Batavia *on the Houtman Abrolhos, off the coast of Western Australia, in 1629.*
From a facsimile of the 1647 Amsterdam edition of Jan Janszoon's
Ongeluckige Voyagie. *Published by the Australian National Maritime*
Museum and Hordern House, Sydney, 1994

him the origin and circumstances of this, why had they practised such cruel-
ties. Said that he also wished to explain how it had been with him in the
beginning, – saying, that the skipper, Jeronimus Cornelisz, the High
Boatswain and still more others, had it in mind to seize the ship *Batavia*
before it was wrecked; to kill the Commandeur and all people except 120
towards whom they were more favourably inclined, and to throw the dead
overboard into the sea and then to go pirating with the ship. Wherefore
Jeronimus and all the people who had been on the island had been certain
that the skipper would have murdered the Commandeur on the way [to
Java] or have thrown him overboard into the sea. So that Jeronimus, having
been for a month on the island after the wrecking of the ship, thought that
one should either murder all the people to 40 or less, or else help them to
some land, so that when the Yacht came, one could seize it, which has been
put into action to that purpose. But they could not fulfil their plan because

> Wiebbe Hayes had been sent with a party of people to a long island, to seek
> water, which they found after a search of 20 days, and therefore they made,
> according to arrangements, 3 fires as signals. But because they were in those
> days busy with the murdering, Jeronimus did not care about the water;
> whereupon several parties from 4 to 5 strong, saved themselves on pieces of
> wood or rafts, and escaped to Wiebbe Hayes's island, at last 45 strong. – As
> they understood what had been decided and that daily so many were being
> murdered, made themselves ready to counter-attack if they should come to
> fight them, and made weapons from hoop-iron and nails, which they bound
> to sticks. – After they had murdered most people, except 30 men and 4
> boys, they decided to go to the high island with 2 flat-bottomed sloops to
> overpower Wiebbe Hayes with his men, for they said, 'If the Yacht comes
> by the inner passage, he will warn them, and our plan will not succeed;
> therefore they must go.' And they had already done three trips against
> them, but they were unable to do any harm to them except on this day when
> they shot some.

The Dutch may have been trying to keep their knowledge of the South
Land to themselves, but there was no way they were going to keep a lid on
this story. Mutiny, murder and a heroic stand led by Wiebbe Hayes made
this one of the most gripping tales of its era. It even had a beautiful heroine,
Lucretia Jansdochter, who had been kept as a concubine by the monstrous
Jeronimus Corneliszoon (she reached Batavia only to find that her husband
had succumbed to the grinding workload, tropical heat and diseases of the
Indies). Pelsaert's journal survived where so many others have been lost,
largely due to the sensational details related above and elaborated at great
length in the ensuing interrogations, trials and executions carried out on the
islands while salvage work on the wreck was carried out. Digests of Pelsaert's
journals were published and became bestsellers.

Most of the mutineers were executed on the islands. Corneliszoon had
both his hands cut off before being hanged. Several others had punishments
carried out on the voyage back to Batavia, such as keel-hauling (being
dragged under the keel from one side of the boat to the other) and flogging.
Two of the mutineers, ringleader Wouter Loos and a mere youngster, Jan
Pelgrom de Bye, were later marooned on the mainland, at an inlet where
Pelsaert also found water (at 27 degrees 51 seconds by his calculation, but
possibly further south, at Hutt River). Despite the water supply, Pelsaert may
already have seen enough of the mainland to believe that leaving them on its
desolate shore was a fate worse than torture and execution back in Batavia.

He did, however, leave them supplies and the hope that they'd be picked up by a passing ship, but they were never seen again.

As he sailed from Batavia's Graveyard on 15 November, Pelsaert finally turned his pen to matters other than the horrors, interrogations and executions he had documented during his time there. He included this description:

> Moreover, on these islands there are large numbers of Cats, which are creatures of miraculous form, as big as a hare; the Head is similar to [that] of a Civet cat, the fore-paws are very short, about a finger long. Whereon there are five small Nails, or small fingers, as an ape's fore-paw, and the 2 hind legs are at least half an ell [about 30 centimetres] long, they run on the flat of the joint of the leg, so that they are not quick in running. The tail is very long, the same as a Meerkat; if they are going to eat they sit on their hind legs and take the food with the fore-paws and eat exactly as the Squirrels and apes do. Their generation or procreation is Very Miraculous, Yea, worthy to note; under the belly the females have a pouch into which one can put a hand, and in that she has her nipples, where have discovered that in there their Young Grow with the nipple in the mouth, and have found lying in it [the pouch] some Which were only as large as a bean, but found the limbs of the small beast to be entirely in proportion, so that it is certain that they grow there at the nipple of the mammal and draw the food out of it until they are big and can run. Even though when they are very big they still creep into the pouch when chased and the mother runs off with them.

This is possibly the first reference to the remarkable fauna of Australia, although it was greatly overshadowed by the horrendous litany of atrocities that occurred around them. What was also overshadowed was ample evidence that, despite the inhospitable aspect of the Houtman Abrolhos and the adjacent coast of the South Land, some 250 people had in fact found enough food and water to survive there. The storm that had almost wrecked the longboat had replenished the water supplies on the islands, which was supplemented by barrels floating in from the wreck site. Boats were built from salvaged timbers, and used for foraging. There was ample food in the form of seals, birds and fish. Not long after Pelsaert had left them to the their fate, the survivors had realised that all they had to do was settle in and wait for rescue. Unfortunately, they never suspected the potential danger from their fellow survivors.

The wreck of the *Batavia* could have demonstrated that the European's first impressions of the South Land were misleading. Closer examination might have revealed, if not an abundance, then certainly sufficient resources to fulfil basic human needs. However, for centuries after the wreck, the notion of being marooned on a 'Desert Island' like those in Houtman Abrolhos, or indeed on the mainland of Australia itself, was associated only with unspeakable cruelty, misery and death.

On 5 December, seven months after the wreck of the *Batavia*, the remaining survivors reached the town of Batavia. There they were met by the new governor general, Jacques Specx. Sara's father had taken command after Coen had died from an unexpected heart attack, during the expected siege of the local sultan. One version of Coen's demise was that he'd collapsed shortly after sighting Specx's squadron approaching Batavia. There are suggestions that the thought of what Specx would do to him upon learning what Coen had done to his daughter was too much even for a man of Coen's calibre.

5

TASMAN

In landing with small craft you will use great circumspection, and your treatment of the natives that should allow you to come to parley, must and ought to be marked by great kindness, wary caution, and skilful judgement; slight misdemeanours on the part of such natives, such as petty thefts and the like, which they should commit against you, you will suffer to pass unnoticed, that by so doing you may draw them unto you, and not inspire them with aversion to our nation. Whoever endeavours to discover unknown lands and tribes, had need to be patient and long suffering, noways quick to fly out, but always bent on ingratiating himself.

The Dutch commander to whom these instructions were given in April 1636 couldn't say he wasn't warned, but at least Gerrit Thomaszoon Pool didn't suffer long. He had only reached the coast of New Guinea with the yachts *Clyn Amsterdam* and *Wesel* when (according to Abel Janszoon Tasman's *Instructions* of 1644) he and 'three of the crew (by the barbarous

inhabitants) was murdered, at the same place where the skipper of the yacht *Arnhem* was killed in the year 1623'.

In the 30 years since the *Duyfken's* crew had first laid eyes on the South Land, only three other organised Dutch explorations had been sent out, and none of them could claim more than limited success. This is despite great ambitions such as those outlined in the instructions given to Pool. 'If the south-land should by you be found to be an island,' he was told, 'you will sail southward along the coast of Nova Guinea, as far as the 32nd degree south latitude, and thence on a westerly course touch at the eastern extremity of the South-Land, which in January 1627 was discovered by the ship *'t Zeepaart.'*

After Pool's death, supercargo Pieter Pieterszoon took over and continued the voyage. He was forced south by strong easterlies, and came upon the South Land in the region of Arnhem Land. There he mapped about 200 kilometres of coast. He had no encounters with the indigenous population, although he saw numerous columns of smoke. After three months he returned to Banda, having added no new information nor, as was later reported, did he discover 'anything of consequence'.

After the wreck of the *Batavia* the glimpses afforded by 'accidental' discoveries continued to provide the Dutch with most of their information about the South Land. In 1631 the *Grooten Broeck* had coasted from Cape Leeuwin to Dirk Hartog Island. In 1636 the *Amsterdam* under Woolebrand Geleynszoon de Jongh improved the charts of the coast near Shark Bay.

At same time, the Dutch were strengthening their grip on the Indies. The English had begun to show an increasing preference for their bases in India since Coen's return to Batavia in 1627. In 1640 the Portuguese managed to revolt against their Spanish overlords and throw them out of Portugal, but in 1641 the Dutch managed to throw the Portuguese out of Malacca. In so doing they effectively gained a monopoly over the East Indies.

Keen to grow their business further they sought new trade opportunities beyond their established territories. The problem was that the desert of the South Land and New Guinea were blocking exploration to the east and south. Only Dutch expeditions to the north met with any success. In 1639, for example, an expedition was sent into the northern Pacific in search of an island reputed to be a source of great wealth. It didn't exist, but the voyage did reach the island of Formosa (present day Taiwan), after nearly half of the crew of 90 had died. More importantly, as far as the discovery of Australia is concerned, the second in command of that voyage was a highly capable 36-year-old from Groningen, Abel Janszoon Tasman.

Tasman had been with the VOC since 1631, rising through the ranks until he was made master of a small ship, the *Mocha*, in July 1634. After the voyage to Formosa, he was sent on voyages to Japan in 1640 and 1641, and to the south of Sumatra in 1642. That same year he was asked to undertake a voyage whose ambition was even greater than the usual comprehensive goals outlined by the governors general of Batavia.

The sailing instructions have not survived to the present day, but it is clear from Tasman's journal of the voyage and subsequent reports, that its intention was to determine the extent of the South Land, and to find a sea route to the Pacific Ocean that would allow Dutch ships to reach South America. The voyage would encompass the findings of the previous 36 years either by ships whose crews more often than not had been speared by natives or by vessels that had been wrecked or blown far off course by storms.

Tasman set out from Batavia on 14 August 1642, with the ship *Heemskerck* and a flute (a small fast coastal sailer) the *Zeehaen*. His ships first sailed across the Indian Ocean, taking advantage of favourable breezes to reach Mauritius, off the coast of Africa, on 4 September. There they took in water and fuel, and prepared as best they could for their epic voyage, before finally getting down to the real business of the expedition on 8 October. From Mauritius the two vessels headed almost due south, towards the roaring forties, which they reached on 23 October. The forties lost no time in living up to their formidable reputation. Wrote Tasman:

Item the 23rd October.
In the morning the wind began to blow stiffly from the west-south-west and south-west so that we had to take in our topsail. At noon Latitude estimated 40 degrees 18 minutes, Longitude 80 degrees 46 minutes [reckoned from Tenerife, which is 16½ degrees west of Greenwich, from where modern longitude is calculated], course kept south-east by south, sailed 40 miles [240 kilometres]; in the afternoon we turned our course to the southeast and had heavy showers of rain from time to time.

Item the 24th.
In the morning we took in our bonnets, lowered our foresail down to the stem, and ran on before the wind with our mainsail only; we dared not try to the wind [turn the ship's bows into the wind to take the waves head on, rather than run with them and risk broaching] because of the strong gale blowing. This gale was attended with hail and rain to such a degree that we feared the ship would not live through it, but at noon the storm somewhat abated so that we hauled to the wind; we could not see the *Zeehaen*, for which reason we hauled to the wind to stay for her. At noon Latitude estimated 40 degrees 42 minutes, Longitude 83 degrees 11 minutes; course kept east by south, sailed 30 miles [180 kilometres]; the wind south-west and south with a violent storm; we kept a sharp lookout for the *Zeehaen* but could not get sight of her.

Item the 25th.
In the morning we sent a man to the masthead to look out for our partner whom he saw astern, of which we were full glad; the weather getting slightly better we again set our bonnets and drew up the foresail. Towards noon the *Zeehaen* again joined us.

Tasman employed a remarkably democratic approach to his command, calling together the officers of both ships whenever possible to consider their plans and to determine the ships' positions, especially their longitude, by averaging the reckonings kept by each officer. This was a practice carried out on other Dutch ships, but it stands out when compared to the journals of other expeditions. The impression is of a leader who valued and encouraged the opinions of his subordinates. As the voyage progressed, they were all sufficiently aware of the objectives and issues to be able to assume command should a fate like Pool's befall Tasman or any other senior members of the expedition.

Consultation also may have served a second purpose. Tasman knew he was sailing in completely unknown waters. However, if any of his crew knew of the Dieppe maps (see Chapter 1), they may well have feared being driven unexpectedly onto the shores of the maps' imagined Terra Australis. If that happened, there was little hope of rescue. So, by bringing all the officers together, and sometimes the mates as well, Tasman was able both to gauge the mood aboard the *Heemskerck* and *Zeehaen*, via the men who commanded every watch and section of the crew, and to transmit to them clear information about where they were going, how they could get there and what they expected to find. Tasman's voyage into the unknown didn't mean his crews had to be kept in the dark.

Tasman maintained a businesslike manner in his daily journal, but there are occasional hints of Tasman the born seaman enjoying the cruise and Tasman the leader not given to panic. At one point he refers to his 'friends of the *Zeehaen*'. At another, noticing the *Zeehaen* had broken its mizzen mast, he wrote: 'We then hoisted our foresail, hailed the *Zeehaen*, and asked her how she was getting on; they replied that they could help themselves until the weather should improve.'

Meanwhile, unfazed by the storm that welcomed them to the forties, the ships continued to steer south-east by south or south-south-east until 31 October. In his journal Tasman wrote:

> Towards noon a drizzling rain came on with fog, while the wind stiffened more and more, so that we took in our topsails; at noon we also took in our main-sail and ran on before the wind with our foresail, wind and sea running very high. At noon Latitude estimated 47 degrees 4 minutes, Longitude 95 degrees 19 minutes; course kept east-south-east, sailed 50 miles; we then had a storm from the west and held our course to the east.

Reduced to a scrap of sail, deep in the forties, a day's run of 50 Dutch mijlen equates to nearly 300 kilometres or an average speed of nearly seven knots for the whole 24 hours. That's pretty respectable in any kind of sailing vessel. In a blunt-bowed old Dutch merchantman, at times it must have been quite a ride.

Tasman was now in a position to traverse the globe at quite a respectable speed, provided the *Heemskerck* and *Zeehaen* could avoid being rolled by enormous seas or broached and sunk by the powerful winds. By 6 November, they were in even higher latitudes, at 49 degrees 4 minutes south. Modern mariners taking supply vessels to Antarctica will tell you that so far south, the weather is always bad. The next day, Tasman's pilot, Francoys Jacobszoon, recommended:

> Our advice is that we should stick to the 44th degree South Latitude until we shall have passed the 150th degree of Longitude [133 degrees 30 minutes east of Greenwich], and then run north as far as the 40th degree South Latitude, remaining there with an easterly course until we shall have reached the 220th degree of Longitude [203 degrees 30 minutes east], after which we should take a northerly course so as to avail ourselves of the trade-wind to reach the Salomonis islands and New Guinea by running from east to west. We cannot but think that, if we find no land up to 150 degrees Longitude, we shall then be in an open sea again, unless we should meet with islands; all which time and experience, being the best of teachers, will no doubt bring to light.

Tasman took his pilot's advice, revising the plan after the weather was calm enough for the officers from the *Zeehaen* to visit the *Heemskerck* for a consultation (it was thought better to turn north for New Guinea a little sooner). From the point of view of the further discovery of the South Land, the overall plan was to prove ideal. The ships reached 150 degrees longitude on 18 November, but the plan to turn north was upset by a storm. By 21 November, however, they were able to steer east-north-east. On 24 November, they estimated they were 42 degrees 25 minutes south latitude, 163 degrees 31 minutes east longitude (157 degrees east of Greenwich). There the lookout cried: '*Landt in zicht!*' Wrote Tasman:

> In the afternoon about 4 o'clock we saw land bearing east by north of us at about 10 miles [60 kilometres] distance from us by estimation; the land we sighted was very high [which explains how it could be seen over the horizon while it was still so far away]; towards evening we also saw, east-south-east

of us, three high mountains, and to the north-east two more mountains, but less high than those to southward.

While not directly recording their excitement upon discovering a new land, Tasman's journal notes that he once again convened his ships' council. In fact he got together everyone down to the second mates. With darkness falling they decided to head back out to sea for most of the night, then turn back towards the coast and approach it in daylight. Morning, however, greeted them with a failing wind, so Tasman convened another meeting. In latitude 42 degrees 30 minutes south the officers averaged the longitudes each of them kept separately and decided that the land at that latitude was at longitude 163 degrees 50 minutes east (147 degrees 20 minutes east of Greenwich).

That day, Tasman also noted in his journal:

> This land being the first land we have met with in the South Sea and not known to any European nation we have conferred on it the name of Anthony Van Diemensland in honour of the Honourable Governor-General, our illustrious master, who sent us to make this discovery.

The actual longitude of what is now Tasmania at this point is closer to 145 degrees 15 minutes east of Greenwich, an error of about 2 degrees 05 minutes or in that latitude about 140 kilometres. Considering the *Heemskerck* and *Zeehaen* had been calculating their longitude by dead reckoning all the way from Mauritius, a sea voyage of nearly 10 000 kilometres that lasted two months and 16 days, it's an excellent piece of navigation.

Van Diemen's Land lay almost due south of the earlier Dutch discoveries at Cape York and the Gulf of Carpentaria, some 3500 kilometres away. It lay well to the south-west of the furthest discoveries on the south coast of the South Land made by *'t Gulden Zeepaert* in 1627. If Tasman suspected that he was at the southern-most tip of a continent touched upon by the previous discoveries, he made no mention of it in his journal.

Ever cautious about a lee shore on which an unfavourable wind might wreck him, he again sailed out to sea for most of the day, favouring courses that carried the vessels to the southward. After dark he turned back towards the land on a course of east-south-east. The next morning he sighted the land again and that night lay under reduced sail for fear of running onto it in darkness. On 28 November the vessels again came in sight of land north-east and north-north-east of them and 'made straight for it; the coast here bears south-east by east and north-west by west; as far as I can see the land here falls off to eastward'. With his latitude of 44 degrees 12 minutes south he was near the southern tip of Van Diemen's Land, in the vicinity of South West Cape. Closing with the land to the east of the Cape, Tasman came upon a group of windswept islands and wild-looking rocks which he named after one of the VOC's governors in Batavia, Joan Maetsuijcker. They are still known as the Maatsuyker Group, including one which 'in shape resembles a lion; this islet lies out into the sea at about 3 miles [16 kilometres] distance from the mainland'.

It was well they'd got south of Tasmania when they did, for the next day they had a top-gallant gale from the west. The wind pushed them east at speed. They passed the fang of stone Tasman named Pedra Branca, some 25 kilometres off the southern capes of Van Diemen's Land, by noon of that day. By five in the afternoon they were off what he soon named Storm Bay. Tasman wrote that it

> Seemed likely to afford a good anchorage, upon which we resolved with our ship's council to run into it … we had nearly got into the bay when there arose so strong a gale that we were obliged to take in sail and to run out to sea again under reduced sail, seeing that it was impossible to come to anchor in such a storm; in the evening we resolved to stand out to sea during the night under reduced sail to avoid being thrown on a lee-shore by the violence of the wind.

The tempest was so severe that wind and current drove them far out to sea. It took all the next day and into the next, 1 December, to reach land again. During a brief calm Tasman gathered his officers and they decided to attempt a landing, finally doing so in the relatively sheltered Frederick Henry Bay, at the north-eastern head of Storm Bay, just east of present day Hobart. As Tasman wrote:

> One hour after sunset we dropped anchor in a good harbour, in 22 fathom [40 metres], white and grey fine sand, a naturally drying bottom; for all which it behoves us to thank God Almighty with grateful hearts.

The next day some of the crew got to stretch their legs for the first time after nearly three months at sea. Tasman sent them to explore, especially to find water and fresh vegetables for the hungry ships' crew. They were the first Europeans to set foot upon Van Diemen's Land, or any part of the south-eastern corner of Australia for that matter.

Early in the morning we sent our Pilot-major Francoys Jacobsz in command of our pinnace, manned with 4 musketeers and 6 rowers, all of them furnished with pikes and side-arms, together with the cock-boat of the *Zeehaen* with one of her second mates and 6 musketeers in it, to a bay situated north-west of us at upwards of a mile [6 kilometres] distance in order to ascertain what facilities (as regards fresh water, refreshments, timber and the like) may be available there. About three hours before nightfall the boats came back, bringing various samples of vegetables which they had seen growing there in great abundance, some of them in appearance not unlike a certain plant growing at the Cape of Good Hope and fit to be used as pot-herbs, and another species with long leaves and a brackish taste, strongly resembling persil de mer or samphire. The Pilot-major and the second mate of the *Zeehaen* made the following report, to wit:

That they had rowed the space of upwards of a mile round the said point, where they had found high but level land covered with vegetation (not cultivated, but growing naturally by the will of God) abundance of excellent timber, and a gently sloping watercourse in a barren valley the said water, though of good quality, being difficult to procure because the watercourse was so shallow that the water could be dipped with bowls only.

That they had heard certain human sounds and also sounds nearly resembling the music of a trump or a small gong not far from them though they had seen no one.

That they had seen two trees about 2 or 2½ fathom [4–4.5 metres] in thickness measuring from 60 to 65 feet [18–19.5 metres] from the ground to the lowermost branches, which trees bore notches made with flint implements, the bark having been removed for the purpose; these notches, forming a kind of steps to enable persons to get up the trees and rob the birds' nests in their tops, were fully 5 feet [1.5 metres] apart so that our men concluded that the natives here must be of very tall stature, or must be in possession of some sort of artifice for getting up the said trees; in one of the trees these notched steps were so fresh and new that they seemed to have been cut less than four days ago.

That on the ground they had observed certain footprints of animals, not unlike those of a tiger's claws; they also brought on board certain specimens of animals' excrements voided by quadrupeds, so far as they could surmise and observe, together with a small quantity of gum of a seemingly very fine quality which had exuded from trees and bore some resemblance to gum-lac.

That at the extremity of the said point they had seen large numbers of gulls, wild ducks and geese, but had perceived none farther inward though they had heard their cries; and had found no fish except different kinds of mussels forming small clusters in several places.

That the land is pretty generally covered with trees standing so far apart that they allow a passage everywhere and a lookout to a great distance so that, when landing, our men could always get sight of natives or wild beasts, unhindered by dense shrubbery or underwood, which would prove a great advantage in exploring the country.

That in the interior they had in several places observed numerous trees which had deep holes burnt into them at the upper end of the foot, while the earth had here and there been dug out with the fist so as to form a fire-place, the surrounding soil having become as hard as flint through the action of the fire.

A short time before we got sight of our boats returning to the ships, we now and then saw clouds of dense smoke rising up from the land, which was nearly west by north of us, and surmised this might be a signal given by our men, because they were so long coming back, for we had ordered them to return speedily, partly in order to be made acquainted with what they had seen, and partly that we might be able to send them to other points if they should find no profit there, to the end that no precious time might be wasted. When our men had come on board again we inquired of them whether they had been there and made a fire, to which they returned a negative answer, adding however that at various times and points in the wood they also had seen clouds of smoke ascending. So there can be no doubt there must be men here of extraordinary stature.

Giants, gum trees and the now-extinct marsupial tiger all in one day; the boat crews clearly suffered nothing to escape their notice. However, they hadn't actually seen the inhabitants, they'd only surmised their stature from notches cut in the enormous trees. Nevertheless, the land was very different to that seen by the Dutch on the rest of the southern, western and northern coasts of the South Land. While they certainly hadn't met with anything that might prevent further exploration, for reasons not detailed by Tasman, they investigated no further.

On 3 December, Tasman sent the boats to collect water. However, all the water they found was brackish, and the rocky shore made digging wells to get fresher water impossible. In the afternoon Tasman went himself with the boats to claim Van Diemen's Land for his country, but the weather had other ideas.

We carried with us a pole with the Company's mark carved into it, and a Prince-flag to be set up there, that those who shall come after us may become aware that we have been here, and have taken possession of the said land as our lawful property. When we had rowed about halfway with our boats it began to blow very stiffly, and the sea ran so high that the cock-boat of the *Zeehaen*, in which were seated the Pilot-major and Mr Gilsemans, was compelled to pull back to the ships, while we ran on with our pinnace. When we had come close inshore in a small inlet which bore west-south-west of the ships the surf ran so high that we could not get near the shore without running the risk of having our pinnace dashed to pieces. We then ordered the carpenter aforesaid to swim to the shore alone with the pole and the flag, and kept by the wind with our pinnace; we made him plant the said pole with the flag at top into the earth, about the centre of the bay … Our master carpenter, having in the sight of myself, Abel Jansz Tasman, Skipper Gerrit Jansz, and Subcargo Abraham Coomans, performed the work entrusted to him, we pulled with our pinnace as near the shore as we ventured to do; the carpenter aforesaid thereupon swam back to the pinnace through the surf. This work having been duly executed we pulled back to the ships, leaving the above-mentioned as a memorial for those who shall come after us, and for the natives of this country, who did not show themselves, though we suspect some of them were at no great distance and closely watching our proceedings. We made no arrangements for gathering vegetables since the high seas prevented our men from getting ashore except by swimming, so that it was impossible to get anything into the pinnace.

That night the ships at anchor rode out yet another storm. And then, despite having started their exploration with commendable zeal, they cut short their visit to the first place they'd discovered. On the morning of 4 December, the storm having abated, the ships left Frederick Henry Bay and turned north to 'seek a better watering-place'. They'd only been there for a little over 48 hours.

That day, however, they simply continued north along the coast, charting Tasman and Maria islands as they went. During the morning they sailed in variable winds, but in the afternoon the gales returned, blowing offshore. During the day they also observed columns of smoke rising along the coast, signs of the human inhabitants they hadn't managed to encounter. In the evening they saw 'a round mountain bearing north-north-west' of them 'at about 8 miles [48 kilometres] distance'.

On 6 December, Tasman wrote:

In the morning, the wind blowing from the north-west by west, we kept our previous course; the high round mountain which we had seen the day before now bore due west of us at 6 miles [36 kilometres] distance; at this point the land fell off to the north-west so that we could no longer steer near the coast here, seeing that the wind was almost ahead. We therefore convened the council and the second mates, with whom after due deliberation we resolved, and subsequently called out to the officers of the *Zeehaen* that, pursuant to the resolution of the 11th ultimo we should direct our course due east, and on the said course run on to the full longitude of 195 degrees of the Salomonis islands ... At noon Latitude estimated 41° 34', Longitude 169°.

That afternoon, Tasman set sail east, away from Van Diemen's Land. In so doing, he left all that lay between it and Cape York undiscovered. Nevertheless, he'd already cemented his place in history, in more ways than one. Van Diemen's Land eventually became known to the world by that name, but ultimately acquired such negative associations due to its brutal penal settlements that the inhabitants sought a new name with more positive connotations. In the mid-19th century they decided to call the place Tasmania.

After leaving the coast, Tasman held his course east until he reached the south island of New Zealand on 13 December. Here he found the Maori people, who more than made up for the retiring nature of the inhabitants of Van Diemen's Land. While the ships were at anchor on 19 December they were approached by Maori in a number of vessels, which began to manoeuvre near the ships. Attempts to exchange gifts with them failed, so the master of the *Zeehaen* sent some men to the Maori in their small boat. As Tasman wrote:

> Those in the prow before us, between the two ships, began to paddle so furiously towards it that, when they were about halfway slightly nearer to our ship, they struck the *Zeehaen's* cock-boat so violently alongside with the stem of their prow that it got a violent lurch, upon which the foremost man in this prow of villains with a long, blunt pike thrust the quartermaster Cornelis Joppen in the neck several times with so much force that the poor man fell overboard. Upon this the other natives, with short thick clubs which we at first mistook for heavy blunt parangs [large knives], and with their paddles, fell upon the men in the cock-boat and overcame them by main force, in which fray three of our men were killed and a fourth got mortally wounded through the heavy blows. The quartermaster and two sailors swam to our ship, whence we had sent our pinnace to pick them up,

which they got into alive. After this outrageous and detestable crime the
murderers sent the cock-boat adrift, having taken one of the dead bodies
into their prow and thrown another into the sea.

Tasman's hopes of establishing friendly relations were dashed, and he set sail
from what he called Murderers Bay almost immediately. He did note,
however, that:

> This is the second land which we have sailed along and discovered. In
> honour of their High Mightinesses the States-General we gave to the land
> the name of Staten Land, since we deemed it quite possible that this land
> is part of the great Staten Land, though this is not certain. This land seems
> to be a very fine country and we trust that this is the mainland coast of the
> unknown South land.

As with Van Diemen's Land, if Tasman had spent longer exploring the
coastline, he'd have discovered that Staten Land was in fact two large islands,
with only a vast expanse of open ocean between them and South America,
rather than a mighty continent. However, time and his failed attempts at
getting fresh supplies must have weighed heavily on him. Being close to
what he considered the longitude of the Solomon Islands, he continued his
course north, eventually discovering Tonga and Fiji before running west and
passing along the northern coast of New Guinea.

In so doing, he established without doubt that there was a good passage
from the Indian Ocean to the Pacific, sailing south of the actual South Land
he'd briefly visited at Van Diemen's Land. As he noted after leaving New
Zealand, on 8 January:

> At noon Latitude observed 32 degrees 25 minutes, Longitude 192 degrees
> 20 minutes; course kept north-east, sailed 21 miles. The great swells now
> come from the south-east. This passage from Batavia to Chili is in smooth
> water [or more appropriately 'open water'] so that there is no objection to
> following it.

Tasman arrived back in Batavia on 15 June 1643. Although his expedition
found few lands considered to be of use to the VOC, it remains one of the
world's great voyages of discovery. He'd only touched on a small section of
the coast of Van Diemen's Land, but his voyage was the first to circle the
South Land (although almost entirely beyond sight of it). By so doing, the
voyage defined the furthest limits that the remaining undiscovered eastern
and southern coasts could possibly extend to.

For those who sought an enormous South Land that counterbalanced the land masses of the northern hemisphere, Tasman's voyage, when it became widely known, was a major setback. The South Land he'd circumnavigated, while very large, was tiny compared to Eurasia. Worse, the only place left where a super-continent might still be found was the expanse of ocean between New Zealand and South America. Tasman thought this might be the case, but tempered this belief by saying 'though this is not certain'. The great navigator wasn't about to sketch coasts he hadn't seen.

Despite finding little that could fill the hold of a VOC ship with profit, Tasman's voyage delighted Governor General Antonio Van Diemen in Batavia. And not just because the governor now had two parts of the South Land named after him (the other was near Arnhem Land). His council reported to the VOC on 19 June 1643:

> Inasmuch as on the 15th instant Commander Abel Janszoon Tasman has again come to anchor on this roadstead (for which God be praised) with the yacht *Heemskerck* and the flute *Zeehaen*, who on the 14th of August of last year had been dispatched from here by way of the island of Mauritius with orders to navigate to and discover the unknown Southern and Eastern lands; as shown by the journals kept on board the said vessels and the reckonings recorded by them, in sailing on an eastern course they found the wind very strong and the seas so high that they did not think it advisable to run farther southward, but thought it better gradually to deviate more to northward of the said course, until they came to 44° Lat and 167° Long, where on the 24th of November last they sighted and discovered a certain great land surrounded by islands, which land they have christened Antonio van Diemen's land, without, however, being aware how far it extends to north-west or north-east, and without communicating with any of the inhabitants, the ships having only sailed along the south-coast of it and onward as far as 189° Long, where in the latitude of from 43 to 35 degrees, on December 13, they sighted and came upon another large land, to which they have given the name of Staten landt, of which latter land they found the natives to be of a malignant and murderous nature, seeing that in a certain large bay these natives came upon them with a number of strongly-manned prows, cut off one of our boats from the ships, and killed four of our men in her with wooden clubs, and wounded another who returned on board swimming; the said land was found to trend to southward in Lat 35° and Long 192°, and consequently a passage from the Indian Ocean into the South Seas has been

found, it having been ascertained that in this parallel, where the westerly trade-wind is blowing, there is a convenient passage to the gold-bearing coast of Chili …

And inasmuch as by the instruments handed to Commander Tasman aforesaid and his Council, we had assured and promised them that, in case in the course of this voyage any rich lands or islands profitable to the Company's commerce should be discovered, or serviceable passages for navigation be found, we should on their return award a handsome recompense to the leaders of the undertaking and the common sailors for extraordinary pains taken and diligence shown by them;

Therefore, although in point of fact no treasures or matters of great profit have as yet been found, but only the lands aforesaid and the promising passage referred to been discovered, whose real situation and nature will have to be further ascertained by a subsequent investigation set on foot for the express purpose.

Yet we have unanimously resolved for the reasons above cited to award a recompense to the said discoverers on behalf of the Honourable Company and in fulfilment of our promise aforesaid; to wit, to the commander, skippers, super-, and sub-cargoes, steersmen and inclusive of the book-keeper, two months' pay each; and to the common sailors and soldiers one months' pay each for which they shall each of them be credited in running account to the debit of the Company, and subsequently be debited again for the amount of the said recompenses, which shall be paid to them in cash.

Done and resolved in the Castle of Batavia, date as above,
(Signed) ANTONIO VAN-DIEMEN,
CORNELIS VAN DER LIJN,
JOAN MAETSUIJCKER,
JUSTUS SCHOUTEN,
SALOMON SWEERS, and
PIETER MESTDAGH, Secretary

Commander Tasman had demonstrated such a capacity for fair dealing that Van Diemen almost immediately sent him on another voyage of discovery to the South Land, to resolve the very questions the explorer's first voyage had raised. Van Diemen's sailing instructions for this voyage have survived (and have been referred to throughout previous chapters) and detail the numerous voyages of discovery that had taken place since the *Duyfken's* expedition of 1606. In several instances his instructions provide the only written evidence that the voyages actually occurred, their original journals and maps having been lost.

As it turned out, the journal of Tasman's second voyage was also lost, but Van Diemen's instructions give a clear outline of his mission, and a surviving map shows how Tasman justified his governor general's confidence. As much as possible, Van Diemen wanted to ascertain whether the discoveries at Cape York and Arnhem Land, on the west coast and to the south were a single land mass. He wrote:

> to obtain a thorough knowledge of these extensive countries, the discovery whereof has been begun (in consequence of the intention of the Company and the recommendation of our masters), now only remains for the future to discover whether Nova Guinea is one continent with that great south land, or separated by channels and islands lying between them; and also whether that New Van Diemen's Land is the same conti-nent with these two great countries, or with one of them; or, if separated from them, what islands may be dispersed between Nova Guinea and the unknown south land, when, after more experience and knowledge of all the said known and unknown countries, we shall be better enabled for further undertakings.

In effect, Tasman was presented with what had been discovered so far, and was asked to fill in the remaining gaps. As with previous expeditions he was asked to pay special attention to the discovery of precious metal. However, by 1644, Governors like Van Diemen were growing increasingly canny in their dealings with the people they encountered. Thus if Tasman did find gold or silver he was told:

> To keep them ignorant of the precious value seem not greedy after it; if they offer to barter for your goods seem not to covet these minerals, but show them copper, zinc, pewter and lead, as if these were of more value to us. If you find them inclined to trade, keep the goods which they seem most greedy after at so high a value that none may be sold nor bartered without great profit, likewise take nothing but what you are convinced will turn out profitable to the Company.

It's a great pity that Tasman's journal hasn't survived, because the charts of his voyage show him first sailing east to Cape York and the frustra-tions of Torres Strait that must have followed (if the previous Dutch attempts to find a route are anything to go by). How long he sought a passage, then still unknown to the Dutch (officially at least), is a mystery. Like Willem Janszoon and the *Duyfken*, Jan Carstenszoon and the *Pera* and *Arnhem*, and Gerrit Thomaszoon Pool's crew in the *Amsterdam* and *Wesel*, he turns south and his track follows the western coast of Cape York. Unlike his predecessors, he kept going, despite the inevitable difficulties of navigation and supply. Tasman charted the whole of the Gulf (naming features such as Groote Eylandt) around to Arnhem Land, then continued across the top of the present-day Northern Territory and on along the north-west coast of the South Land to present-day North West Cape.

This was the most extensive voyage along the coastline made to-date, and it established that the coast from Cape York to North West Cape was continuous. Previous voyages had established with reasonable certainty that both the west coast of the South Land and the south coast (from Cape Leeuwin across the Great Australian Bight to present-day Ceduna) were continuous. Had Tasman continued his voyage along the coast after North West Cape, he'd have had to pass several thousand kilometres of previously explored coast before he came to anywhere new (between Ceduna in South Australia and the southern Van Diemen's Land). Prudently, he left such exploration to later voyagers.

It is also from Tasman's second voyage that the South Land gained a new name. On his 1644 chart of the Australian coast, which includes the discoveries of all earlier voyages, the continent is referred to as New Holland. The inspiration for the name is unclear, particularly since the two places have almost nothing in common.

Despite the excellent work Tasman had done in further mapping the New Holland coast, when the Heren 17 of the VOC learned of this second great voyage of exploration, they wrote to Van Diemen in remarkably blunt terms:

> [We] see that Your Worships have again taken up the exploration of the coast of Nova Guinea in hopes of discovering silver- and gold-mines there. We do not expect great things of the continuation of such explorations, which more and more burden the Company's resources, since they require increase of yachts and sailors. Enough has been discovered to carry

on trade, provided the latter be attended with success ... These plans of Your Worships somewhat aim beyond our mark.

It was an extraordinary point of view, but as Jan Ernst Heeres points out in *The Part Borne by the Dutch in the Discovery of Australia*, it highlighted the fundamental difference between the commercial priorities of the Heren 17 and their representatives in the Indies. The VOC was a trading company, a business set up to buy, transport and sell goods. However, the governor general in the Indies was also a ruler, responsible for policy affecting almost every aspect of life within his jurisdiction. This included military operations (as has been seen in earlier chapters) and required intelligence regarding potential threats gathered by ships sent on exploratory voyages.

As it turned out, however, Antonio Van Diemen didn't live to endure the censure of his masters. He died before their letter arrived at Batavia. Nevertheless, it marked the end of the brief period of exploration and accidental encounters that had revealed to the world the existence of an entirely new continent. And while the Dutch may have endeavoured to keep their discoveries secret, they were also so proud of them that they couldn't resist celebrating their successes. The Australian coast was included in a map showing both of the world's hemispheres, constructed in marble and copper, and laid on the floor of the Great Citizen Hall of the Town Hall at Amsterdam between 1648 and 1655 (it's now in the Royal Palace of Amsterdam, while another map based on a lithograph of Tasman's 1644 map adorns the floor of the Mitchell Library in Sydney, incidentally including the incorrect position of Trial Rocks). Copies of this map of the Australian coast eventually accompanied later voyagers to Australia, among them Lieutenant Matthew Flinders of HMS *Investigator*.

Tasman, meanwhile, continued to serve the company in the Indies, although in 1649 he was sacked after hanging one of his crew without trial. He was soon reinstated, after compensating the crewman's family, and eventually died a wealthy landowner in Batavia in October 1659.

As for New Holland, the Dutch hadn't found gold nuggets strewn along the beaches, nor rich kingdoms with which to trade. With our benefit of hindsight, to say of it that 'enough has been discovered' may seem incredibly short-sighted, yet it shouldn't be forgotten that the Dutch experience along such a great extent of coastline had been almost uniformly disappointing, to say the least. There had been violent encounters with the indigenous inhabitants, horrific shipwrecks accompanied by unprecedented barbarity, and voyages along shores that presented the most arid and dismal prospects that European explorers had ever encountered. After 38 years, the Dutch were sure that if this new continent had anything of value to Europeans, it wasn't about to yield it easily.

6

WRECK AND RESCUE REVISITED

SCIENCE AND WAR • THE SEARCH FOR *DE VERGULDE DRAECK* • ENCOUNTERS AT CAPE LEEUWIN • THE ANGLO–DUTCH WARS • THE DUTCH JOINED BY THE FRENCH • THE LESSER OF TWO EVILS • *DE VLIEGENDE ZWAAN* AND *THE LONDON* SIGHT THE WEST COAST • FRENCH SHIP *L'OISEAU* SIGHTS THE WEST COAST • THE DUTCH AND ENGLISH UNITED •

After Abel Janszoon Tasman's great voyage of 1644, New Holland languished for more than a century at the fringes of the global consciousness. Having disappointed its early discoverers and the senior officials of the VOC, both in terms of its extent and its potential for trade, the vast continent was all but written off by all bar the dreamers and adventurers. It's tempting, therefore, to leap forward to the next great wave of exploration (from the 1760s until the early 1800s); yet to do so would be to arrive at the destination without knowing how the great seafarers got there. From the 17th to the 18th centuries there were great shifts in the global geo-political balance and with them a growing awareness of the world beyond the shores of Europe. During that time, the South Land continued to provide enough episodes of drama, tragedy and even piracy to ensure that it was never quite forgotten.

In the 1640s, Europe began its steady march towards globalism. For

example, in 1645, just after Tasman's second great voyage of exploration, the Invisible College was formed in London. Despite its sinister-sounding title, it was in fact an organisation of scientists, soon to be renamed the Royal Society. It would become one of the most respected scientific bodies; its spirit of enquiry reaching to the four corners of the world. It's no coincidence that in the following year (as mentioned in Chapter 3), Sir Robert Dudley published the first English map (written in Latin) to show any part of the Australian coastline. Not that English ships were in much peril; only the Dutch ships came across the Australian coastline when they overshot the Brouwer Route. There was another encounter in 1648, when Jan Janszoon Zeeuw in the VOC ship *Leeuwerik* mapped the already well-visited west coast in the region of 25–26 degrees south.

The concern with the perils of the Australian coast were soon overshadowed by events in Europe. In 1651 the protracted English Civil War ended.

Shortly after, a cash-strapped English government passed the *Navigation Act*. The Act imposed trade restrictions that only permitted English ships and crews to carry goods between England and her colonies. The effect on the sea-faring Dutch was not dissimilar to the effect of having Lisbon closed to them half a century earlier. In fact, the Act was so severe that the following year war broke out. The firefights between EEIC and VOC ships over the Spice Islands notwithstanding, it was one of the first wars that England fought on purely economic grounds. In 1652 the English navy inflicted a defeat on a Dutch fleet off Dover, and again in 1653 in the English Channel.

The war so weakened the Dutch, who secured a peace in 1654 with the Treaty of Westminster, that the Portuguese took the opportunity to drive them out of Brazil. The Dutch dependence on trade, its increasingly global nature, and its consequent vulnerability, was not lost on the victorious and increasingly versatile English navy.

Meanwhile, the Heren 17's efforts to curtail the exploration of New Holland were only partially successful. On 28 April 1656, the VOC ship *De Vergulde Draeck* (*The Gilt Dragon*), Pieter Albertszoon master, was nearing the end of a voyage from Texel to Batavia carrying a cargo of trade goods and 185 000 guilders worth of silver. Despite the bitter lessons of the ship *Batavia*, Albertszoon managed to miscalculate his position, and the ship became the second Dutch vessel known to have run aground on New Holland (on a reef five kilometres offshore and 100 kilometres north of present-day Perth, between Guilderton and Ledge Point).

The ship soon broke up, but not before 75 of the 193 passengers and crew made it ashore. Their position was dire, but like the *Batavia* they had a small boat that was able to make the voyage to Java to summon assistance. Unlike *Batavia's* Francisco Pelsaert, however, skipper Albertszoon remained with the bulk of the survivors and sent seven of his crew to summon help.

As the governor general wrote to the VOC on 4 December 1656:

> On the 7th June there arrived here ... from the South-land the cock-boat of the yacht *den Vergulden Draeck* with 7 men, to our great regret reporting that the said yacht had run aground on the said South-land in 30½° [it was actually considerably further south than that position], on April the 28th, that besides the loss of her cargo, of which nothing was saved, 118 men of her crew had perished, and that 68 men who had succeeded in getting ashore, were still left there. For the purpose of rescuing these men, and of

attempting to get back by divers or others any part of the money or the merchandises that might still be recoverable, we dispatched thither on the said errand on the 8th of the said month of June, the flute *De Witte Valk* [a small armed transport vessel], together with the yacht *De Goede Hoop*, which after staying away for some time were by violent storms forced to return without having effected anything, and without having seen any men or any signs of the wreck, although the said *Goede Hoop* has been on the very spot where the ship was said to have miscarried.

In fact, of the two yachts, *De Goede Hoop* had been unable to get near the mainland because of the stormy weather. However, her crew persevered and eventually search parties were able to reach shore in *De Goede Hoop's* boats. They were unable to find any trace of survivors, or the wreck itself, though not for want of trying. It is perhaps a measure of their determination that 11 men from *De Goede Hoop* were also lost ashore during the search effort, and not seen again.

Vessels that were homeward-bound also left messages at the newly-established Dutch settlement of Cape Town (founded in 1652) for outward-bound ships to join the search. In 1657, one of them, the flute *Vinck*, sailed from the Cape to New Holland and attempted to search for survivors. According to the *Daily Register* of Batavia for that year:

The skipper [of the *Vinck*] further reports that, according to the order and instructions handed him by Commander Riebeeck [at the Cape of Good Hope], he had touched at the South-land, but it being the bad monsoon on the said coast, they had found it impossible to sail along the coast so far as to look after the wreck and the men of the lost ship *den Draeck*; for in the night of June 8 (having the previous day seen all signs of land, and the weather being very favourable) they had come to anchor in 29°7'S L and the estimated Longitude of 130°43' [just north of present day Dongara], in 25 fathom coarse sandy bottom mixed with coral; the following morning at daybreak they saw the breakers on the reef at the end of which they were lying at anchor, and on one side ahead of them, the South-land, where there showed as a low-lying coast with dunes; upon which they weighed anchor and continued sailing along the coast in order to keep near the land, which was still in sight the day following; but the weather began to become so much worse and the breakers on the coast were so violent, that it was a fearful sight to behold, upon which they shaped their course a little more to seaward. On the 10th and 11th they kept sailing along the coast in 40 or 50 fathom, but seeing their chances of touching at the coast this time get less and less, and the weather continuing very unruly with violent storms of thunder and lightning, they resolved to keep off the coast, and drifted on without sail.

The search continued in 1658, when the galliots (essentially fishing boats able to carry cargo) *De Waekende Boey* and *Emeloort* were again sent from Batavia. Under the command of Samuel Volckersen and Aucke Pieterszoon Jonck respectively, the vessels landed both on the mainland and an island later named Rottnest (Rat's Nest), for the large numbers of 'rats' found there (actually small marsupial quokkas, see Chapter 8). This search was also notable for the presence of an artist who made the first European images of Australia.

The governors in Batavia wrote to the VOC on 14 December 1658:

The said ships returned to this place on the 19th of April following, after exploring the coast about the place of the disaster each of them for herself, since they had got separated; having in different places sent manned boats ashore, and fired many cannon-shots time after time both by day and night, without, however, discovering any Netherlanders or any traces of the wreck, excepting a few planks [etc] ... which must undoubtedly be looked upon as remnants of the said ship.

Volckersen also gave a brief account of the country in the vicinity of Perth, and the island offshore:

The South-land has sandy dunes forming many points on the sea-side; the dunes all consist of loose sand overgrown with grass into which a man will sink up to his ankles, and leave deep footprints on withdrawing his feet. About a mile [6 kilometres] more or less off shore, there is as a rule a rocky reef, on which the breakers may be seen to dash violently in many places, the depth above the reef being in several places 1, $1^{1}/_{2}$ and even 2 fathom [1.8 to 3.6 metres], so that pinnaces and boats may get over it for the purpose of a landing, there being deeper water close inshore ... Inward the land is pretty high, with hills of even height, but barren and wild to look at, except near the island where a great many trees are seen. In slightly under 32°S Lat there is a large island, at about 3 miles [18 kilometres] distance from the mainland of the South-land; this island has high mountains, with a good deal of brushwood and many thornbushes, so that it is hard to go over; here certain animals are found, since we saw many excrements, and besides two seals and wild cat, resembling a civet-cat, but with browner hair.

As with *De Goede Hoop*, the *Waekende Boey* lost 14 of its crew on the coast. However, the 14, led by upper steersman Abraham Leeman, had a boat. They managed to raise its freeboard using sealskins and set sail for Batavia. Despite a longer voyage than that of the *Batavia's* longboat, in a much smaller vessel, the tough Dutchmen reached the south coast of Java, but not before several died of thirst on the way. Desperate for water, the surviving men tried to get ashore on a treacherous section of Java's southern coast, but in doing so the boat was wrecked. They then faced a gruelling journey through the jungles of Java. Eventually four of them made it to a VOC base, including the upper steersman Leeman.

Even as the fruitless search for *De Vergulde Draeck* continued, more ships were having accidental encounters with the coast of New Holland. In 1658 Jacob Pieterszoon Peereboom and the VOC ship *Elburgh* encountered the coast between Cape Leeuwin and Geographe Bay. Unlike the sailors who encountered the rugged coast further north, Peereboom and his men were able to land, as the governors in Batavia reported:

> In 33°14′S L, round a projecting point, they have found a good anchoring place, where they have been at anchor in 20 fathom, and where the skipper, together with one of the steersmen, the sergeant and 6 soldiers landed round Leeuwinnen Cape, finding there three black men, hung with skins like those at Cape de Bonne Esperance, with whom, however, they could not come to parley.
>
> On the spot where the blacks had been sitting, our men found a burning fire, near which there lay a number of assagays [spears], together with three small hammers, consisting of a wooden handle to one end of which a hard pebble was fastened by means of a kind of wax or gum, the whole strong and heavy enough to knock out a man's brains.
>
> A little farther inward they came upon a number of huts, without any persons in them, and in various spots they found rills of fresh water, and here and there large quantities of the wax or gum aforesaid, of which we beg leave to hand you a small sample herewith, together with one of the said hammers, the wax or gum being of a red colour, and emitting an agreeable smell after being rubbed for some time …

The encounters with the indigenous population on the coast of Western Australia differ from those with people on Cape York Peninsula. While those in the west tended to flee on the approach of Europeans, those on Cape York tended to be more aggressive. In part this may be explained by the hard lessons learned by the Wik people of Cape York in the earliest encounters with the Dutch.

Those in the west may also have regarded the Europeans as 'ghosts'; Aboriginal ancestors returned from the dead. As such they may not have considered the white men a threat as much as objects of fear. In either case, first encounters with Aboriginal Australians often tended to leave the Europeans baffled and frustrated.

The Europeans, on the other hand, were only too familiar with invasion, and the need to vigorously defend territory and rights. In 1660, the English brought in their *Second Navigation Act*, despite the fact that the first had precipitated war with the Dutch. As if the first Act wasn't restrictive enough, the second went even further. Only ships built in England would be allowed to trade between England and her colonies, and her American colonies were not permitted to sell their sugar and tobacco directly to foreign countries; it all had to go through England. It was a move that made few friends, even disillusioning many Americans whose loyalties lay with the mother land. It was followed in 1663 by the *Staple Act*, which also required European goods bound for England's colonies to pass through England first.

Not surprisingly, enforcing such restrictive trade measures required increased naval power. So 1663 was also the year the English established their dockyard at Sheerness, bolstering their ability to build and maintain their increasingly active navy. Over 100 new ships were built in the years immediately after 1663, armed with the latest and heaviest cannon.

The following year, the English attacked and took the Dutch colony of New Amsterdam, on Manhattan Island in America. The triumphant English renamed the town New York. Thus assailed, the Dutch had little choice but to return to war. The Second Anglo–Dutch War broke out off the coasts of Africa in 1665, then moved closer to home, the English defeating the Dutch in a naval engagement off Lowestoft. During the fight the magazine of the Dutch flagship was hit by cannon fire from the *Royal Charles*, the subsequent explosion blowing the entire ship clear out of the water.

While England and the Netherlands squabbled, a new player entered the global battlefield: France. In 1666 she came in on the Dutch side, tipping the balance against the emerging power of the English. The Dutch were victorious off North Foreland, the English off the Dutch coast, while French warships succeeded in capturing Antigua and Montserrat, in the Americas, from the English. France, a country of 20 million compared to England's five million, was the obvious candidate to fill the power vacuum being left by a slowly declining Spain.

As the war escalated, the financial strain was felt by the Dutch and English alike. However, the English also had to endure the Great Plague of 1665 and the Great Fire of London of 1666. In 1667, commonsense prevailed with the Dutch, French, English and Danes concluding the Treaty of Breda, in which the Dutch retained Surinam in the Indies, while the English kept New York.

The French, meanwhile, continued to build their power. Under the imprimatur of the Catholic King Louis XIV they'd formed their own East and West Indies companies in 1664. In 1670 the Catholic French made the secret and somewhat questionable Treaty of Dover, pledging to support the Protestant English against the Protestant Dutch and the Catholic Spanish. The French navy, meanwhile, was rapidly expanding, numbering 200 ships in 1671.

Amid these manoeuvres, science continued to forge ahead. In 1670 Frenchman Jean Picard made the first exact measurement of the arc of the meridian, a key element in determining the earth's exact size and shape. William Clement in England invented the anchor escapement, which reduced the drag and recoil of verge-and-recoil escapements in pendulum clocks, making time-keeping almost ten times more accurate. Both were significant steps on the long journey towards improved instruments for use in navigation at sea.

In Europe, hardly anyone noticed as once again, in 1672, yet another war broke out with the Dutch; France and England both declaring war on the beleaguered nation. The Dutch, however, weren't to be taken lightly. On 7 June 1672 they caught the French and English fleets at anchor in Sole Bay, off Suffolk. Those on shore had grandstand seats as dozens of ships mounting thousands of cannon engaged on both sides. The Duke of York's flagship, the *Prince*, was surrounded and battered by several Dutch ships. When it was a wreck, the Duke moved his flag to the *St Michael*. The Dutch shot that out from under him, forcing the Duke to retreat to the *London*. The Dutch only withdrew after suffering heavy losses themselves. But they'd inflicted a defeat on the Anglo–French force. In 1673 they won again at Schooneveld Banks and retook New York. The only English victory was the seizing of St Helena, in the South Atlantic, a handy base for ships bound for the Cape and the Indies beyond. France, meanwhile, attacked the Dutch on land. The Dutch didn't stand a chance but rallied behind Willem III of Orange. Crying, 'we can die in the last ditch', the young nobleman ordered the gates of the country's dykes opened, flooding the countryside and stopping the French advance. A joyful populace made him head of state.

Only then did the trading nation of Protestant England come to recognise its true enemy: the French. England might have had a major commercial rival in the Protestant Dutch, but the growing Catholic French power threatened the safety of the nation itself. When fighting among the three combatant nations abated in 1674, and the Treaty of Westminster was signed, it signified much more than just peace between England and the Netherlands. In 1677, Mary, the daughter of England's future King James II (who had declared himself Catholic), married Willem III despite the opposition of Dutch commercial interests. Nevertheless, it was the foundation of a new alliance, and one that defined France as the new enemy.

Science, meanwhile, continued its less tumultuous progress, with Greenwich Observatory founded in 1675, the site through which the prime meridian for English vessels was soon to run. Dutchman Christiaan Huygens invented the balance wheel for watches. And in 1677 the brilliant young astronomer Edmund Halley observed the transit of Venus (as James Cook would do a century later, as described in Chapter 10). Two years before he'd also travelled to the newly seized St Helena to catalogue the stars of the southern hemisphere. These achievements may mean little in isolation, but each was a key step towards the better navigation of the world's oceans.

Indeed, navigation was already improving. Between 1658 and 1678, Dutch vessels were taking the hazards of New Holland to heart and managing to avoid it entirely. All that is known of a 1678 voyage along the north-west coast by Jan Van der Wall in *De Vliegende Zwaan* (*The Flying Swan*) comes from a surviving chart of the coastline that extends from North West Cape to Roebuck Bay. The chart itself was rudimentary as far as details were concerned. Most significant is the absence of the Monte Bello Islands. Had Van der Wall charted them at all, and especially if he'd done so accurately, he might have revealed the true position of the (still elusive) Trial Rocks.

It was only three years later, however, that the English once again appeared in the vicinity of New Holland. In June 1681, Captain Daniel and the ship *London* became the second Englishman to sight part of Australia, the northern section of the Houtman Abrolhos, where the *Batavia* had been wrecked. As with Brookes and the *Trial*, he described and charted what he saw, the difference being that he was correct about his position. In his journal, Daniel wrote:

> With the wind SW by W steering by compass NE by E, at 10 am the water was discoloured: a man at the foretop saw a breach rise ahead of us. We put our helm hard a starboard [turned to port] and stood away NW by W and weathered the NW end of it about ½ a mile [1 kilometre, the then English mile being about a third of a Dutch mile]: at that distance the depth was 35 fms [65 metres] white corally ground with some red mixed: next depth (about 2 hours after we tacked) was about 40 fms, the same ground, and at 9 pm having run off by log on a NW by W course had no ground at 65 fms … The breach which we first saw happened to be the northernmost of all, there being several and by our computation are 20 miles [32 kilometres] in length. Within the breaches several small white sandy islands were seen with some bushes on them: a very heavy sea broke against the south part of these. When close to them the mainland was not seen.

In her book, *Early Explorers in Australia*, English historian Ida Lee notes that Daniel named the Abrolhos 'Dangerous Rocks' and may also have given the name of Maiden's Isle to Rottnest Island (further to the south), 'as it is so called in many old atlases'. He charted the Abrolhos Shoal, imperfectly, becoming only the second Englishman to chart any part of Australia or its islands or reefs.

The French, meanwhile, were also spreading their wings. Their envoys were turning up in the Indies and starting to trade in their own right; and they were enjoying the favours of the rulers of countries like Siam. In 1686, their territorial ambitions took a more concrete form, when they annexed Madagascar. A year later, their ships were off the coast of Australia. On 4 August 1687, the French ship *L'Oiseau* (*The Bird*), commanded by Captain Duquesne-Guitton, was en route from the Cape of Good Hope to Siam with French Ambassador Claude Ceberet when they sighted the coast of Western Australia, near the Swan River.

The first recorded sighting of Australia by the French was only a fleeting glimpse. As with many previous sightings its nature was more accidental than deliberate, yet its significance cannot be overlooked. For it was the vanguard of the French presence in the South Seas, a presence that was to extend the field of European war to the seven seas.

The redrawing of the battle lines is most clearly illustrated by events that were gathering momentum even as the crew of *L'Oiseau* were peering at the Australian coast. Back in Europe, English and Dutch interests were becoming so entwined that some Englishmen were advancing plans to install the heroic Dutchman, Willem III, on the English throne. In 1688, the prospect of King James II's newborn Catholic son eventually ascending to the throne was too much for the Protestants of his realm. Willem III of the Netherlands, on the other hand, was a relative of James (by marriage to his daughter Mary), grandson of Charles I, a Protestant and a popular figure on both sides of the English Channel. In an extraordinary move made with the support of powerful English nobles, the Dutchman Willem invaded England with 14 000 Dutch troops, forcing James to flee to France. The following year an English Convention offered Willem and Mary the throne, which they jointly ascended as William III and Mary II. As Winston Churchill notes in *A History of the English-Speaking Peoples*, despite their commercial differences the English and Dutch were now united and were seldom divided again in European affairs. Indeed, they both went to war with their new common enemy, France, in the very same year. It was the beginning of an Anglo–French rivalry that was to last for more than a century, and give New Holland an importance far beyond the considerations of trade and commerce.

7

THE BUCCANEER'S HIDEOUT

'We will bring our commissions on the muzzles of our guns, at which time he should read them as plain as the flame of gunpowder could make them.' Thus spoke the buccaneer Captain Sawkins, dismissing the enquiry of the President of Panama as to whether the swashbuckler's impending attack (in 1679) was entirely legal. At the time, only privateering under a commission from one of the world's governments was strictly legitimate, but few of the buccaneers concerned themselves with such trifles.

The end of the 17th century was an exciting time to be alive. Treasure laden galleons plied the world's oceans, ripe for plunder by anyone bold enough to risk their cannon and the gallows. So tempting were the promises of riches, that ships voyaging to the Americas often saw entire crews run away to become buccaneers. (The name 'buccaneer' derives from the French hunters in the Caribbean who rebelled against the Spanish and happened to cook their meat on wooden frames called *boucans*.) One such buccaneer was

a colleague of the colourful Captain Sawkins, a young adventurer named William Dampier.

Dampier is one of the most fascinating characters ever to set foot on Australia's shores. Born in 1652, he was raised on an English farm, but orphaned at only 16. He ran away to sea three years later. At 27, while on a voyage to Jamaica, he fell in with a squadron of buccaneering ships, and embarked on an extraordinary voyage that would take him around the world over 12 tumultuous years. Dampier kept a journal the whole way, thus we know that when he reached Australia, early in 1688, he did so aboard an English trading vessel, the *Cygnet*. We also know that the *Cygnet* was stolen (by her own crew, who left their skipper on Guam, where he drowned, possibly at the hands of the local ruler). Dampier and his mates were on the run from just about everybody, having also attacked and taken both Spanish and Dutch vessels, having no regard for enemy or friend.

Before reaching New Holland, Dampier had already considered its location. While discussing the size of the Pacific and Indian oceans, he referred to the conversations of seamen who told him

> that ships sailing from the Cape of Good Hope to New Holland (as many ships bound to Java or thereabouts keep that latitude) find themselves there (and sometimes to their cost) running aground when they have thought themselves to be a great way off; and it is from hence possibly that the Dutch call that part of this coast the Land of Indraught (as if it magnetically drew ships too fast to it) and give cautions to avoid it: but I rather think it is the nearness of the land than any whirlpool or the like that surprises them.

William Dampier, image by Charles Sherwin published in 1791, after a portrait by Thomas Murray. nla.pic-an12653785, National Library of Australia

Dampier's explanation shows how gossip had passed from the Dutch to the English across the language barrier, the world's oceans and the 72 years since the ship *Eendracht* (which ironically means 'concord') became the first European vessel to sight Western Australia in 1616. However, from Dampier the English were now about to get their first detailed account of the mysterious South Land.

'The 4th day of January 1688 we fell in with the land of New Holland in the latitude of 16 degrees 50 minutes,' Dampier wrote. Finding nowhere to anchor, the *Cygnet* sailed north-east by east until it reached the island-dotted King Sound (on Australia's north-west coast) and within it what is now known as Cygnet Bay, where they anchored on 5 January. Dampier noted its geography.

> New Holland is a very large tract of land. It is not yet determined whether it is an island or a main continent; but I am certain that it joins neither to Asia, Africa, nor America [Abel Janszoon Tasman having established as much]. This part of it that we saw is all low even land, with sandy banks against the sea, only the points are rocky, and so are some of the islands in this bay.
>
> The land is of a dry sandy soil, destitute of water except you make wells; yet producing divers sorts of trees; but the woods are not thick, nor the trees very big … There was pretty long grass growing under the trees; but it was very thin. We saw no trees that bore fruit or berries.
>
> We saw no sort of animal nor any track of beast but once; and that seemed to be the tread of a beast as big as a great mastiff-dog. Here are a few small land-birds but none bigger than a blackbird; and but few sea-fowls. Neither is the sea very plentifully stored with fish unless you reckon the manatee [actually a dugong] and turtle as such. Of these creatures there is plenty but they are extraordinary shy; though the inhabitants cannot trouble them much having neither boats nor iron.

The inhabitants he regarded as 'the miserablest people in the world … who have no houses, and skin garments, sheep, poultry, and fruits of the earth, ostrich eggs, etc'. Though his European ideas about quality of life rendered his impressions of them unfavourable, his description of them was quite detailed.

> They are tall, straight-bodied, and thin, with small long limbs. They have great heads, round foreheads, and great brows. Their eyelids are always

half-closed to keep the flies out of their eyes; they being so troublesome here that no fanning will keep them out of their eyes … They have great bottle-noses, pretty full lips, and wide mouths. The two fore-teeth of their upper jaw are wanting in all of them, men and women, old and young; whether they draw them out I know not: neither have they any beards.

He noted that they tended to live in companies of 20 or 30, and that their staple diet consisted of small fish caught in fish traps; stone weirs usually built across small inlets. He also noted the communal sharing of their scarce food back at their camps.

There the old people that are not able to stir abroad by reason of their age and the tender infants wait their return; and what providence has bestowed on them they presently broil on the coals and eat it in common. Sometimes they get as many fish as makes them a plentiful banquet; and at other times they scarce get everyone a taste: but be it little or much that they get, everyone has his part, as well the young and tender, the old and feeble, who are not able to go abroad, as the strong and lusty … There is neither herb, root, pulse, nor any sort of grain for them to eat that we saw, nor any sort of bird or beast that they can catch, having no instruments to do so.

In these observations Dampier wasn't quite correct. The fact that he didn't see the Aboriginal people catch birds and beasts, or make use of herbs, roots and pulses, doesn't mean that they didn't do so. Nevertheless, Dampier was impressed by how tough life was for the Aboriginal people he encountered. In that observation he was neither the first nor the last. Unlike the Dutch, who often found that the indigenous Australians fled at their approach, Dampier gained his insights partly by putting himself close to their food sources.

These poor creatures have a sort of weapon to defend their weir or fight with their enemies if they have any that will interfere with their poor fishery. They did at first endeavour with their weapons to frighten us, who lying ashore deterred them from one of their fishing-places. Some of them had wooden swords, others had a sort of lance. The sword is a piece of wood shaped somewhat like a cutlass [probably a boomerang, used for hunting rather than fighting, which suggests fishing wasn't the only food source]. The lance is a long straight pole sharp at one end, and hardened afterwards by heat.

He had more luck when he and the *Cygnet's* crew went to one of the many islands in King Sound that now form part of the Buccaneer Archipelago. They found a group of 40 local people of all ages, some of whom were too old or too young to flee the approach of the Europeans. There was nowhere for anyone to hide, so the warriors made a stand. After the crew of the *Cygnet* fired a warning shot, chaos ensued. 'The lustiest of the women, snatching up their infants, ran away howling,' wrote Dampier,

> and the little children ran after squeaking and bawling; but the men stood still. Some of the women and such people as could not go from us lay still by a fire, making a doleful noise as if we had been coming to devour them: but when they saw we did not intend to harm them they were pretty quiet, and the rest that fled from us at our first coming returned again.

As mentioned in Chapter 6, it's quite likely that the Europeans were considered the ghosts of Aboriginal people who had died; the language barrier the result of a confusion of mind caused by the passage into the afterlife. However, language wasn't the only barrier to understanding. Finding water on the island, Dampier and his colleagues gave a few men some clothes in return for help carrying water barrels to the boat. The Aboriginal people being accustomed to sharing all their resources (as evidenced by Dampier's reference to the sharing of food) couldn't begin to comprehend an exchange of goods in return for services rendered. With the barrels on their shoulders, the men didn't move. When Dampier and the others gave up the attempt, the locals took the clothes off and left them.

While in King Sound, the crew beached the *Cygnet* in a sandy cove to work on the worm-riddled hull. In doing so, Dampier noted the size of the tide, which rose and fell some nine metres, leaving the ship high and dry a kilometre from the water. 'All the neap tides we lay wholly aground,' wrote Dampier, 'for the sea did not come near us by about a hundred yards [90 metres]. We had therefore time enough to clean our ship's bottom which we did very well.' The *Cygnet* certainly did get a good cleaning, remaining in King Sound for over two months.

Other members of the crew hunted turtle and dugong, which formed the major part of the Europeans' diet, a good-sized dugong able to supply about a tonne of meat. According to Ida Lee in *Early Explorers in Australia*, 'Part of the flesh resembles beef and other portions would easily be mistaken for pork.' It should be noted, however, that dugong are now a protected species, which can only be legally hunted by indigenous Australians.

While on Australia's shores, and possibly beforehand, Dampier harboured hopes of escaping the *Cygnet's* erratic voyage. As he wrote:

> While we lay here I did endeavour to persuade our men to go to some English factory [in the Indies]; but was threatened to be turned ashore and left here for it. This made me desist and patiently wait for some more convenient place and opportunity to leave them than here: which I did hope I should accomplish in a short time; because they did intend, when they went from hence, to bear down towards Cape Comorin [on the southern tip of India].

On 12 March the *Cygnet* set sail from New Holland, bound for Cocos Island and from there intending to proceed to the Red Sea. It wasn't until the ship reached Nicobar Island, near India, in May 1688, that Dampier was able to escape. From Nicobar Dampier and others who had also left the *Cygnet* took to the open ocean in a canoe, weathering a storm that threatened to sink them. Dampier voyaged around the East (including Malacca, Sumatra and Tonkin) for several years until he finally returned to England on 16 September 1691. By that stage he was no longer a wealthy buccaneer; all he had was a share in a tattooed native named Joely, which he was forced to sell.

His great asset, however, was his journal, which took six years (interrupted by several short voyages) to prepare for publication. When *A New Voyage Around the World* came out in 1697, it became an instant bestseller and made Dampier a celebrity. Australian historian Sir Ernest Scott wrote in *Australian Discovery*:

> Leading men of affairs were glad to converse with him [Ida Lee maintains he was 'brought under the notice of King William III by the Earl of Pembroke'], and he used his opportunities to promote a voyage of discovery to New Holland under his own command. He had influential patrons, the Admiralty were convinced that there was advantage in the project, and in 1699 the ship ROEBUCK was placed at his disposal for the purpose.

This is all the more remarkable because Dampier's book included admissions that he'd been a buccaneer. Under English law it was a crime, but while stealing a sheep might get an offender hung, piracy was only punishable by fines and imprisonment. In Dampier's case, it got him a job in the navy.

The *Roebuck*, a 12-gun vessel, was Dampier's first command. He was given this position despite having no previous experience of command or demonstrable ability as a leader of men. What is also striking is the argument Dampier put forward to justify the expedition, especially in light of what little he had found on his previous voyage. It bears a remarkable similarity to the instructions given to the several Dutch expeditions which preceded it. As he explained in his subsequent book, *A Voyage to New Holland*:

> This large and hitherto almost unknown tract of land is situated so very advantageously in the richest climates of the world, the torrid and temperate zones; having in it especially all the advantages of the torrid zone, as being known to reach from the equator itself (within a degree) to the Tropic of Capricorn, and beyond it; that in coasting round it, which I designed by this voyage, if possible, I could not but hope to meet with some fruitful lands, continent or islands, or both, productive of any of the rich fruits, drugs, or spices (perhaps minerals also, etc) that are in the other parts of the torrid zone, under equal parallels of latitude; at least a soil and air capable of such, upon transplanting them hither, and cultivation. I meant also to make as diligent a survey as I could of the several smaller islands, shores, capes, bays, creeks, and harbours, fit as well for shelter as defence, upon fortifying them; and of the rocks and shoals, the soundings, tides, and currents, winds and weather, variation, etc, whatever might be beneficial for navigation, trade or settlement; ... As there is no work of this kind brought to perfection at once I intended especially to observe what inhabitants I should meet with, and to try to win them over to somewhat of traffic and useful intercourse, as there might be commodities among any of them that might be fit for trade or manufacture, or any found in which they might be employed.

Even better, Dampier intended to commence his exploration on the 'eastern and least known side of the Terra Australis'. He planned to reach it by what he considered the fastest route: rounding South America via the Strait of Magellan or Tierra del Fuego, then crossing the Pacific. However, events worked against him. Almost from the time the *Roebuck* left England, on 14 January 1699, she wasn't a happy ship. The vessel was barely seaworthy; her crewmen were almost as mutinous as those on the *Cygnet*. Dampier, unaccustomed to command, also quarrelled with his senior officer, Lieutenant Fisher. The situation deteriorated to the point that Dampier feared Fisher would lead a mutiny and altered course for Bahia de Todos Santos (the Bay of All Saints on the coast of Brazil at 13 degrees south) where he

> hoped to have the governor's help, if need should require, for securing my ship from any such mutinous attempt; being forced to keep myself all the way upon my guard, and to lie with my officers, such as I could trust, and with small arms upon the quarter-deck; it scarce being safe for me to lie in my cabin by reason of the discontents among my men.

Dampier ended up putting Fisher in irons and having him imprisoned by the Portuguese governor.

While he resupplied for the next leg of the voyage, Dampier was also aware that the crew and remaining officers were reluctant to go further, especially as they were facing the prospect of rounding Cape Horn in winter. The hapless Dampier was forced to amend his plans, and head directly to the much-explored Western Australian shore. When he finally set sail on 23 April, he headed east for Africa's Cape of Good Hope, which he passed without stopping on 3 June.

He arrived off the western coast of Australia at the beginning of August 1699. On 2 August, 'When it was day we steered in east-north-east with a fine brisk gale; but did not see the land till 9 in the morning, when we saw it from our topmast-head.'

Despite being keen to get ashore to search for water after more than three months at sea, bad weather and the shoals off the coast (in latitude 26 degrees 10 minutes south) prevented him from coming to anchor until 6 August. 'In the morning we saw an opening in the land and we ran into it,' Dampier wrote, 'and anchored in 7-and-a-half fathom [13.5 metres] water, 2 miles [3 kilometres] from the shore, clean sand. It was somewhat difficult getting in here, by reason of many shoals we met with: but I sent my boat sounding before me. The mouth of this sound, which I called Shark's Bay, lies in about 25 degrees south latitude.'

Dampier sent a boatload of men to search for water, but they returned empty casked. The next day Dampier went to look himself, with the same result. Shark Bay, as it is now called, had already proved to earlier Dutch visitors to be a particularly parched section of the coast of Western Australia. However, Dampier had been sent from England in order to make valuable discoveries. Under the circumstances, it's not hard to understand why he might try to make the place sound better than it was:

> The grass grows in great tufts as big as a bushel, here and there a tuft being
> intermixed with much heath, much of the kind we have growing on our
> commons in England. Of trees or shrubs here are divers sorts ... Some of
> these trees were sweet-scented, and reddish within the bark, like the
> sassafras, but redder. Most of the trees and shrubs had at this time either
> blossoms or berries on them. The blossoms of the different sort of trees
> were of several colours, as red, white, yellow, etc, but mostly blue: and these
> generally smelt very sweet and fragrant, as did some also of the rest. There
> were also beside some plants, herbs, and tall flowers, some very small
> flowers, growing on the ground, that were sweet and beautiful, and for the
> most part unlike any I had seen elsewhere.

It sounds like paradise, and tourists still flock to Western Australia to view
the spectacular annual displays of wild flowers. Yet in reality, Shark Bay is
arid year round, starkly beautiful in its way, but as different from leafy
England as it's possible to get. Next, Dampier turned his attention to the
fauna.

> There were but few land-fowls; we saw none but eagles of the larger sorts
> of birds; but 5 or 6 sorts of small birds. The biggest sort of these were not
> bigger than larks; some no bigger than wrens, all singing with great variety
> of fine shrill notes; and we saw some of their nests with young ones in them.
> The water-fowls are ducks (which had young ones now, this being the
> beginning of the spring in these parts) curlews, galdens, crab-catchers,
> cormorants, gulls, pelicans; and some waterfowl, such as I have not seen
> anywhere besides.
>
> The land animals that we saw here were only a sort of raccoon, different
> from those of the West Indies, chiefly as to their legs; for these have very
> short forelegs; but go jumping upon them as the others do (and like them
> are very good meat) and a sort of iguana, of the same shape and size with
> other iguanas described, but differing from them in 3 remarkable particu-
> lars: for these had a larger and uglier head, and had no tail: and at the rump,
> instead of the tail there, they had a stump of a tail which appeared like
> another head; but not really such, being without mouth or eyes: yet this
> creature seemed by this means to have a head at each end and, which may
> be reckoned a fourth difference, the legs also seemed all 4 of them to be
> forelegs, being all alike in shape and length, and seeming by the joints and
> bending to be made as if they were to go indifferently either head or tail

foremost. They were speckled black and yellow like toads, and had scales or knobs on their backs like those of crocodiles, plated onto the skin, or stuck into it, as part of the skin. They are very slow in motion; and when a man comes nigh them they will stand still and hiss, not endeavouring to get away. Their livers are also spotted black and yellow: and the body when opened has a very unsavoury smell. I did never see such ugly creatures anywhere but here. The iguanas I have observed to be very good meat: and I have often eaten of them with pleasure; but though I have eaten of snakes, crocodiles and alligators, and many creatures that look frightfully enough, and there are but few I should have been afraid to eat of if pressed by hunger, yet I think my stomach would scarce have served to venture upon these New Holland iguanas, both the looks and the smell of them being so offensive.

The raccoons were small wallabies, the iguana most likely the stump-tailed skink, *Trachydosaurus rugosus*. No other writer appears to have furthered the research into its edibility. Having dealt with the land creatures, Dampier turned to the waves. Here, at least, there was plenty to justify the region's modern World Heritage Listing. Dampier identified skates, thornbacks, various stingrays, garfish and bonito, as well as an abundance of shellfish including edible oysters and pearl oysters. They caught two turtles and plenty of sharks

> which our men eat very savourily. Among them we caught one which was 11 foot [3.3 metres] long. The space between its two eyes was 20 inches [50 centimetres], and 18 inches from one corner of his mouth to the other. Its maw was like a leather sack, very thick, and so tough that a sharp knife could scarce cut it: in which we found the head and bones of a hippopotamus; the hairy lips of which were still sound and not putre-fied, and the jaw was also firm, out of which we plucked a great many teeth, 2 of them 8 inches [20 centimetres] long and as big as a man's thumb, small at one end, and a little crooked; the rest not above half so long.

The hippopotamus to which Dampier referred demonstrates the kind of confusion that led to all manner of fanciful creatures appearing on maps of the South Land. In fact, the creature was most probably a dugong which Dampier had encountered on his previous voyage and referred to as a manatee. It may also have been a southern elephant seal, which are still occasionally found in the vicinity.

Dampier charted the bay, drew pictures of the plants and creatures he saw, and collected botanical specimens which are now in the herbarium of Oxford University. This while the *Roebuck* edged about the shallow waters of Shark Bay, trying to find water. After a week without finding a single drop, Dampier moved on. He decided to turn north, along shores that had already been seen by numerous Dutch vessels throughout the 17th century. In *A Voyage to New Holland*, he felt compelled to explain his decision:

> Should it be asked why at my first making that shore I did not coast it to the southward, and that way try to get round to the east of New Holland and New Guinea; I confess I was not for spending my time more than was necessary in the higher latitudes; as knowing that the land there could not be so well worth the discovering as the parts that lay nearer the Line and more directly under the sun. Besides, at the time when I should come first on New Holland, which was early in the spring, I must, had I stood southward, have had for some time a great deal of winter weather, increasing in severity, though not in time, and in a place altogether unknown; which my men, who were heartless enough to the voyage at best, would never have borne after so long a run as from Brazil hither.

The weather notwithstanding, visiting 'a place altogether unknown' was actually the point of the exercise. Heading north, however, Dampier noted sea snakes, whales and dolphins before again coming in sight of land on 17 August. The *Roebuck* was well off the land when the soundings showed they were over a shoal. That night, still over the shoal, the ship was surrounded by a pod of whales,

> some ahead, others astern, and some on each side blowing and making a very dismal noise; but when we came out again into deeper water they left us. Indeed the noise that they made by blowing and dashing of the sea with their tails, making it all of a breach and foam, was very dreadful to us, like the breach of the waves in very shoal water, or among rocks.

The *Roebuck* sailed on until, four days later on 21 August, land was again sighted from the masthead during the afternoon. The ship anchored at sunset among a chain of islands, now known as the Dampier Archipelago, named by a Frenchman, Louis de Freycinet, a century later. Dampier thought the chain of islands might extend all the way back to Shark Bay, but the archipelago is actually limited to the area offshore from the present day town of Dampier. Islands do dot the coast to the south-west as far as North West Cape, including the Monte Bello Islands and the nearby Trial Rocks.

It was here that Dampier expressed doubts that New Holland was a solid landmass.

> By the great tides I met with a while afterwards, more to the north-east, I had a strong suspicion that here might be a kind of archipelago of islands and a passage possibly to the south of New Holland and New Guinea into the great South Sea eastward; which I had thoughts also of attempting in my return from New Guinea (had circumstances permitted) and told my officers so: but I would not attempt it at this time because we wanted water and could not depend upon finding it there.

Describing what was to become the Dampier Archipelago, he commented on Tasman's mapping of 55 years before. Dampier found the islands in latitude 20 degrees 21 minutes south:

> But in the chart that I had of this coast, which was Tasman's, it was laid down in 19 degrees 50 minutes, and the shore is laid down as all along joining in one body or continent, with some openings appearing like rivers; and not like islands, as really they are … which inclines me to think that he came not so near the shore as his line shows, and so had deeper soundings, and could not so well distinguish the islands …

Still hoping to find water, Dampier edged the *Roebuck* further into the archipelago, sending the ship's boat ahead to take soundings. The boat's instructions were to return if it found shallows, but to go ashore if it suspected there was water on any of the islands. The ship followed, finding depths from 35 metres to only seven. It was in seven metres that they anchored and signalled the boat to return.

> My boat came immediately aboard and told me that the island was very rocky and dry, and they had little hopes of finding water there. I sent them to sound, and bade them, if they found a channel of 8 or 10 fathom [14 or 18 metres] water to keep on, and we would follow with the ship. We were now about 4 leagues [20 kilometres] within the outer small rocky islands, but still could see nothing but islands within us; some 5 or 6 leagues [28 or 33 kilometres] long, others not above a mile round. The large islands were pretty high; but all appeared dry and mostly rocky and barren. The rocks

looked of a rusty yellow colour, and therefore I despaired of getting water on any of them.

He ventured a few kilometres more before the sea shoaled again and he was forced to drop anchor. However, he was now well inside the archipelago, describing his position as being on the inner side of an island 'on whose outside is the bluff point'. Again Dampier went ashore and dug for water, finding none. So, as at Shark Bay, he botanised.

> There grow here 2 or three sorts of shrubs, one just like rosemary; and therefore I called this Rosemary Island. It grew in great plenty here, but had no smell. Some of the other shrubs had blue and yellow flowers; and we found 2 sorts of grain like beans: the one grew on bushes; the other on a sort of creeping vine that runs along on the ground, having very thick broad leaves and the blossom like a bean blossom, but much larger, and of a deep red colour, looking very beautiful. We saw here some cormorants, gulls, crab-catchers, etc, a few small land-birds, and a sort of white parrot, which flew a great many together. We found some shellfish, namely limpets, periwinkles, and abundance of small oysters, growing on the rocks, which were very sweet. In the sea we saw some green-turtle, a pretty many sharks, and abundance of water-snakes of several sorts and sizes. The stones were all of rusty colour, and ponderous.

According to Ida Lee, the description of the island probably mistakenly joins what Captain Philip Parker King named Rosemary and Malus islands. The mistake was probably due to the direction from which Dampier approached, which makes them appear joined. As for the fauna, she maintains that the deep red bean 'looking very beautiful' is probably Dampier's Glory Pea (*Clianthus Dampieri*); a specimen of which is in the Dampier Herbarium at Oxford. Unfortunately, history didn't settle on Dampier's Glory Pea, the name Sturt's Desert Pea (*Swainsona formosa*) was substituted, and this now-protected member of the pea family is the floral emblem of South Australia. Dampier's luck was no better with the white parrot. It was known as Dampier's cockatoo (*Licmetis pastinator*) but is now either the Western cockatiel or long-billed corella. Six other plants were collected and eventually named in the Oxford Herbarium as *Casuarina equisetifolia* (beach she-oak), *Melaleuca gibbosa* (the slender honey-myrtle), *Solanum orbiculatum* (bush tomato), *Tripolona Dampieri*, *Dammara alba*, and *Trachymene pusilla* (the last three not having common names). Dampier did have quite a number of other flora named after him, particularly the *Dampiera* genus of 60–70 species including *Dampiera purpurea*, *Dampiera scottiana* and *Dampiera stricta*.

Again failing to find water the *Roebuck* edged its way back out to sea and continued north. At night, in a calm, they managed to catch a considerable number of fish including 'snapper, bream, old-wives, and dogfish'. On 28 August they saw more sea snakes and whales. They also managed to catch a 'noddy-bird' which Dampier dutifully described.

> It had a small long bill, as all of them have, flat feet like ducks' feet; its tail forked like a swallow, but longer and broader, and the fork deeper than that of the swallow, with very long wings; the top or crown of the head of this noddy was coal-black, having also small black streaks round about and close to the eyes; and round these streaks on each side a pretty broad white circle. The breast, belly, and underpart of the wings of this noddy were white; and the back and upper part of its wings of a faint black or smoke colour.

It was turning into a pleasant enough cruise for a naturalist, the increasingly dire water situation notwithstanding. On 30 August the *Roebuck* again sighted land in latitude 18 degrees 21 minutes south, in the vicinity of Cape Villeret, just south of what Phillip Parker King later named Roebuck Bay, after Dampier's ship. The bay is overlooked by the present-day pearling and resort town of Broome. The *Roebuck* anchored well offshore due to the shallow nature of the coastline, and the following day Dampier and a party of men armed with shovels, pick-axes, muskets and cutlasses went ashore to search for water.

The water situation must have been causing increasing concern, as Dampier's actions suggest. Rowing ashore they saw three Aboriginal men on the beach ahead of them, who left at their approach. Dampier and his crew went after them, only to find the locals had been joined by eight or nine more on top of a hill. Again the Aborigines retreated from the Europeans. From the top of the hill Dampier saw a plain with what looked like the houses 'just like the Hottentots' houses at the Cape of Good Hope' but they turned out to be boulders. Finding the plain otherwise deserted, Dampier returned to the beach to dig for water. While his crew worked, the Aborigines returned, but despite Dampier's best efforts, they couldn't be induced to stay and talk. So Dampier took two of his men and tried to catch one of them. The Aborigines seemed to have had the same idea. As Dampier relates:

> We knew by what rencounter we had had with them in the morning that we could easily outrun them; so a nimble young man that was with me, seeing some of them near, ran towards them; and they for some time ran away before him. But he soon overtaking them, they faced about and fought him. He had a cutlass, and they had wooden lances; with which, being many of them, they were too hard for him. When he first ran towards them I chased two more that were by the shore; but fearing how it might be with my young man, I turned back quickly, and went up to the top of a sandhill, whence I saw him near me, closely engaged with them. Upon their seeing me, one of them threw a lance at me, that narrowly missed me. I discharged my gun to scare them but avoided shooting any of them; till finding the young man in great danger from them, and myself in some; and that though the gun had a little frighted them at first, yet they had soon learnt to despise it, tossing up their hands, and crying pooh, pooh, pooh; and coming on afresh with a great noise, I thought it high time to charge again, and shoot one of them, which I did. The rest, seeing him fall, made a stand again; and my young man took the opportunity to disengage himself, and come off to me; my other man also was with me, who had done nothing all this while, having come out unarmed; and I returned back with my men, designing to attempt the natives no farther, being very sorry for what had happened already. They took up their wounded companion; and my young man, who had been struck through the cheek by one of their lances, was afraid it had been poisoned: but I did not think that likely. His wound was very painful to him, being made with a blunt weapon: but he soon recovered of it.

Having resorted to shooting a man while engaged in what would normally be the routine matter of finding water, Dampier had added to the growing number of incidents of first contact with Aboriginal people that had ended in bloodshed. He clearly regretted it and while his circumstances may have driven him to it, he was also unable to recognise that he was in an area where any water supply was considered precious, especially in those parts of the year when it was dry. In his retreat, he went on to note the details of the people he had encountered, in particular their leader.

Among the New Hollanders whom we were thus engaged with, there was

> one who by his appearance and carriage, as well in the morning as this after-
> noon, seemed to be the chief of them, and a kind of prince or captain
> among them. He was a young brisk man, not very tall, nor so personable as
> some of the rest, though more active and courageous: he was painted (which
> none of the rest were at all) with a circle of white paste or pigment (a sort
> of lime, as we thought) about his eyes, and a white streak down his nose
> from his forehead to the tip of it. And his breast and some part of his arms
> were also made white with the same paint; not for beauty or ornament, one
> would think, but as some wild Indian warriors are said to do, he seemed
> thereby to design the looking more terrible; this his painting adding very
> much to his natural deformity; for they all of them have the most
> unpleasant looks and the worst features of any people that ever I saw,
> though I have seen great variety of savages.

Dampier also noted the features of the people he referred to as 'New Hollanders', which implies that he recognised them as the occupants of the land. As he had done a decade earlier at King Sound, now only a short voyage from Roebuck Bay, he described them in largely unflattering terms. He also thoroughly examined the surrounding country, mostly in search of water, but noting the creatures and habitations he encountered.

Back on board the *Roebuck*, Dampier again documented the large tidal variation of about nine metres, but assumed it meant there was a passage through to the Pacific Ocean. From his experience of the tides in both places, he decided it must lie between his Rosemary Island and the site of his previous voyage's visit, King Sound. In fact no such passage exists; the tides are caused by the sea squeezing between mainland Australia and the chain of islands of the Indonesian Archipelago. The only passage was that found by Luis Vaéz de Torres, far to the north-west at Cape York, 93 years earlier.

His men, meanwhile, had dug a well nearly three metres deep without finding water. The next day, 1 September, he sent his boatswain to dig deeper, but they had no success. The following day the men dug further inland and found brackish water fit only for boiling their oatmeal. Even then it made some of them ill, but it did extend their water supply slightly. The lack of water severely limited Dampier's options regarding the continuation of his voyage, although he still hoped to get around to King Sound, where he knew he could find water as he'd done with the buccaneers of the *Cygnet*. Before leaving the environs of Roebuck Bay, he summarised his observations, not forgetting to mention 'yellow flowers or blossoms, some blue and some white, most of them of a very fragrant smell'. His men also sighted 'two or three beasts like hungry wolves, lean like so many skeletons, being nothing but skin and bones [probably dingoes]. We saw a raccoon or two [wallabies], and one small speckled snake.' He mentioned crows that differed little from those in England and turtledoves that made good eating.

In five weeks at New Holland, Dampier sailed along some 1500 kilometres of coastline, stopping at Shark Bay (which he named), Dampier Archipelago (named after him) and near Roebuck Bay (named after his ship). In that time he found only a scant amount of brackish water, not surprisingly since it was the dry season when he visited that coast, which gets little water at the best of times anyway. He had found little of commercial value for the sponsors of the voyage, and surmised the existence of a passage from the Dampier Archipelago across to the Pacific Ocean, which wasn't actually there. In considering another possibility he continued in his erroneous notions about the Dutch Land't d'Eendracht, writing that there was a passage 'unless the high tides and great indraught thereabout should be occasioned by the mouth of some large river; which has often low lands on each side of its outlet, and many islands and shoals lying at its entrance'.

As he continued his voyage north on 5 September, he attempted to reach King Sound, but found more shoals that forced him further from the coast. At last, he felt himself in a position where he had to choose between King Sound and Timor.

> I began to bethink myself that a great part of my time must have been spent in being about a shore I was already almost weary of, which I might employ with greater satisfaction to my mind, and better hopes of success, in going forward to New Guinea. Add to this the particular danger I should have been in upon a lee shore, such as is here described, when the north-west monsoon should once come in; the ordinary season of which was not now far off, though this year it stayed beyond the common season; and it comes on storming at first, with tornadoes, violent gusts, etc. Wherefore quitting the thoughts of putting in again at New Holland, I resolved to steer away for the island Timor; where, besides getting fresh water, I might probably expect to be furnished with fruits and other refreshments to recruit my men,

who began to droop; some of them being already to my great grief afflicted with the scurvy.

With that, Dampier departed the coasts of New Holland, engaging in extensive justifications presumably for the benefit of those who had furnished him with so much and were to receive a modest collection of botanical specimens in return. Dampier continued his voyage in the increasingly fragile *Roebuck*, and while he had intended to resume his voyage on the eastern side of New Guinea, circumstances worked against him. After reaching Timor Dampier passed along the north coast of New Guinea to its eastern tip, where he found and named the island of New Britain. He was then forced to turn back. The *Roebuck* was falling apart, his shrinking crew wanted to go home, and the prospect of entering uncharted waters in such a reduced state was too much to ask. Dampier headed for Batavia to resupply before heading on to the Cape.

He was homeward bound when the *Roebuck* sprang a leak and finally foundered in the Atlantic, just off the Ascension Islands, on 21 February 1701 (the wreck was found 300 years later, in April 2001). He and the remaining crew were eventually picked up and Dampier returned to England in the East India ship *Canterbury* in 1701. There, rather than being met with more fame and adulation, he was court-martialled.

Lieutenant Fisher had preceded Dampier, having been released from the prison where he'd been left without any money to support himself. A naval inquiry found Dampier guilty of 'very hard and cruel usage' towards one of their own. The court decided there were no grounds for his conduct, fined him all the pay he'd earned while on his voyage and declared him 'not a fit person to be employed as commander of any of His Majesty's ships'.

It should have ended his career. However, in 1701, after the War of the Spanish Succession broke out, two privateer vessels, the *St George* and the *Fame*, were fitted out and in 1702 Dampier was made commander of the *St George*. He was introduced to the Queen by the Lord High Admiral, before going off on yet another voyage of legalised piracy. It proved just as quarrelsome as the *Roebuck* voyage. The *Fame's* captain abandoned the voyage while still in sight of England, his replacement died and the ship's lieutenant took over. The lieutenant eventually marooned one of his seamen, Alexander Selkirk, on the island of Juan Fernandez, in the Pacific. The voyage itself achieved little in terms of enemy ships taken, and Dampier again had his ship sink beneath him, after it had become so unseaworthy that it had to be abandoned. He eventually made it back to England in 1707, having circumnavigated the world a second time.

In 1708, it appears his lack of ability as a commander was finally recognised. He couldn't command the loyalty of his crews, nor motivate them to the high-risk activity of exploration. He'd then struggled to get them to go privateering. However, he was still highly regarded as a navigator. He was invited to join a privateering expedition to the Pacific as a pilot for two vessels, the *Duke* and *Duchess*. Under the command of a highly respected captain Dampier appears to have been more in his element. During the voyage, Selkirk (the marooned seaman from the *Fame*) was rescued from the island of Juan Fernandez, having been marooned for four years, and went on to become the inspiration for Defoe's Robinson Crusoe. The voyage itself also succeeded in capturing prizes worth £170 000. With his share Dampier returned from the voyage that was to be his last, and settled in London where his health soon deteriorated. He died in March 1715.

Dampier's career may have started with a bang, but it didn't entirely end with a whimper. His legacy may not have been fully appreciated during his lifetime, but it grew in stature after his death. Admiral Smythe in the *United Service Journal* of 1837 noted that

> he was the first who discovered and treated of the geological structure of sea coasts; and though the local magnetic attraction in ships had fallen under the notice of seamen, he was among the first to lead the way to its investigation since the facts that 'stumbled' him at the Cape of Good Hope, respecting the variations of the compass, excited the mind of Flinders, his ardent admirer, to study the anomaly.

Ida Lee noted that 'after Dampier's return from this voyage in 1702 more than ever before was known in England concerning the South Land'. That knowledge included the description of a successful voyage from England to Brazil, then on past the Cape of Good Hope to New Holland. It was the sea route to New Holland that was eventually found by the English to be the easiest. It also included a realisation that the objectives of voyages of exploration could include more than just the discovery of valuable commodities for trade; especially if you were a scientist.

All this and the life of a buccaneer to boot. William Dampier unified a sense of adventure with an enquiring observant mind, and while he might have become far more famous if he'd turned south at Shark Bay instead of north, he still became an inspiration for the generations that were to follow him. And for them, as the 18th century dawned, the mysteries of a largely unexplored continent, the South Land, still beckoned.

8

THE MISERABLE
SOUTH LAND

THE SEARCH FOR THE *RIDDERSCHAP*
VAN HOLLAND •DE VLAMINGH FAREWELLS
'THE MISERABLE SOUTH LAND' •
COMMERCE VERSUS EXPLORATION •
ARNHEM LAND EXPLORED • THE THEORY OF
ISLANDS • THE *ZUYTDORP* WRECKED • WAR
AND PEACE, A PRIZE FOR LONGITUDE, THE
SOUTH SEA BUBBLE • THE *ZEEWIJK*
WRECKED • THE FRENCH IN ASIA • THE
DUTCH SEARCH FOR TORRES STRAIT •

While William Dampier was making the most detailed discoveries of any Englishman who had trod the shores (or islands) of Australia to that date, the Dutch were following their usual pattern of putting ships 'on the bricks' and sending others to search for them. In 1694, it was the turn of the *Ridderschap Van Holland*, Dirck de Lange master. She was en route from the Cape of Good Hope to the East Indies with 326 people aboard, including a VOC director, James Couper, and somewhere in that great expanse, disappeared. The consensus was that she became yet another casualty of the west coast of New Holland.

As with previous incidents, outbound ships were alerted to keep watch for the missing vessel and her crew. However, unlike previous incidents, a search was initiated by the Heren 17 back in the Netherlands. The Dutch appear to have transcended pure commercial interest (as did the English with Dampier) as they assembled a fleet of three vessels – the ship

Geelvinck (133 hands), the hooker *Nijptang* (*The Nipper* a two-masted fishing boat, 50 hands) and the galliot *'t Weseltje* (*The Little Weasel*, 14 hands) – to conduct the search under the command of Willem de Vlamingh. At least one of the Heren 17, Nicolaas Corneliszoon Witsen, the mayor of Amsterdam, hoped the expedition would achieve more than search and rescue. 'I have directed a draughtsman to join the expedition,' he wrote, 'that whatever strange or rare things they meet with, may be accurately depicted.' Witsen, a traveller and writer himself, and a friend of the missing Couper, pressed upon the expedition the need to explore not only the coast, but to press inland as far as possible.

De Vlamingh's fleet reached New Holland on 29 December 1696, more than two years after the *Ridderschap Van Holland* went missing. They immediately found 'strange or rare things', as recorded in the journal of Gerrit Colaert, skipper of the *Nijptang*, published in Richard Henry

Major's *Early Voyages to Terra Australis*. 'Our people observed a remarkable fish here, about two feet [60 centimetres] long, with a round head and a sort of arms and legs and even something like hands,' wrote de Vlamingh, although the ship's artist appears not to have thought what was probably a young dugong worthy of depiction.

They anchored off the island that they would soon name Rottnest (Rat's Nest Island), after the quokkas they encountered when they went exploring on 30 December. 'There are very few birds there and no animals,' wrote Colaert,

> except a kind of rat as big as a common cat, whose dung is found in abundance over all the island. There are also very few seals or fish, except a sort of sardine and grey rock bream. In the middle of the island, at about half an hour's distance, we found several basins of excellent water, but brackish, and six or seven paces further a fountain of fresh water fit to drink. In returning to the shore, the crew found a piece of wood from our own country, in which the nails still remained. It was probably from a shipwrecked vessel.

De Vlamingh, responsible for finding things of note to the company, wrote 'Nature has denied nothing to make it pleasurable beyond all islands I have ever seen.'

The following day, more wood was found. If it was from the *Ridderschap Van Holland*, it wasn't much to go on. More intriguing were columns of smoke, rising on the mainland. Hoping they might be signals from survivors, several boats were dispatched there the next morning. It was here that the expedition, in following its instructions to explore New Holland, went further than any previous maritime exploration had done, penetrating deep inland along the river that de Vlamingh named the Swan.

'At sunrise on the morning of the 4th,' wrote Colaert,

> I, in company with the skipper, put off to the mainland with the boats of the three South Land navigators. We mustered, what with soldiers and sailors, and two of the blacks that we had taken with us at the Cape, eighty-six strong, well armed and equipped. We proceeded eastwards; and, after an hour's march, we came to a hut of a worse description than those of the Hottentots. Further on was a large basin of brackish water [Melville and Perth Waters, now overlooked by the Perth business district], which we afterwards found was a river; on the bank of which

were several footsteps of men, and several small pools, in which was fresh water, or but slightly brackish. In spite of our repeated searches, however, we found no men.

The shore party decided to camp ashore, around a fire lit by the elusive locals. The next day, they divided into three smaller groups and went in separate directions with hopes of encountering some of the inhabitants. Around midday, they rendezvoused back at the river, none of them having found more than basic camps and footprints.

They had, however, found a fruit tree. Its nuts tasted like Dutch beans, the younger ones like walnuts. However, wrote Colaert:

> After an interval of about three hours, I and five others who had eaten of these fruits began to vomit so violently that we were as dead men; so that it was with the greatest difficulty that I and the crew regained the shore, and thence, in company with the skipper, were put on board the galliot, leaving the rest on shore.

The nuts were probably from Zamia palms. They're edible, but need to be well soaked first, to get rid of their poison. It took most of the men a couple of days to recover, during which the exploration of the Swan River continued by boat for some 90 kilometres of its length. This was the furthest any European had been recorded as having gone inland. As the Dutch went, they saw more abandoned campfires and noted large numbers of swans. In true antipodean fashion, they were black, the opposite of the northern hemisphere's white swans.

The exploration continued until 11 January, when the Swan River became too shallow for navigation and de Vlamingh had 'discovered nothing of importance'. He was in fact near what is now renowned wine-growing and wheat country. The sailors, meanwhile, tried taking some of the indigenous inhabitants by surprise during the hours of darkness, but met with failure. In summarising, Colaert wrote in his journal: 'The best of it is that no vermin is found there; but in the day time one is terribly tormented with the flies.'

On 13 January, a fortnight after their arrival, the vessels sailed north, examining the coastline as they went. They landed frequently, finding tracks of men and animals, but encountering no human or other living creature. They found few watering places or safe anchorages. As they went north, the land became increasingly barren.

On 21 January, sailing along the shore between 28 degrees and 29 degrees south, the chief pilot went ashore to explore, returning late in the day. He reported seeing three or four men on the shore, and several more inland

> all quite naked, black, and of our own height; but that he had not been
> able to get near them on account of the current; that afterwards, rowing a
> little further, they had landed and found a lake, which extended far into
> the country like a river. It was of brackish taste, and though white had a
> reddish tinge caused by the bottom, which was of red sand and mud.

This was the estuary of the Murchison River, site of present-day Kalbarri, at 27 degrees 42 minutes south. Anchoring offshore in Gantheaume Bay, on 25 January de Vlamingh and a party of officers and 31 soldiers went ashore and again pushed inland. Late January being nearly the hottest part of summer, and especially so in that part of Australia, the Europeans soon found themselves in some distress. Colaert wrote:

> We put ourselves in marching order, but from the fatigue occasioned by
> the excessive heat, and the obstructions on the road from brushwood, we
> were obliged occasionally to rest ourselves, till we reached the mountains,
> where we took our rest. But if the road had been difficult, a greater trouble
> was yet in store for us; for, finding no fresh water, we thought we should
> have fainted with thirst. From this point we could see our vessels, and
> wished a thousand times over that we were on board again.

They called a halt while three men, led by the soldiers' commandant, searched for water. They eventually found a brackish pool, beside which they camped for two days. While there they noted footprints 45 centimetres long, although when they tracked them they somehow changed to ordinary ones.

Once more, exploration encountered nothing of the people except for their abandoned campsites. The following day the party returned to the ships and continued their voyage north, close to shore along the steep cliffs the longboat of the *Batavia* had passed 68 years earlier. On 30 January they reached Dirck Hartog's Reede, the gulf that would be named Shark Bay by William Dampier just 18 months later. Again they explored some 40 kilometres inland, de Vlamingh finding a large bird's head and two nests three fathoms (5.4 metres) in circumference, probably belonging to ospreys.

De Vlamingh wrote in his journal that the bay

was the best roadstead of all where we have lain so far. It is very large and wide and have the north shore at least five miles [30 kilometres] from us … one can anchor here as near the shore as one likes and good sandy bottom is everywhere at 10 to 12 fathoms [18–20 metres]. The land here is very dry and sandy without trees and at night one can catch or turn over as many turtles as one likes, and get as many turtle's eggs as one desires.

The chief pilot also explored what turned out to be Dirk Hartog Island, locating the tin plate Hartog had fixed there 81 years earlier. It had fallen from the badly-weathered post but the pilot was able to find the plate and read the inscription (see Chapter 3). The expedition took the plate with them, and fixed a new plate to a new pole. The translation is:

AD 1697, on the 4th of February there arrived here the ship *de Geelvinck*, skipper Willem de Vlaming, of Vlieland; assistant Joennes van Bremen, of Copenhaguen; upper-steersman Michiel Blom, of Bremen; the hooker *de Nijptang*, skipper Gerrit Collart, of Amsterdam; assistant Theodorus Heermans, of do; upper-steersman Gerrit Gerrits, of Bremen, the galiot *'t Weseltje*, master Cornelis de Vlaming, of Vlieland; steersman Coert Gerrits, of Bremen; the whole of our flotilla sailed from here on the 12th do, in order to explore the South-land with destination for Batavia.

This dish was afterwards recovered by Louis de Freycinet on an expedition with *L'Uranie* and *La Physicienne* 120 years later. De Vlamingh's men, meanwhile, continued their exploration of the bay, taking soundings with their boats for a distance of some 25 kilometres. Apart from finding oysters, turtles, ducks and a fish that could feed more than 50 men and tasted like a stingray, a storm gave them their first rain since sighting New Holland more than a month before. Steering for the mainland on 9 February, they encountered a coast that was 'steep, the sand of a reddish colour, rocky, dry and forbidding'. Searching for water, even after rain, they found all of the watercourses were dry.

As their pewter plate noted, they set sail from Shark Bay on 12 February. They continued north until 19 February, when they rounded North West Cape and entered Williams River (actually Exmouth Gulf). Finding poor anchorage, they set sail again and then took council on what to do. On 21 February, according to Colaert:

In the morning, we put to sea towards the NW Latitude 21 degrees. Held once more a council. Received from De Vlamingh three half barrels of water. Half an hour after sun-rise, our captain came from on board De Vlamingh's vessel, from which five cannon shot were fired and three from our vessel, as a signal of farewell to the miserable South Land; and we steered our course NNW, in 135 degrees of longitude from the South Land.

Phillip Playford's *Voyage of Discovery to Terra Australis* reports de Vlamingh's point of view, on the fufilment of his instructions:

I had obtained sufficient information to pass on to [the company's direc-tors] to enable them to send another expedition to this coast, without holding any fear for their vessels, which is a rather important indication of the success of my voyage.

The reality was that, as so many voyagers along the West Australian coast had found before them, the land offered almost nothing in terms of discov-eries of value to the company, be they commercial or scientific. The charts made of the coast were among the best done by the Dutch to that date, but there was little apart from these maps to show for the time, trouble and expense the Dutch had taken. Apart from the charts and journals, the governor general reported to the VOC on 30 November 1697:

In general in this part of the South-land, which in conformity with their instructions they have diligently skirted, surveyed and observed, they have found little beyond an arid, barren and wild land, both near the shore and so far as they have been inland, without meeting with any human beings, though now and then they have seen fires from afar, some of the men fancying that two or three times they have seen a number of naked blacks, whom however they have never been able to come near to, or to come to parley with; nor have they found there any peculiar animals or birds, excepting that especially in the Swaene-rever they have seen a species of black swans, three of which they have brought to Batavia alive, which we should have been glad to send over to Your Worships, but that shortly after their arrival here they all of them died one after another. Nor, so far as we know, have they met with any vestiges of the lost ship *de Ridderschap van Hollant* or of any other bottoms, either in those parts or near the islands of Amsterdam and St Paul, so then in sum nothing of any impor-tance has been discovered in this exploratory voyage.

Despite de Vlamingh's best efforts, VOC director Witsen accused him of failing to carry out instructions, and not spending more than a couple of days at any of his anchorages, although de Vlamingh had spent upwards of a fortnight in the Perth region, and almost as long in Shark Bay. Witsen may well have been bitter about such a dismal result for an expedition he'd played such a large part in organising. All he got from it were a couple of shells (though they were excellent specimens). Wrote Ida Lee in *Early Explorers in Australia*:

> The first specimens of any kind to reach Holland from New Holland were two shells which had been given to Burgomaster Witsen of Amsterdam in 1698 by a sea captain in the service of the Dutch East India Company. This was William Vlamingh, who had visited Western Australia in the previous year; and, in a letter to Dr Lister of the Royal Society Witsen says 'he found them on the seaside, and I make bold to send you the draught of them, the shells themselves being twice as long and as broad as the draught'. He adds the courteous message 'I could not bestow them better than on one who hath the best knowledge of these and all other sea products.' A description of the shells, with illustrations, was afterwards published in Lister's *Synopsis Conchyliorum* – one being the first nautilus [*Nautilus pompilius*], the other then named the *Concha persica clavicula radiata*.

Witsen's deference to the pre-eminence of England's Royal Society is significant in terms of the future European exploration of Australia. For in the same year that the nautilus and conch shell reached Lister, Dampier had set sail for the South Land, and would soon return with his drawings and collection of dried plants. Despite his voyage being the first deliberate exploration by the English, it had yielded the best collection of flora and fauna from the continent at the far side of the world.

Meanwhile, Witsen could only regret the opportunity lost, as the VOC tightened its purse strings once more. Some historians have noted that if he'd wanted the exploration executed to his satisfaction, he should have gone himself. As it was, after his retirement he was still writing to friends about the company's policy, 'It is money only, not learned knowledge, that our people go out to seek over there, the which is sorely to be regretted.'

While Dampier and de Vlamingh were having indifferent experiences on the coasts of New Holland, Europe was once more preparing for war. In

1696, the war that had seen the English and Dutch united against the French had ended, but peace was short-lived. Spain's King Carlos II (also known as Charles II) was childless, and the question of a successor divided Europe's great powers. Key to the succession was the ability to counterbalance the growing power of France's Louis XIV. In 1700, King Carlos II named Louis' grandson as his heir. A Treaty of Partition for the declining Spanish empire failed to stop the arguments over his succession, and when Carlos died, the question of his successor remained unresolved. In 1701 the War of Spanish Succession was declared. It was to last more than a decade, during which it became apparent that a country's ability to supplement its wealth with the profits from its empire was increasingly crucial to survival.

Survival was also the name of the game when it came to avoiding the elusive Trial Rocks. In 1703, they put in an appearance in John Thornton's *Lists of Latitudes,* located in latitude 19 degrees 45 minutes south with a lengthy description of their extent and shape. However, Thornton and his hydrographic colleagues soon had more tangible rocks to chart. In 1704 the English and Dutch stormed and took the Rock of Gibraltar. Despite the best efforts of the Spanish and French to retake it, the English and Dutch clung to it like limpets. For the English, it was to become the cornerstone of a presence in the Mediterranean that was to be of great strategic value down to the present day.

The Dutch meanwhile, continued to dabble with their explorations in New Holland. In 1705, they instructed yet another fleet to explore the landmass south of Java. However, the objectives for the flute *Vossenbosch,* sloop *Waijer* and *patsjallang* or pinnace *Nova Hollandia* under the command of Maarten Van Delft were purely navigational. The governor general in Batavia instructed Van Delft on 20 January 1705:

> You will in the first place have diligently to observe, whether there is anywhere a passage from the outside to the inside, and this not only as regards Nova Guinea, but also as concerns Hollandia Nova, so that these orders … will have to be acted up to not only by the officers of the *Geelvinck* [which didn't make the voyage], but also by those of the *Vossenbosch*; and you should take special care, in case you should find such real or seeming passage, not to run too far into it, lest you should be carried away by currents in the same, and run the risk of accidents; on which account the examination of such passages should nowise be under-

taken by the frigate or by the flute, but only by a pinnace or *patchiallang*, never to any farther distance than the experienced sailors in the same shall deem advisable to enable a safe return out of the said passages, and in no case so far as to get out of anchoring depth ...

The hope was to find a shortcut through the centre of New Holland, or the long-sought-for strait between New Guinea and Australia. The instructions are remarkably similar to those of many expeditions which had gone before them. However, the new attempt may have been due to Dampier's opinion in the just-published *Voyage to New Holland*, which discussed the possibility of a passage somewhere on the section of coast he thought Abel Janszoon Tasman had poorly mapped. In any case it's hard not to admire the Dutch persistence, especially in light of the trials the three ships soon underwent.

From 2 April 1705, the fleet was in sight of the New Holland coast in the region of north-eastern Arnhem Land (though they reckoned they were in northern Van Diemen's Land). They explored the bays, headlands and rivers according to their instructions until 12 July. Their discoveries were not considered remarkable, although they did manage to have much more success in their contacts with the locals. As the governors reported from Batavia Castle (see Chapter 3) on 6 October 1705, the fleet saw columns of smoke, and shortly after adults and children fleeing the sight of their vessels. A closer contact soon took place, as the governors reported:

> Some natives were met by the men on the thirty-first of April, who did not retire, but ran hastily to an eminence, and with signs and gestures attempted to drive them away. No one was able to understand their language, which, according to the skipper Martin van Deift, seems to resemble in some respects that of Malabar; but even this is by no means clear.

The description of the inhabitants that followed is not dissimilar to that penned by William Dampier, especially in terms of its attention to detail. While it may reflect an increasing scientific interest in the ethnography of the world, it also provides valuable insights into first contacts between Europeans and indigenous Australians. Unfortunately, it also followed the established pattern of bloodshed, as the governors reported:

> The colour and stature of these men, appears from the description given to resemble most that of the Indians of the east; but they go stark naked

without any regard to age or sex, as was constantly observed by our sailors from the above-mentioned date, until their departure. The only exception to this rule were the women who had children with them, these alone wearing a slight covering of leaves or such-like over their middle. The whole number of these islanders did not exceed fourteen or fifteen men; seeing that our people could not be induced by their grimaces, violent gestures, yelling and flourishing of *assegais* [spears], and all kinds of weapons, to retreat from the shore, they were imprudent enough to throw some of their *assegais*, or rather sharpened sticks, at our men, with the intention of wounding and intimidating them; but their chief, or one who at least appeared to be so, being hit by a ball from the single musket which was fired at them in return, the rest began to run quickly away, being very agile and well made.

The women are tall and slim, with very large mouth and small eyes; the head of both sexes is curly, like that of the Papuan islanders, and a yellow or red ointment, prepared with turtle fat, seems to be used as an ornament. The nature of these tribes is foul and treacherous, as was apparent at the last moment, when our people were on the point of departing. Eight islanders attacked and wounded two sailors, with the hope of seizing upon their clothes, and that after having conversed with these men for weeks, eaten and drunk with them, visited them on board, and being allowed to examine everything to their great admiration, after having received presents, and also on their part regaled our people with fish and crabs. Besides this, their bad disposition came to light in the case of the man who had been previously wounded by our party as before mentioned; when he afterwards was assisted and bandaged, and had every possible attention shown him by our men, he tore the linen to pieces and threw it away into a corner; notwithstanding that at other times these natives appeared particularly greedy after linen, knives, beads, and such toys.

They however possess nothing which is of value themselves, and have neither iron nor anything like mineral ore or metal, but only a stone which is ground and made to serve as a hatchet. They have no habitations, either houses or huts; and feed on fish, which they catch with harpoons of wood, and also by means of nets, putting out to sea in small canoes, made of the bark of trees, which are in themselves so fragile, that it is necessary to strengthen them with cross-beams.

Some of them had marks on their body, apparently cut or carved, which, as it seemed to our people, were looked upon by them as a kind of ornament. They eat sparingly and moderately, whereby they grow up always active and nimble; their diet seems to consist of fish, and a few roots and vegetables, but no birds or wild animals of any kind are used as food, for though animal food exists, and was found by our men in abundance, the natives appeared to be indifferent to it.

The governors went on to report that, according to the skipper of *Waijer*, around 14 June, upwards of 500 men, women and children were seen gathered at several campfires inland. This suggests that the Dutch were in the vicinity of a significant ceremony, but could make nothing of it. It was also noted that, while the expedition had instructions to bring back any indigenous New Hollanders who wanted to come, because of the language difficulties it hadn't been clear whether they had any willing takers. Despite being able to grab two or three locals who came aboard their vessels daily, the Dutch scrupulously avoided taking prisoners.

They also managed to explore some of the rivers inland, the currents of which raised hopes of the sought-after passage through the continent. Exploring one such river the crew of the *Nova Hollandia* found a powerful tide that was as salty as seawater. Taking soundings, the inlet remained deep, and the bottom didn't change in composition, even though the vessel may have travelled 50–60 kilometres inland. Despite the fact that New Holland, be it an island or a mainland, extended for thousands of kilometres to the south, the governor general in Batavia concluded:

> The South Land in a great measure consists of islands, – a supposition not at all improbable, considering how on its south side, from the point called Leeuwin, or the land visited by the Leeuwin in the year 1622, to Nuyts-land, discovered in 1627, it is entirely girt and surrounded by innumerable islands, although these things had better be left to a more accurate examination of the country, and a more matured judgment. But there is another consideration in favour of this supposition, namely, the rude and barbarous character, and malicious disposition of the above-mentioned islanders, as it has been frequently remarked, that such serious defects are much more generally found among islanders, than among the inhabitants of continents.

The possibility that they were meeting people who were surviving as best they could on one of the toughest landmasses on earth doesn't seem to have entered the Dutch mind. This is despite the fact that their crews got into all manner of distress when they couldn't find any sustenance on shore. As the Dutch mariners noted: 'Many men on board began to suffer and also to die, from severe sickness, principally fever, acute pains in the head and eyes, and above all, dropsy, so that they were compelled to resolve upon returning.'

On the return voyage only the *Nova Hollandia* made it to Banda. The crews of the *Vossenbosch* and *Waijer* were too weak to make that landfall, and were swept on to Macassar (Indonesia). Along the way, the skipper, upper and under steersman, and most of the petty officers of the *Vossenbosch* died.

The year the remnants of this fleet limped home, the search for Trial Rocks continued. An English vessel, the frigate *Jane*, found herself in their supposed vicinity and while keeping a lookout for them, her commander noted in the journal 27 June (reported by Ida Lee):

> Hove to, according to custom, on account of the Tryal Rocks (if such exist), for although they are reported to extend 20 leagues [100 kilometres] in length I was informed by the Commodore of the Dutch ships ... that he never heard of these rocks being seen. If they exist they must lie much farther east than in the route toward Java Head.

His scepticism was amply justified, as no ship had seen the rocks in their supposed location since the ship *Trial* foundered on them in 1622. And he was right about them being further east. Exactly how far? That question was still unanswered.

For the Dutch, their encounters with the Australian coast continued in the form of one more shipwreck. In 1712, the VOC ship *Zuytdorp*, Marinus Wijsvliet master, became the first to be wrecked on the coast of the mainland itself. The ship went aground at the base of the line of cliffs that extend south of Shark Bay. They're now known as the Zuytdorp Cliffs.

Many of those aboard managed to make it ashore. Relics on the cliffs above the wrecksite found by locals in 1927, helped in locating the wreck itself. In the 1960s, when divers visited the remote location, they found that the sea floor where the *Zuytdorp's* chests of silver coins had spilled open had become fused into a solid mass of silver. It became known as the

Carpet of Silver, just before it was plundered, although many coins and relics have since become part of the collection of the Western Australian Maritime Museum. Of the fate of the *Zuytdorp* survivors, nothing is known. While they survived the wreck, and left signs of their presence above the wrecksite and in its immediate vicinity, they then disappeared into the wasteland south of Shark Bay, leaving no trace.

Back in Europe, the War of Spanish Succession was drawing to its end, not because it had resolved the issues at stake, but due to the exhaustion of the nations involved. Nevertheless, for the English, it had been a defining moment. With the help of the Dutch, they had won stunning victories on land and sea, adding the island of Minorca to their base at Gibraltar, thereby securing their position in the Mediterranean.

The country had long been a maritime power, but the successes of the Spanish war provided a platform for the creation of a truly global empire. Even the setbacks of the war provided benefits. In 1707, after supporting the attack on Gibraltar and laying siege to French bases on Toulon, Admiral Sir Cloudesley Shovell was returning to England with his fleet when he was shipwrecked on the Scilly Isles (Cornwall). Two men-of-war and a frigate were lost, along with 1500 sailors. Shovell was among the dead. The disaster was attributed to a navigational error and led to the Admiralty offering a prize of £20 000 to anyone who could devise a practical method for calculating longitude at sea.

While the Admiralty sought innovations in science, the English government was finding novel ways to finance the enormous debt from the war, estimated at £50 million at the time. In return for a charter to trade in the South Seas, the South Sea Company took on a portion of the national debt. The arrangement benefited all concerned, and immediately increased the value of South Sea Company stock. It seemed miraculous. All it took was smoke, mirrors and long sea voyages to turn debt into profit, and soon speculative ventures were springing up all over England. People sank their life savings into the South Sea Company and other ventures, and some grew dizzily rich. The South Sea Company eventually took on the entire national debt, and the value of its stock increased more than twenty-fold.

However, you didn't need to be able to calculate longitude, or get close to the reefs of New Holland, to know the English were sailing in dangerous waters. The Dutch might have been able to warn the English about what was to happen, having been spectacularly burned by speculation in tulips during the 1630s. However, when the South Sea bubble finally burst, in 1720, thousands lost everything. Suicides were recorded daily; the Postmaster-General of England poisoned himself. Many in the English parliament had profited from the speculation, and angry crowds thronged outside their chambers. Such was the lure of riches in the South Seas and their fabled lands of gold that the English economy now teetered on the brink of ruin.

Amid the chaos, science and technology marched inexorably forward. In 1721, an Englishman, George Graham, invented the cylinder escapement for watches, another step towards more accurate timepieces, and the calculation of longitude at sea. Alas, it didn't come soon enough for the Dutch ship *Zeewijk*. As the governor general in Batavia wrote to the VOC on 31 October 1728:

On the 26th of April there arrived here quite unexpectedly with the patchiallang *de Berrmen* a note from the ex-skipper and the subcargo of the Zealand ship *Zeewijk*, Jan Steijns and Jan Nebbens, written from Sunda Strait ... informing us that the said ship, after sailing from the Cape of Good Hope on April 21 [1727], had on June 9 following run aground on the reef situated before the islands called Fredrik Houtmans Abriolhos near the South-land in 29° S L, also known as the Tortelduijf Islands; that favoured by good weather the men had saved from the wreck all kinds of necessaries, and with the loosened woodwork had constructed a kind of vessel, with which they had set out from there on the 26th of March, and arrived in the aforesaid strait on the 21st of April last ...

[We] have found ... not only that the ex-skipper Jan Steijns has, against his positive instructions and against the protests of the steersmen, too recklessly sailed near the South-land, and thereby been the cause of this disaster, but also that he has attempted to impose upon his superiors by falsified journals, hoping thereby, if possible, to conceal his grievous mistake ...

The situation of the islands on whose outermost reef the ship *Zeewijk* has run aground, is shown by the annexed small chart. They lie out of sight of the South-land, and are partly overgrown with brushwood, edible vegetables, etc ... here have been discovered not only a number of wells dug by human hands, but also certain vestiges of a Dutch ship, presumably lost on the reef aforesaid ...

Despite their navigational failings, the ingenious Dutch sailors had constructed Australia's first sailing vessel, the *Sloepie* (*Little Sloop*) from the wreck. When it came to their work on improving navigation, the Europeans were no less capable. In 1731 the Englishman John Hadley demonstrated the octant, forerunner of the sextant, an improved instrument for navigation at sea. In 1735, John Harrison built the first chronometer. Harrison 1, as it is known, was a masterpiece of engineering, though a large and unwieldy instrument, and it embodied many of the principles of highly accurate time-keeping devices that would make the calculation of longitude at sea at last feasible. Also in 1735, the great Swedish naturalist Carl Linnaeus published his *Systema Naturae*, the foundation for the modern classification, and formal study of, plants and animals. Both were becoming an increasingly popular interest among the affluent, educated and worldly classes of England and the continent.

While they may have lacked an exact means of determining longitude at sea, the improved instruments they did have seem to have made avoiding New Holland easier. In the decades after the loss of the *Zeewijk*, few vessels voyaged there, accidentally or otherwise. In 1738 the English ship *Prince of Wales* was 200 kilometres off the coast of New Holland, in the latitude of the Trials, but saw nothing of them. In 1743 the English ship *Haeslingfield* sighted Cloates Island, as a protrusion of North West Cape had been mistakenly described (possibly in 1719 and 1739 by other English ships). Over the next century it was to be as erroneously mapped as the elusive Trials.

The following year, 1744, an English hydrographer, John Campbell, in a book *Navigantum atque Ininerantium Bibliotheca*, suggested that the English East India Company send a ship to circumnavigate New Holland to assess its commercial potential. It was a call that had been made in various forms since Queen Elizabeth's time, and it suggests enough people had forgotten the details of the fruitless voyage of Dampier and the popping of the South Sea bubble. That, or they still harboured hopes of finding lands of gold.

Adding to the interest, the French were extending their dominion beyond European waters. In 1746 they managed to take Madras, in India, from the English. In 1747, the English defeated the French in a sea battle off Cape Finisterre, and set about extending their far flung bases into an empire. In 1751 and 1752, they took Arcot and Trichinopoly in India from France. Two years later the French withdrew their governor general from India. In effect, they relinquished the sub-continent to the English (and the Indian potentates, who were progressively subdued). It was a fabulous jewel of empire, and gave the English dominion over a vast swathe of the world's oceans. However, there were gaps, especially in the unexplored South Pacific.

During the same decade, in 1755, an earthquake struck the Portuguese city of Lisbon. It suffered tremendous devastation, with more than 30 000 dead, while fires completed the destruction of buildings, and many of the records of the Portuguese government were lost. The earthquake had major implications for the European discovery of Australia. As mentioned in Chapter 2, the Portuguese may have predated the Dutch as the first European discoverers of Australia. However, without any records to prove it, as Jan Ernst Heeres noted in *The Part Borne by the Dutch in the Discovery of Australia*, 'all is mere surmise and conjecture'. What records there were may have been lost in 1755.

As it happens, the last chapter in the Dutch maritime exploration of Australia came the following year. In 1756, the small ships *Rijder* and *Buijs*, JE Gonzal and LL Asschens masters, once more visited the Gulf of Carpentaria and Cape York. Once again, they failed to discover the strait between Cape York and New Guinea. However, the manner of the failure is poignant. During their voyage the two ships had become separated, but the *Buijs* had sailed on, until she was forced to drop anchor in the shallows at the western entrance to the Endeavour Strait. According to a report from the governors in Batavia:

> On the 30th of April the wind was SE by E and SE in the morning and forenoon, with a fresh breeze. They got the boat ready for the purpose of taking soundings ahead. At noon their estimated latitude was 10°56' [at the western entrance to the Endeavour Strait]; at 4 o'clock they had nearly lost sight of the boat, and fired a gun charged with ball in order to recall the same, but the boat not returning, they kept a light burning at the top-mast, and during the night fired a gun now and then. In this way they waited for the boat until the 12th of May, when they finally resolved to depart from there, since their stock of water and firewood would not

allow of their waiting longer. On board the missing boat were two steersmen, to wit, Hendrick Snijders and Pieter Van Der Meuelen, one quarter-master and five common sailors.

It's most likely that the boat suffered some kind of mishap and the men soon drowned. However, there's the tantalising possibility that it was swept through the Strait. As such, Snijders, Van Der Meuelen and the crew may have become only the second European group after Luis Vaéz de Torres to get through the Strait. They may even have been the first Europeans to set eyes on the east coast of Australia, and to knowingly do so. Alas, they didn't return to tell the tale. Like so many Dutchmen and their ships strewn across the first 150 years of the maritime exploration of Australia, their fate lay shrouded among the many mysteries that enveloped the South Land.

At the end of that time, four ships were known to lie broken on its shores: the *Batavia*, *Vergulde Draeck*, *Zuytdorp* and *Zeewijk* (all have since been located by divers). The *Ridderschap Van Holland* may also have been lost there, but its wreck has not been found. Then there are those who were marooned. The first among them were Wouter Loos and Jan Pelgrom de Bye of the *Batavia*, but there were 68 lost from the *Vergulde Draeck* and more from the vessels that searched for it, and the entire group of survivors, total number unknown, from the *Zuytdorp*.

Is it possible that at least some of them survived? Could they have befriended the local indigenous population, into which they were gradually absorbed? Subsequent European settlement has obscured any clear evidence that may have existed, but considerable academic study suggests that some Dutch shipwreck victims may have thrived on the coasts of Australia. In *And Their Ghosts May Be Heard*, Rupert Gerritsen collates much of this evidence, including European artifacts, rudimentary agricultural practices, fishing methods, boatbuilding techniques, reports of anomalous hair and eye colouring in the indigenous population (seen by the first European land explorers), linguistic anomalies and even hereditary diseases that may have had Dutch origins.

It is in some ways fitting that there remain vestigial traces of Dutch exploration of Australian shores. However, after 1756, the Dutch fade from the story of the maritime exploration of Australia. After the *Buijs* gave up its fruitless wait for the return of the boat, the ship made sail and turned west, away from the South Land. It picked its way through the shallows of Endeavour Strait and out into the Timor Sea, taking with it the last hope the Dutch might have had of finding a passage into the Pacific. The Strait would soon be found, but not by them. That honour would go to another country just 14 years later.

9

THE BRITISH
ARE COMING

**THE ENGLISH ROUTE TO NEW
HOLLAND • THE SEVEN YEARS' WAR
AND ENGLAND'S GLOBAL STRATEGY •
ENGLAND SEEKS THE GREAT SOUTH
LAND • UNREST IN THE AMERICAN
COLONIES •ENGLAND'S SECOND VOYAGE
• BOUGAINVILLE SCORNS THE EAST
COAST • THE TRANSIT OF VENUS •
A SUITABLE CAPTAIN •**

There's nothing a sailor hates more than the wind in their teeth. For evidence, behold the southern Pacific Ocean. If there was a truly large landmass (other than Australia) to counter-balance the continents of the Northern Hemisphere, the South Pacific Ocean was the only place left where it could be found. But in the years since Abel Janszoon Tasman had made his epic voyage of 1642 (see Chapter 5) not one European vessel had voyaged there. The problem was the prevailing wind. Ships sailing due west from Cape Horn found themselves slogging into the roaring forties and fifties that blew relentlessly from the direction they wanted to go. Gigantic seas and a wall of wind inevitably forced them north.

Tasman, it will be remembered, had sailed east from the Indian Ocean, with the wind at his back, covering a prodigious amount of ocean to discover the southern tip of what would become Tasmania and part of the west coast of what he named New Zealand. William Dampier had hoped to explore the east coast

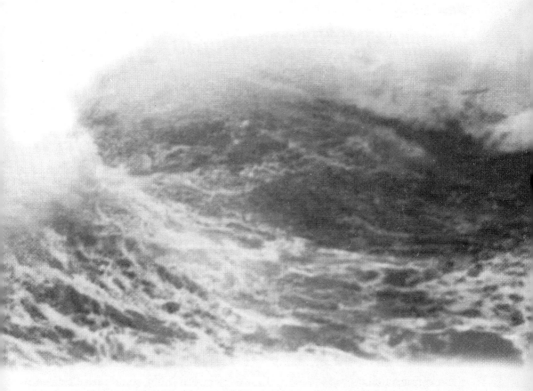

of Australia but had proposed approaching from Cape Horn. When he realised the seasons would be against him, he gave up the idea and instead took the Brouwer Route to the familiar west coast of New Holland. Thus his chance of making new discoveries of Australian coasts ended before it had even begun.

With these two navigators' experiences in mind, and the benefit of hindsight, the easiest route to Australia was obvious: sail for South America or the Cape of Good Hope. From there head east, but instead of turning north 1000 mijlen (6000 kilometres) east of the Cape of Good Hope, just keep going until you reach Tasmania. Unfortunately, by the 1760s, the English preferred the direct approach.

By that time, the English government was convinced that the discovery of the South Land was an enterprise worth considerable effort. The reason was the Seven Years' War. In 1756, the English fight was led by Prime Minister William Pitt, The Elder, using a global strategy. With the lessons of history at hand, plus a far-flung empire and an indomitable navy, Pitt knew that it wasn't enough to defeat one's enemies in a single theatre of war. This would merely allow them to regroup. Only by attacking enemies wherever they could be found could you hope to disperse their power and defeat them. Indeed, a later English prime minister, Winston Churchill, believed Pitt's strategy made this the first true world war.

Thus in the terrible struggle between England and France (and their allies) the Atlantic became a strategic pond. In the French West Indies the English fleet bombarded the fortifications of Grenada, Martinique and St Vincent in 1762 taking them by storm with sailors and marines. The navy also took Cuba from Spain (which had joined with the French), giving them domination of the routes of the Spanish treasure fleets. In the same year, in the Far East theatre, an English squadron sailed from Madras in India, attacking and taking Manila from the Spanish, whereupon hydrographer Alexander Dalrymple availed himself of the files relating to Luis Vaéz de Torres' voyage through the elusive strait that would soon bear Torres' name. Even in the Mediterranean, English bases at Gibraltar and Port Mahon on Minorca (lost and regained during the war) helped to ensure British ascendancy in that sea. Taken all together, the British navy gave the mother land just cause to boast that she ruled the waves, and many of the adjoining coasts.

Thus when the English turned their gaze to the Pacific and Indian oceans, they perceived the shadowy outlines of New Holland. They realised that a base there, not much more than a month's voyage from India, could provide a centre for naval operations that could dominate much of the eastern hemisphere. This viewpoint represents a revolution in thinking compared to that of the Dutch. They had looked at the southern continent solely through the prism of commercial possibilities, and seen nothing. When the English looked at New Holland, they saw a strategic pivot for their empire. And if they didn't take advantage of it, surely the French would.

Despite the fact that the Seven Years' War had, like so many wars before, nearly bankrupted the country (it eventually brought about Pitt's demise), in 1764 the English Admiralty fitted out the ships *Dolphin* (a sixth-rate, 24-gun, man-of-war with 150 crew) commanded by John Byron and the *Tamar* (a sloop of 16 guns and a crew of 90), under the command of Patrick Mouat, for an exploration to the Pacific. Sailing in June Byron first assessed the Falklands as a base for English ships bound for the South Seas. Then from the Strait of Magellan he decided 'to make a NW course til we get the true Trade wind, and then shape a Course to the Wtward in hopes of falling in with Solomons Islands if there are such, or else to make some new Discovery'.

His orders had been to sail west as far south as he could, hopefully discovering the Great South Land that some still hoped lay between New Zealand and Cape Horn. However, the westerlies had other ideas. Byron was forced further north and ended up sailing only in latitude 23 degrees south (New Zealand is in the 30s and 40s). He sailed clear across the Pacific without seeing land until he reached the Ladrones (now known as the Marianas) in July 1765. He then returned to England via Batavia.

Undaunted, the Admiralty immediately started making plans for a new expedition. Two voyages in as many years was quite an undertaking, considering the English nation had only sponsored one other expedition to the same waters in the 160 years since any European had laid eyes on Australia. It is even more noteworthy considering the reduced state of England's finances. To help pay for the Seven Years' War, England had turned once again to her colonies in North America. In 1763 the new prime minister, George Grenville, had introduced taxation for the Americans and enforced the old *Navigation Acts*, restricting trade between England and her colonies in order to increase the revenues for the English Treasury. In 1764 he brought in the English *Sugar Act* and *Colonial Currency Acts*, further taxing the American colonies. In 1765 the *Stamp Act* (a tax on American documents and postage) was introduced along with the *Quartering Act* (whereby cities were compelled to maintain the English troops they garrisoned). Riots ensued.

English policy may have been sound in appreciating the strategic value of a colony in New Holland (indeed its far-reaching value can be seen in Australia's later use as a platform for Allied counter-offensives in the Pacific during World War II), but it was counter-balanced by short-sighted policy that threatened the stability of the precious colonies of America. In New York the Americans met, created and published the Declaration of Rights and Liberties. The English were forced to repeal the *Stamp Act* in 1766, but responded with the equally provocative *Declaratory Act*, which effectively gave the English Parliament the right to overrule the fledgling local legislatures.

In the same year, the second English expedition set sail for Australian waters. It went with the urging of hydrographers John Callander and Alexander

Dalrymple, who made a case for the discovery of the Great South Land similar to that of John Campbell in 1744 (see Chapter 8). With no evidence to support his opinion, Dalrymple pronounced (in a book published in 1770) that: 'The scraps from its inhabitants' economy would be sufficient to maintain the power, dominion, and sovereignty of Britain by employing all its manufactures and ships.' Dalrymple hoped that this fabled continent's discoverer would be him (he wasn't), and believed also that it extended from New Zealand almost to Cape Horn (it didn't).

The new voyage involved the *Dolphin* (now a veteran of such journeys) and the *Swallow* (an almost derelict 14-gun sloop with a crew of 90) under Samuel Wallis and Philip Carteret respectively. Once again, the two were directed to search for the southern continent due west of the Strait of Magellan. However, they weren't voyaging alone. In 1766 Louis Antoine de Bougainville and Chesnard de la Giraudais also set sail. With the ships *Boudeuse* and *Etoile* they headed for the Pacific, intent on exploration and discovery, too.

Upon reaching the Straits of Magellan (in 1767) the *Dolphin* and the beleaguered *Swallow* soon found themselves battling to make headway even through the windswept sinuous passage. The two vessels eventually became separated, but both struggled on until they finally left the Strait behind, fought their way through the tumult of wind, waves and countercurrents, and reached the Pacific.

The difficulties the ships endured were matched by events in the American colonies. In New York the Colonial Assembly was suspended for not enforcing the *Quartering Act*. Not content with that, the English Parliament then introduced another tax. It applied to all the lead, paint and tea entering America.

Down in the South Pacific, despite Wallis' best efforts the *Dolphin* was forced north by the prevailing westerlies. He eventually discovered the island of Otaheite (now Tahiti), in latitude 17 degrees 37 minutes south, before returning to England in May 1768. The plucky Carteret drove his leaky boat further south, discovering Pitcairn Island in latitude 25 degrees. The battering the vessel took from storms didn't help the 20-year-old *Swallow*. In his journal of the voyage Carteret wrote:

> It was now the depth of winter in these parts, and we had hard gales and high seas that frequently brought us under our courses and low sails: The winds were also variable, and though we were near the tropic, the weather was dark, hazy, and cold, with frequent thunder and lightning, sleet and rain. The sun

was above the horizon about ten hours in the four-and-twenty, but we frequently passed many days together without seeing him; and the weather was so thick, that when he was below the horizon the darkness was dreadful.

After leaving Pitcairn, which he'd found on 2 July 1767, Carteret wrote matter-of-factly about his situation:

> While we were in the neighbourhood of this island, the weather was extremely tempestuous, with long rolling billows from the southward, larger and higher than any I had seen before. The winds were variable, but blew chiefly from the SSW and WNW. We had very seldom a gale to the eastward, so that we were prevented from keeping in a high south latitude, and were continually driving to the northward.
>
> On the 4th, we found that the ship made a good deal of water, for having been so long labouring in high and turbulent seas, she was become very crazy; our sails also being much worn, were continually splitting, so that it was become necessary to keep the sail-maker constantly at work. The people had hitherto enjoyed good health, but they now began to be affected with the scurvy.

And Bougainville? By 6 June 1768 his ships were just 100 kilometres east of the Australian coast. It had been his intention to sail west on the latitude of 15 degrees south, a course which would have seem him take the honour of being the first European in recorded history to sight the east coast of Australia. However, his progress was blocked by a line of coral reefs, now known as Bougainville Reef. So he turned his course north. It was a fateful decision. The Frenchman justified the course change by saying that if he'd persisted he would eventually reach the east coast of New Holland. However, from what Dampier had written about the west coast in similar latitudes, it wouldn't have been worth the trouble. 'Unimportant and inhospitable,' he said. Kerr, in his *General History and Collection of Voyages and Travels* (Volume 13), offers another explanation:

> The judicious reader, however, will allow far greater weight to the circumstances of his deficiency for an uncertain navigation, than to such hypothetical reasoning. He had only bread for two months, and pulse for forty days; and his salt meat had become so bad, that the crew preferred the rats to it, whenever they were fortunate enough to catch them.

Bougainville and the French had fallen just short of discovering the east coast of Australia. Instead, he passed through the Solomon Islands and around the north coast of New Guinea, missing Torres Strait as well. On his voyage back to France, three weeks out of Cape Town, he passed the battered *Swallow* and the resilient Carteret. Carteret finally limped back to England in May 1769. By then, yet another voyage had set sail for the Pacific.

In 1770, a once in a lifetime astronomical event was due to take place: a transit of Venus across the face of the sun. It was an excellent opportunity to refine navigational techniques and measurements. The astronomers anticipated that it would be best observed from the Pacific Ocean, and members of the Royal Society pressed the government to support an expedition for that purpose.

The government saw the expedition as an excellent cover for yet another search for the South Land. Even better, Wallis' discovery of Tahiti (which he'd reported on his return early in 1768) provided an island perfectly placed for observing the transit, (as the astronomer Halley had done a century before on St Helens, as mentioned in Chapter 6). After that, the Royal Society's scientists could document any discoveries on the coasts of the South Land. Thus the alignment of astronomical bodies neatly matched an alignment of scientific, maritime and political interests that had been over a century in the making.

The first choice for the command of the expedition was the persistent hydrographer Dalrymple. He'd long been agitating to write his name in the history books and saw the voyage as his big chance. There was only one problem; he wasn't a naval officer. Yet Dalrymple had a solution. He requested that the navy give him a 'brevet commission' as captain (the rank and privileges without the pay) so that the crew would respect him. Unfortunately, the British navy already had experience of civilians taking command of their vessels and crews, Dampier being a notable example. In his compendium of volumes of voyages and travels Robert Kerr notes that:

> Sir Edward Hawke, at that time at the head of the Admiralty, did not give his consent to this demand, saying, that his conscience would not permit him to entrust any of his majesty's ships to a person not educated as a seaman; and declaring, in consequence, that he would rather have his right hand cut off than sign any commission to that effect.

The forthright Admiral was as immovable as the rock of Gibraltar, despite Dalrymple's vehement protests. Eventually, another name was put forward for the command, that of a young ship's master of already proven abilities in navigation, maritime survey and the command of men. The man's name was James Cook.

10

COOK

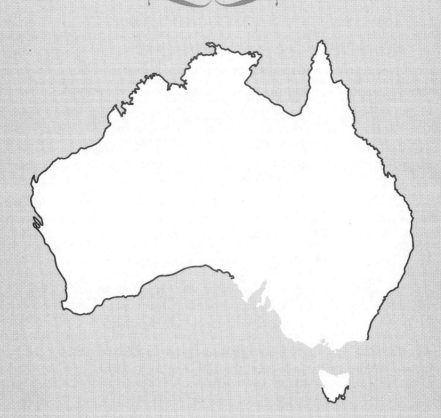

Whenever I want a thing well done in a distant part of the world, when I want a man with a good head, a good heart, lots of pluck, and plenty of common sense, I always send for a Captain of the Navy.

The sentiment belongs to Lord Palmerston and the 19th century, but the man who most embodied it belongs to the 18th century. In 1770 Lieutenant James Cook was the tall, handsome 41-year-old commander of His Majesty's ship *Endeavour* (a 370-tonne former collier with a crew of 85), the man chosen to conduct the observation of the transit of Venus at Tahiti, but also given secret instructions to search for the Southern Continent and 'take possession of convenient situations in the country in the name of the King of Great Britain'.

Born in 1728, Cook had already shown his skills as a navigator during the maritime survey of the St Lawrence River and elsewhere in the North American station. He'd been at sea since he was a youth, apprenticed on a collier, the 450-tonne *Freelove*. At the age of only 27 he became master of

another collier, the *Friendship*, before joining the navy in 1755.

In Tahiti, the observation of the transit went well, although the young commander and the *Endeavour's* astronomer, Charles Green, found a slight variation in the times each observed. They later realised it was caused by the shimmering of solar radiation that rendered the observation slightly inexact. While a superb navigator himself during the *Endeavour's* voyage much of the day-to-day navigational grind was done by Green. Some historians have noted that Green was rather taciturn, but it may have resulted from plotting the ship's longitude using 'lunars', a method that involved meticulous observations, complex tables and laborious calculations.

Unfortunately, the horologist John Harrison was only just completing his fourth chronometer, Harrison 4, the year the *Endeavour* sailed (1769). This chronometer, slightly larger than a pocket watch, was the embodiment of his genius and the beating heart of a practical method for calculating longitude at sea.

Cook, meanwhile, resumed his search for the South Land, having earlier sailed south-west from Cape Horn as far as 60 degrees 10 minutes south without sighting land. He first tracked west from Tahiti to the Society Islands, before heading south once more. When he reached the roaring forties, he was greeted with weather that made him think twice about proceeding. His reluctance was reinforced by the size of the waves he encountered. They were 'mountains high' as the seamen of the time were apt to describe them, and the seaman in Cook knew they could only get that big if they had a large expanse of open ocean in which to build up.

On Saturday 2 September 1769, he wrote:

At 4 pm, being in the Latitude of 40 degrees 22 minutes South, and having not the least Visible signs of land, we wore, and brought too under the Foresail, and reef'd the Mainsail, and handed it. I did intend to have stood to the Southward if the winds had been Moderate, so long as they continued Westerly, notwithstanding we had no prospect of meeting with land, Rather than stand back to the Northward, on the same Track as we came, but as the weather was so very Tempestious I laid aside this design ...

James Cook by Nathaniel Dance. In 1770 the captain of the Endeavour
charted the entire east coast of the continent from Cape Hicks to Cape York.
A1200, L24702 National Archives of Australia

(It should be noted that Cook's journal entries follow 'ship's time', starting at noon the day before, and ending at noon on the day referred to. Thus 4 pm on 2 September is actually 4 pm on 1 September.)

In fact he dealt with the westerlies by angling north-west, then south-west, until he reached New Zealand. This, as mentioned in Chapter 5, was hoped to be an extremity of the Great South Land. Abel Janszoon Tasman had only charted part of the west coast, leaving open the possibility that the land extended far to the west and south, but Cook spent six months producing detailed charts of New Zealand, proving beyond question that it wasn't part of any south land.

When this work was completed, Cook was of the opinion that he'd carried out the basic requirements of his voyage. It was now a matter of deciding the best way home. Cook's Journal of 31 March 1770 (actually 1 April as Cook also retained ship's time after passing the 180th meridian of longitude, now the International Date Line, until reaching Batavia), explains his decision to sail for New Holland's east coast.

> Being now resolv'd to quit [New Zealand] altogether, and to bend my thought towards returning home by such a rout as might Conduce most to the Advantage of the Service I am upon, I consulted with the Officers upon the most Eligible way of putting this in Execution. To return by the way of Cape Horn was what I most wished, because by this rout we should have been able to prove the Existance or Non-Existance of a Southern Continent, which yet remains Doubtfull; but in order to Ascertain this we must have kept in a higher Latitude in the very Depth of Winter, but the Condition of the Ship, in every respect, was not thought sufficient for such an undertaking. For the same reason the thoughts of proceeding directly to the Cape of Good Hope was laid aside, especially as no discovery of any Moment could be hoped for in that rout. It was therefore resolved to return by way of the East Indies by the following rout: upon Leaving this Coast to steer to the Westward until we fall in with the East Coast of New Holland, and then to follow the direction of that Coast to the Northward, or what other direction it might take us, until we arrive at its Northern extremity; and if this should be found impracticable, then to Endeavour to fall in with the Land or Islands discovered by Quirós [see Chapter 2].

So the further maritime exploration of Australia was Cook's Plan C. The decision seems almost serendipitous, but it was to have far reaching consequences, not least because Cook also had on board botanist Joseph Banks (later Sir Joseph) and his entourage (including botanist Dr Daniel Solander (protégé of Carl Linnaeus, see Chapter 8) and draughtsman Stanley Parkinson). Banks would later become president of the Royal Society, an adviser to the British government on matters such as convict resettlement, and sponsor of several notable naval careers. There's no question that as the *Endeavour* edged towards Van Diemen's Land, she was carrying more talent than any previous expedition to Australia's shores. Willem de Vlamingh had a draughtsman, William Dampier was interested in the natural world, but there was nothing like the navigational and scientific skill aboard the little collier that lay in 39 degrees 40 minutes south, 22 degrees west of her last sight of land at Cape Farewell in New Zealand on Tuesday, 17 April 1770.

For most historians, the European discovery of Australia's east coast begins three days later. Indeed, Ernest Favenc, in his *History of Australian Exploration* notes that:

> The maritime exploration of our coast may be said to have fairly commenced on the morning of the 19th of April, 1770, [calendar date 20 April] when Captain Cook first sighted land. True we had many visitors before, but none had given the same attention to the work, with an eye to future colonisation, nor sailed along such an extent of shore.

However, those who have voyaged through this volume might take a different view. Tasman, for example, had sailed from Cape York to North West Cape. Jan Pieterzoon Coen had sent expeditions to look closely at the north coast with a keen eye for colonisation, and was duly disappointed by what was found. In fact, the Dutch had mapped nearly three-quarters of the coastline with all the accuracy the technology of their time would allow. Alas they'd been uniformly disappointed by the 'miserable South Land'. Meanwhile, Cook's journal entry of 16 April (calendar date 17 April), shows he was just as good as the best Dutch skippers when it came to recognising the tell-tale signs of land.

> In the PM saw an Egg Bird, and yesterday a Gannet was seen; these are Birds that we reckon never to go far from land. We kept the lead going all night, but found no soundings with 100 and 130 fathoms line.

Cook didn't need to see land to know it was near, yet it says something about his ability that he had three days warning of its approach. On 16 April (calendar 17 April), Banks' journal (based on a regular, rather than a 'ship's' day) also noted the signs of land. He remarked that the second lieutenant had sighted a small butterfly, and at night a small land bird the size of a sparrow. The next day Banks noted a gannet that flew steadily north-west 'as if he knew the road that he was going led to the shore'.

However, this wasn't the only information Cook had at his disposal. As he wrote in his journal of 18 April (calendar 19 April):

> By our Longitude we are a degree to the Westward of the East side of Van Diemen's Land. According to Tasman, the first discoverer's, Longitude of it, who could not err much in so short a run as from this land to New Zealand; and by our Latitude we could not be above 50 or 55 Leagues to the Northward of the place where he took his departure from.

Cook was using the observations made by the Dutchman 128 years earlier to guide him. Cleverly, he was relying on the fact that even by dead reckoning Tasman couldn't be far wrong about the relative positions of Van Diemen's Land and New Zealand. It's no wonder Cook was considered a capable navigator. For one thing, he respected the navigators who'd gone before him. According to them, he should have reached land already. Cook finally did so, according to his journal, on 19 April (calendar 20 April).

> At 5 [am], set the Topsails close reef'd, and 6, saw land, extending from North-East to West, distance 5 or 6 Leagues, having 80 fathoms, fine sandy bottom. We continued standing to the Westward with the Wind at South-South-West until 8, at which time we got Topgallant Yards a Cross, made all sail, and bore away along shore North-East for the Easternmost land we had in sight, being at this time in the Latitude of 37 degrees 58 minutes South, and Longitude of 210 degrees 39 minutes West.

Cook judged that the most southerly land he could see (which he named Point Hicks after Lieutenant Hicks, the *Endeavour's* officer who first sighted it) was in 38 degrees south, 148 degrees 53 minutes east. The lighthouse that now stands there is at 37 degrees 48 minutes south, 149 degrees 16 minutes east. Cook was actually in Bass Strait, on its eastern side, and despite the fact that it wasn't 'discovered' until 27 years later, Cook noted that:

> To the Southward of this point we could see no land, and yet it was clear in that Quarter, and by our Longitude compared with that of Tasman's, the body of Van Diemen's land ought to have bore due South from us, and from the soon falling of the Sea after the wind abated I had reason to think it did;

but as we did not see it, and finding the Coast to trend North-East and South-West, or rather more to the Westward, makes me Doubtfull whether they are one land or no.

He was, of course, entirely correct. In turning away from Bass Strait Cook was following his earlier plan. And while much of what lay to the west had already been discovered; all that lay to the north was a mystery.

The new discoveries came the same day. Cook wrote that: 'What we have as yet seen of this land appears rather low, and not very hilly, the face of the Country green and Woody.' The following day, he added: 'The weather being clear gave us an opportunity to View the Country, which had a very agreeable and promising aspect, diversified with hills, ridges, plains, and Valleys, with some few small lawns.'

The botanist Banks concurred, writing that, 'The countrey this morn [of calendar 21 April] rose in gentle sloping hills which had the appearance of the highest fertility, every hill seemed to be cloth'd with trees of no mean size.'

These descriptions of New Holland are unlike any that preceded them. Indeed, the south-east of the continent presented a verdant contrast to the parched landscapes to the west and north. It remained so as *Endeavour* tracked along the coast, Cook naming Cape Howe, the prominent Mount Dromedary and the striking Pigeon House Mountain. All the way, the *Endeavour* journals note columns of smoke indicating human habitation.

On 22 April (calendar 23 April) Cook noted the presence of the East Coast Current. Trying to sail north with only light winds at night, he found in the morning that he'd been swept south. In fact this current can flow at nearly four knots [6 kilometres per hour] and those heading north (with charts to help them avoid any hazards) hug the coast to avoid the current as much as possible (yachties call it rock-hopping).

As they sailed north, Cook tried to land at several locations – Bateman's Bay, Jervis Bay and a beach near present-day Bulli – without success. Finally, on 29 April, the *Endeavour* spotted another promising entrance to a bay. The next day a favourable breeze allowed Cook to take the ship in. He wrote:

In the PM wind Southerly and Clear weather, with which we stood into the bay and Anchored under the South shore about 2 miles [3 kilometres] within the Entrance in 5 fathoms [9 metres] … Saw, as we came in, on both points of the bay, several of the Natives and a few hutts; Men, Women, and

Children on the South Shore abreast of the Ship, to which place I went in the Boats in hopes of speaking with them, accompanied by Mr Banks, Dr Solander, and Tupia [a native from Tahiti]. As we approached the Shore they all made off, except 2 Men, who seem'd resolved to oppose our landing. As soon as I saw this I order'd the boats to lay upon their Oars, in order to speak to them; but this was to little purpose, for neither us nor Tupia could understand one word they said. We then threw them some nails, beads, etc, a shore, which they took up, and seem'd not ill pleased with, in so much that I thought that they beckon'd to us to come ashore; but in this we were mistaken, for as soon as we put the boat in they again came to oppose us, upon which I fir'd a musquet between the 2, which had no other Effect than to make them retire back, where bundles of their darts [spears] lay, and one of them took up a stone and threw at us, which caused my firing a Second Musquet, load with small Shott; and altho' some of the shott struck the man, yet it had no other effect than making him lay hold on a Target. Immediately after this we landed, which we had no sooner done than they throw'd 2 darts at us; this obliged me to fire a third shott, soon after which they both made off.

The first contact between the Europeans and the indigenous population was typical of those elsewhere on the continent. Nevertheless, Cook and his party strove to establish good relations. After landing they found several small children abandoned in an encampment, and left them with 'strings, beads, etc'.

Cook also found fresh water on the north point of the bay in which they landed. The next day more plentiful water was found, and in the morning a party was sent ashore to cut firewood. Banks was already busy botanising. As he wrote:

The Soil wherever we saw it consisted of either swamps or light sandy soil on which grew very few species of trees, one which was large yeilding a gum much like *Sanguis draconis*, but every place was coverd with vast quantities of grass. We saw many Indian houses and places where they had slept upon the grass without the least shelter; in these we left beads ribbands &c. We saw one quadruped about the size of a Rabbit, My Greyhound just got sight of him and instantly lamd himself against a stump which lay conceald in the long grass; we saw also the dung of a large animal that had fed on grass which much resembled that of a Stag; also the footsteps of an animal clawd like a dog or wolf and as large as the latter; and of a small animal whose feet were like those of a polecat or weesel. The trees over our heads abounded very much with Loryquets and Cocatoos of which we shot several; both these sorts flew in flocks of several scores together.

On 3 May (calendar 4 May) Banks wrote: 'Our collection of Plants was now grown so immensely large that it was necessary that some extrordinary care should be taken of them least they should spoil.' And on 6 May (calendar 7 May) Cook wrote that: 'In the evening the Yawl return'd from fishing, having Caught 2 Sting rays weighing near 600 pounds. The great quantity of plants Mr Banks and Dr Solander found in this place occasioned my giving it the Name of Botany Bay.'

In fact he named the location Stingray Bay, and appears to have changed his mind at some later point. The Admiralty plan of the bay has it as Stingray. The bay was charted and explored until 8 May, when the *Endeavour* sailed and Cook summarised his observations. What he didn't say was that this was the first voyage to New Holland to find water, wood and reasonable fishing, all in a safe harbour. Criticism was eventually levelled at Cook and Banks for overstating the quality of what they found at Botany Bay, but considered in the light of the preceding chapters, their descriptions were justified.

On his way north Cook noted Port Jackson, Broken Bay, and Cape Three Points. Here the *Endeavour* was again swept south on the East Coast Current, but Cook found that by staying closer to shore, he could reduce its effect. Thus Cook became the first sailor to rock-hop north.

On 12 May *Endeavour* was off Point Stephens, in latitude 32 degrees 45 minutes south. Cook named the adjacent Port Stephens after another secretary of the Admiralty, and a high point with two hillocks he named Cape Hawke. This honoured Sir Edward Hawke, the First Lord of the Admiralty, who said he'd rather cut off his hand than have the hydrographer Alexander Dalrymple command one of his ships. His preference for Cook was proving well justified.

On 15 May Cook passed the Solitary Islands, after which he wrote:

A Tolerable high point of land bore North-West by West, distant 3 Miles [five kilometres]; this point I named Cape Byron. It may be known by a remarkable sharp peaked Mountain lying in land North-West by West from it.

In naming Cape Byron, Cook was honouring the skipper of the *Dolphin* who had discovered Tahiti only two years earlier (see Chapter 9). As for the remarkable peak, on 16 May Cook named it Mount Warning, because in the sea east of it he was almost wrecked on a shoal, twice. The culprit was the East Coast Current. After sighting the shoal, Cook managed to weather it, naming a nearby landmark Point Danger. However the current carried him back to the south, and again he had to claw his way past.

Mount Warning (known as Wollumbin, the cloudmaker, among the local indigenous population) is the central plug of one of the largest volcanic calderas in the world. Banks wrote of it on 15 May (calendar 16 May), 'At sun set a remarkable peakd hill was in sight 5 or 6 Leagues [20 or 25 kilometres] off in the countrey, which about it was well wooded and lookd beautifull as well as fertile.' In fact the area is now on the World Heritage List for its incredible diversity of flora and fauna. Had Banks managed to get ashore here, he'd have been able to collect enough specimens to sink the *Endeavour*.

Banks also noted people on the shore among whom, 'Not one was once observd to stop and look towards the ship; they pursued their way in all appearance intirely unmovd by the neighbourhood of so remarkable an object as a ship must necessarily be to people who have never seen one.'

Those who would like to style Cook after fiction's Jack Aubrey in *Master and Commander* (perched at the masthead, hair streaming) need look no further than Cook's journal of 17 May (calendar 18 May). For here he writes of spying the lie of the land in Moreton Bay, 'in the Bottom of which the land is so low that I could but just see it from the Topmast head'. The bay itself was named after James, Earl of Morton, president of the Royal Society in 1764 and one of the Commissioners of Longitude. Here also Cook named the striking Glass Houses, more volcanic plugs visible from the sea at 26 degrees 53 minutes south.

On 24 May the *Endeavour* came to anchor again in an open bay Cook named after its bird-life, Bustard Bay. One of the nearby towns is so proud of its historical connection that it's now called 1770, although Cook described the terrain as poorer though similar to that of Botany Bay. Wrote Banks:

> The Soil in general was very sandy and dry: tho it producd a large variety of Plants yet it never was coverd with a thick verdure. Fresh water we saw none, but several swamps and boggs of salt water; in these and upon the sides of the lagoon grew many Mangrove trees in the branches of which were many nests of Ants, one sort of which were quite green. These when the branches were disturbd came out in large numbers and revengd

themselves very sufficiently upon their disturbers, biting sharper than any I have felt in Europe. The Mangroves had also another trap which most of us fell into, a small kind of Caterpiler, green and beset with many hairs: these sat upon the leaves many together rangd by the side of each other like soldiers drawn up, 20 or 30 perhaps upon one leaf; if these wrathfull militia were touchd but ever so gently they did not fail to make the person offending them sensible of their anger, every hair in them stinging much as nettles do but with a more acute tho less lasting smart.

The hapless Banks and the *Endeavour* continued north the following day, and on 25 May Cook named Cape Capricorn, on the eastern side of Curtis Island, as it was almost on the tropic line at 23 degrees 26 minutes 22 seconds south. Cook soon found himself among islands and shoals, little knowing he was entering the waters of the Great Barrier Reef.

It wasn't long before Banks was beholding some of the area's wonders. He wrote on 26 May (calendar 27 May):

> Before I went out we tried in the cabbin to fish with hook and line but the water was too shoal (3 fhm) [5.4 metres] for any fish. This want was however in some degree [supplied] by Crabs of which vast numbers were on the ground who readily took our baits, and sometimes held them so fast with their claws that they sufferd themselves to be hawld into the ship. They were of 2 sorts, *Cancer pelagicus* Linn. and another much like the former but not so beautifull. The first was ornamented with the finest ultra-marine blew conceivable with which all his claws and every Joint was deeply tingd; the under part of him was a lovely white, shining as if glazd and perfectly resembling the white of old China.

Over the next few days the ship was repeatedly forced to anchor and sound ahead with her boats before proceeding. On 30 May Cook went ashore near Cape Townshend (named after the Chancellor of the Exchequer in 1767) to find water and lay the ship ashore to clean her hull. Banks went with him and found,

> Insects in general were plentifull, Butterflies especialy: of one sort of these much like *P Similis* Linn. the air was for the space of 3 or 4 acres [1–1.5 hectares] crowded with them to a wonderfull degree: the eye could not be turnd in any direction without seeing milions and yet every branch and twig was almost coverd with those that sat still: of these we took as many as we chose, knocking them down with our caps or any thing that came to hand. On the leaves of the gum tree we found a Pupa or Chrysalis which shone

almost all over as bright as if it had been silverd over with the most burnishd silver and perfectly resembled silver; it was brought on board and the next day came out into a butterfly of a velvet black changeable to blue, his wings both upper and under markd near the edges with many light brimstone colourd spots, those of his under wings being indented deeply at each end.

There were even more remarkable things on the shore. Again Banks wrote:

> Here was also a very singular Phaenomenon in a small fish [the Queensland lungfish] of which there were great abundance. It was about the size of a minnow in England and had two breast finns very strong. We often found him in places quite dry where may be he had been left by the tide: upon seeing us he immediately fled from us leaping as nimbly as a frog by the help of his breast finns: nor did he seem to prefer water to land for if seen in the water he often leapd out and proceeded upon dry land, and where the water was filld with small stones standing above its surface would leap from stone to stone rather than go into the water: in this manner I observd several pass over puddles of water and proceed on the other side leaping as before.

The ship, meanwhile, continued groping through the shoals and reefs, passing through the Whitsunday Passage on 5 June. On that day (calendar 6 June) Banks noted two men and a woman with a canoe fitted with an outrigger. It was noticeably better made than those of Botany Bay (he actually refers to Stingray Bay), which led him to hope that 'the people were something improved'.

Five days later, Cook went ashore at Green Island, near present-day Cairns. He named Trinity Bay, which the city faces. Its northern end he named Cape Tribulation for as he put it, 'here began all our troubles'.

Thus on the evening of 11 June, when he encountered reefs blocking his progress north along the coast, he put out to sea, thinking that heading offshore he was safe. As he wrote:

> Having the advantage of a fine breeze of wind, and a clear Moon light Night in standing off from 6 until near 9 o Clock, we deepned our Water from 14 to 21 fathoms [25–38 metres], when all at once we fell into 12, 10 and 8 fathoms [22, 18 and 14 metres]. At this time I had everybody at their Stations to put about and come to an Anchor; but in this I was not so fortunate, for meeting again with Deep Water, I thought there could be no danger in standing on. Before 10 o'Clock we had 20 and 21 fathoms [36–38 metres], and Continued in that depth until a few minutes before

11, when we had 17 [31 metres], and before the Man at the Lead could heave another cast, the Ship Struck and stuck fast. Immediately upon this we took in all our Sails, hoisted out the Boats and Sounded round the Ship, and found that we had got upon the South-East Edge of a reef of Coral Rocks, having in some places round the Ship 3 and 4 fathoms [5.4 and 7.2 metres] Water, and in other places not quite as many feet, and about a Ship's length from us on the starboard side (the Ship laying with her Head to the North-East) were 8, 10, and 12 fathoms [14, 18 and 22 metres].

Cook makes the disaster seem almost routine. Banks reveals it was anything but. In his version:

Scarce were we warm in our beds when we were calld up with the alarming news of the ship being fast ashore upon a rock, which she in a few moments convincd us of by beating very violently against the rocks. Our situation became now greatly alarming … we were upon sunken coral rocks, the most dreadfull of all others on account of their sharp points and grinding quality which cut through a ship's bottom almost immediately. The officers however behavd with inimitable coolness void of all hurry and confusion; a boat was got out in which the master [Robert Molineux] went and after sounding round the ship found that she had ran over a rock and consequently had Shole water all round her. All this time she continued to beat very much so that we could hardly keep our legs upon the Quarter deck; by the light of the moon we could see her sheathing boards &c floating thick round her; about 12 her false keel came away.

In Banks' opinion, the *Endeavour* was a wreck: 'I intirely gave up the ship and packing up what I thought I might save prepard myself for the worst.' Cook concentrated on saving his ship.

As soon as the Long boat was out we struck Yards and Topmast, and carried out the Stream Anchor on our Starboard bow, got the Coasting Anchor and Cable into the Boat, and were going to carry it out in the same way; but upon my sounding the 2nd time round the Ship I found the most water a Stern, and therefore had this Anchor carried out upon the Starboard Quarter, and hove upon it a very great Strain; which was to no purpose, the Ship being quite fast, upon which we went to work to lighten her as fast as possible, which seem'd to be the only means we had left to get her off. As we went ashore about the Top of High Water we not only started water, but threw overboard our Guns, Iron and Stone Ballast, Casks, Hoop Staves, Oil

Jarrs, decay'd Stores, etc; many of these last Articles lay in the way at coming at Heavier. All this time the Ship made little or no Water.

At 11 am, being high Water as we thought, we try'd to heave her off without Success, she not being afloat by a foot or more, notwithstanding by this time we had thrown overboard 40 or 50 Tuns [tonnes] weight. As this was not found sufficient we continued to Lighten her by every method we could think off; as the Tide fell the ship began to make Water as much as two pumps could free.

Cook and his crew could only prepare for the next high tide, on the night of 12 June. By then, the ship had been grinding her hull on the reef for nearly a day. There was every chance that if they got her off, she'd promptly go to the bottom.

As Cook noted:

At 9 oClock the Ship righted and the leak gaind upon the Pumps considerably however I resolv'd to resk all and heave her off in case it was practical and accordingly turnd as many hands to the Capstan & windlass [manually operated winches used to haul on the anchor chains] as could be spared from the Pumps.

A more pessimistic Banks wrote:

The dreadfull time now aproachd and the anziety in every bodys countenance was visible enough: the Capstan and Windlace were mannd and they began to heave: fear of Death now stard us in the face; hopes we had none but of being able to keep the ship afloat till we could run her ashore on some part of the main where out of her materials we might build a vessel large enough to carry us to the East Indies.

According to Cook: 'About 20' past 10 oClock the Ship floated and we hove her into deep water having at this time 3 feet 9 Inches [1.1 metres] water in the hold.'

As he hauled in his anchors, the water gained on the pumps. He recovered some, but others were cut away so the crew could concentrate on keeping the crippled *Endeavour* afloat. Cook started running for the mainland, her boats sounding ahead and searching for a place to beach. With the water flowing in at up to 35 centimetres an hour, they pumped all through 13 June until one of the midshipmen, Monkhouse, suggested fothering the leak (using a sail sewn with oakum and tied over the hole), having seen it done on another ship he'd served on. The technique worked, buying the ship time, and the men some respite.

Finally, the boats reported they'd found a river where *Endeavour* could be beached and repaired. Bad weather kept Cook from entering the river for several days, but after going aground twice, on 18 June Cook got the stricken vessel into Cook Harbour, at the site of present-day Cooktown.

Her crew immediately went to work. Everything that could be taken off was unloaded, then *Endeavour* was run ashore (on 22 June) to provide access to the leak at low tide. The carpenters soon found just how lucky *Endeavour* had been. A large chunk of coral had broken off the reef and wedged in the hole caused by the impact. It had plugged enough of the leak for the ship to remain afloat.

While the carpenters worked on the hull, the crew foraged for food and the scientists fanned out over the countryside. They noted signs of inhabitants, but found them extremely elusive. And where Banks mentioned seeing one 'alligator', draughtsman Parkinson notes: 'There were many alligators on the coast, some of them very large, and we frequently saw them swimming round the ship.' These were in fact saltwater crocodiles.

Kangaroos were seen, and Cook noted that, 'These kangaroos were the first seen by Europeans. The name was obtained [later] from the natives by Mr Banks.' The reader may recall, however, that in Chapter 4 Francisco Pelsaert described wallabies on the Abrolhos, although it was eclipsed by the horror surrounding the wreck of the *Batavia*.

One of the most startling descriptions of an animal came from a seaman who thought he'd seen the devil. Banks noted: 'It was (says he) about as large and much like a one gallon cagg [about the size of the average bucket], as black as the Devil and had 2 horns on its head, it went but Slowly but I dared not touch it.' It was most likely a young or injured fruit bat.

By 27 June, the hull was patched as well as possible. Attempts were made to refloat the ship, using empty casks lashed to the sides, but failed. After another attempt, on 28 June, they realised they'd have to wait for the next spring tide (the highest, a week later). Banks, meantime, found to his horror that when the ship had filled with water, many of his plant specimens had been ruined.

On 1 July, hoping he'd soon be ready for sea, Cook ascended a nearby hill to examine the prospects. He saw shoals extending all the way to the horizon. As he wrote on 30 June (calendar 1 July):

The only hopes I have of getting clear of them is to the Northward [the coast here trended to the north-west], where there seems to be a Passage, for as the wind blows constantly from the South-East we shall find it difficult, if not impractical, to return to the Southward.

Further attempts to refloat the ship followed, and on 5 July the *Endeavour* swam again. The reloading began on 7 July. On 8 July Banks and Lieutenant Fore went on an expedition inland. Banks wrote:

> We walkd many miles over the flats and saw 4 of the animals [kangaroos], 2 of which my greyhound fairly chas'd, but they beat him owing to the lengh and thickness of the grass which prevented him from running while they at every bound leapd over the tops of it. We observd much to our surprize that instead of Going upon all fours this animal went only upon two legs, making vast bounds just as the Jerbua (*Mus Jaculus*) does.

Jerboa include 25 species of hopping rodents found in Africa and Asia.

On 11 July Cook finally saw a group of the local inhabitants, nearly a month after they'd landed at Endeavour River. The first people they saw ran away, but soon they managed to exchange some gifts and sit down with the locals. Cook wrote that:

> One of these Men was something above the Middle Age, the other 3 were young; none of them were above 5½ feet high, and all their Limbs proportionately small. They were wholy naked, their Skins the Colour of Wood soot, and this seem'd to be their Natural Colour. Their Hair was black, lank, and cropt short, and neither wooly nor Frizled; nor did they want any of their Fore Teeth, as Dampier has mentioned those did he saw on the Western side of this Country. Some part of their Bodys had been painted with red, and one of them had his upper lip and breast painted with Streakes of white, which he called Carbanda. Their features were far from being disagreeable; their Voices were soft and Tunable, and they could easily repeat any word after us, but neither us nor Tupia could understand one word they said.

The locals visited again the following day, and the day after, when Cook noticed with some dismay that even the women were naked: 'We could very clearly see with our Glasses that the Woman was as naked as ever she was born; even those parts which I always before now thought Nature would have taught a woman to Conceal were uncovered.'

On 15 July Lieutenant Gore managed to shoot one of the elusive kangaroos, the body of which provided Banks with an opportunity to give a fuller description:

> To compare it to any European animal would be impossible as it has not the least resemblance of any one I have seen. Its fore legs are extreemly short and of no use to it in walking, its hind again as disproportionaly long; with these it hops 7 or 8 feet [2.1 or 2.4 metres] at each hop in the same manner as the Gerbua, to which animal indeed it bears much resemblance except in Size, this being in weight 38 lb and the Gerbua no larger than a common rat.

It provided the crew with a meal the next day.

Many of the local Aboriginal people were now becoming familiar with the crew of the *Endeavour*. However, on 20 July it led to trouble. The *Endeavour's* crew had been catching turtle, which was prized highly by the Aboriginal people. When the locals tried to take part of the catch, the crew stopped them. The Aboriginal people retaliated by setting fire to the grass around the crew on shore. Cook shot one of them at long range, not thinking him badly injured, after which the situation settled down. However, Cook noted his good fortune in having his ship mostly stowed, as the wildfire might have consumed everything, especially his gunpowder.

Though the *Endeavour* was ready for sea, the trade winds blew so hard they couldn't get the ship out of the harbour for several weeks. While they waited, other incidents occurred on shore. On 23 July, a lone man came unexpectedly upon a group of Aboriginal people. He had enough sense not to run. Wrote Cook, 'After he had set a little while, and they had felt his hands and other parts of his body, they suffer'd him to go away without offering the least insult, and perceiving that he did not go right for the Ship they directed him which way to go.'

Banks also noted that, 'No Indians came near us but all the hills about us for many miles were on fire and at night made the most beautiful appearance imaginable.' On 27 July, with the ship still contained by the trade winds, Banks made another discovery.

> In botanizing to day I had the good fortune to take an animal of the Opossum (*Didelphis*) tribe: it was a female and with it I took two young ones [thought to be the common brushtail, *Trichosurus vulpecula*]. It was not unlike that remarkable one which De Bufon has decribd by the name of Phalanger as an American animal; it was however not the same, for De

Buffon is certainly wrong in asserting that this tribe is peculiar to America; and in all probability, as Pallas has said in his *Zoologia*, the Phalanger itself is a native of the East Indies, as my animal and that agree in the extrordinary conformation of their feet in which particular they differ from all the others.

What Banks had found was a clue to the existence of Gondwana, a supercontinent that had once comprised Australia, Africa and South America. They had drifted apart millions of years before, but the existence of related species on each continent showed that these had not always been separate lands.

Not long after, on 5 August 1770, the *Endeavour* finally was warped out of Endeavour River in a brief calm. She was forced to anchor on 7 August, confronted by shoals onto which the returned trade winds threatened to drive her. When the gales abated Cook continued north, until he thought he'd cleared the shoals, in the vicinity of Cape Flattery, which he named because he soon discovered how wrong he was.

On 12 August a landing party climbed a hill on what Cook named Lizard Island, 'Where, to my Mortification, I discover'd a Reef of Rocks laying about 2 or 3 Leagues [10 or 15 kilometres] without the Island, extending in a line North-West and South-East, farther than I could see, on which the sea broke very high.'

This was the outer edge of the reefs, but Cook noted several breaks which might be channels. Cook stayed all night on Lizard Island (which he named for its abundance of lizards, although he recorded that it also afforded good water, fuel and anchorage), hoping to get a clearer view of the shoals in the morning. On 13 August, he noted passages out of the reefs, and resolved to quit the coast, in particular because he was now running perilously low on supplies (he was down to three months on short rations), and if the north-west trade kicked in early (it normally starts around November) it would prevent him reaching Batavia to resupply.

On 14 August he managed to get out of the reefs by way of Cook's Passage, near Lizard Island. Summarising what he'd been through, Cook noted:

The moment we were without the breakers we had no ground with 100 fathoms of Line, and found a large Sea rowling in from the South-East. By this I was well assured we were got with out all the Shoals, which gave us no small joy, after having been intangled among Islands and Shoals, more or less, ever since the 26th [calendar 27] of May, in which time we have sail'd above 360 Leagues [1700 kilometres] by the Lead without ever having a Leadsman out of the Chains, when the ship was under sail; a Circumstance that perhaps never hapned to any ship before, and yet it was here absolutely necessary. I should have been very happy to have had it in my power to have keept in with the land, in order to have explor'd the Coast to the Northern extremity of the Country, which I think we were not far off, for I firmly believe this land doth not join to New Guinea.

Of more pressing concern, he found the ship was more damaged than he thought. It required a pump to be working around the clock to keep the ship afloat, though it was considered a small danger compared to what she'd been through. The *Endeavour's* condition may have prompted Cook to head back towards the coast on 16 August, Cook 'being fearful of over shooting the passage, supposing there to be one, between this land and New Guinea'. This is a clear indication that Cook was looking for Torres Strait, his information coming perhaps from the disgruntled Dalrymple's studies, the Dieppe maps, or even the suspicions of the Dutch. He certainly seemed to know that the Strait was in the vicinity of 11 degrees south, where it would provide a short cut he badly needed.

On the afternoon of 16 August the *Endeavour's* crew sighted land, but again there lay before her the fearful outer reefs swept by massive breakers. While the trade winds might throw the ship onto such a terrible lee shore, they at least gave the ship enough steerage to avoid danger. Alas, as *Endeavour* closed on the line of reefs, the trade wind faded. As evening fell the ship was becalmed, drifting at the mercy of the currents. Cook detailed in his journal of 16 August (calendar 17 August) the horror that grew as dawn approached:

A little after 4 o'clock the roaring of the surf was plainly heard, and at daybreak the Vast foaming breakers were too plainly to be seen not a mile [1.6 kilometres] from us, towards which we found the ship was carried by the Waves surprisingly fast. We had at this time not an air of Wind, and the depth of water was unfathomable, so that there was not a possibility of anchoring. In this distressed Situation we had nothing but Providence and the small Assistance the Boats could give us to trust to; the Pinnace was under repair, and could not immediately be hoisted out. The Yawl was put in the Water, and the Longboat hoisted out, and both sent ahead to tow, which, together with the help of our sweeps abaft, got the Ship's head round to the Northward, which seemed to be the best way to keep her off the

Reef, or at least to delay time. Before this was effected it was 6 o'clock, and we were not above 80 or 100 yards [70–90 metres] from the breakers. The same sea that washed the side of the ship rose in a breaker prodidgiously high the very next time it did rise, so that between us and destruction was only a dismal Valley, the breadth of one wave, and even now no ground could be felt with 120 fathom [216 metres] … All the dangers we had escaped were little in comparison of being thrown upon this reef, where the Ship must be dashed to pieces in a Moment. A reef such as one speaks of here is Scarcely known in Europe. It is a Wall of Coral Rock rising almost perpendicular out of the unfathomable Ocean, always overflown at high Water generally 7 or 8 feet [2.1 or 2.4 metres], and dry in places at Low Water. The Large Waves of the Vast Ocean meeting with so sudden a resistance makes a most Terrible Surf, breaking Mountains high, especially as in our case, when the General Trade Wind blows directly upon it.

While Cook was contemplating imminent destruction the faintest of breezes curled the *Endeavour's* sails. It was almost nothing; so small, Cook commented, 'that at any other Time in a Calm we should not have observed it'. It lasted barely ten minutes, but it pushed *Endeavour* 200 metres from the breakers. When the breeze faded, so did *Endeavour's* chances of survival.

Then the breeze returned, at about the same time an opening in the reef was spotted. It was 400 metres away, and beyond it was calm water. However, the opening was scarcely as wide as the ship was long. Taking *Endeavour* into such a gap with such fickle zephyrs toying with her was fraught. Yet Cook had little choice:

> Into this place it was resolved to Push her if Possible, having no other Probable Views to save her, for we were still in the very Jaws of distruction, and it was a doubt wether or no we could reach this Opening. However, we soon got off it, when to our Surprise we found the Tide of Ebb gushing out like a Mill Stream, so that it was impossible to get in.

One might conclude the elements were conspiring against him, but not Cook.

> We however took all the Advantage Possible of it, and it Carried us out about a ¼ of a Mile [400 metres] from the breakers; but it was too Narrow for us to keep in long. However, what with the help of this Ebb, and our Boats, we by Noon had got an Offing of 1½ or 2 Miles [2.4–3.2 kilometres], yet we could hardly flatter ourselves with hopes of getting Clear, even if a breeze should Spring up, as we were by this time embay'd by the Reef, and the Ship, in Spite of our Endeavours, driving before the Sea into the bight.

It was then that the tide turned. Where a few moments before it had pushed them away from the reefs, now it started drifting them towards the jagged coral. Then another, wider opening in the reef was seen, 1.6 kilometres to the west. Lieutenant Hicks was sent in a dinghy to sound its depth.

His commander, meanwhile,

> struggled hard with the flood, sometime gaining a little and at other times loosing. At 2 o'Clock Mr Hicks returned with a favourable Account of the Opening. It was immediately resolved to Try to secure the Ship in it. Narrow and dangerous as it was, it seemed to be the only means we had of saving her, as well as ourselves. A light breeze soon after sprung up at East-North-East, with which, the help of our Boats, and a Flood Tide, we soon entered the Opening, and was hurried thro' in a short time by a Rappid Tide like a Mill race.

Inside the reef they at last found bottom and Cook dropped anchor, having had quite enough nautical adventure for one day. Cook named the channel Providential Channel, while his journal entry of 17 August (calendar 18 August) shows all the signs of someone who needed to debrief.

> It is but a few days ago that I rejoiced at having got without the Reef; but that joy was nothing when Compared to what I now felt at being safe at an Anchor within it. Such are the Visissitudes attending this kind of Service, and must always attend an unknown Navigation where one steers wholy in the dark without any manner of Guide whatever. Was it not from the pleasure which Naturly results to a man from his being the first discoverer, even was it nothing more than Land or Shoals, this kind of Service would be insupportable, especially in far distant parts like this, Short of Provisions and almost every other necessary. People will hardly admit of an excuse for a Man leaving a Coast unexplored he has once discovered. If dangers are his excuse, he is then charged with Timerousness and want of Perseverance, and at once pronounced to be the most unfit man in the world to be employ'd as a discoverer; if, on the other hand, he boldly encounters all the dangers and Obstacles he meets with, and is unfortunate enough not to succeed, he is then Charged with Temerity, and, perhaps, want of Conduct. The former of these Aspersions, I am confident, can never be laid to my Charge, and if I am fortunate to Surmount all the Dangers we meet with, the latter will never be brought in Question; altho' I must own that I have engaged more among the Islands and Shoals upon this Coast than perhaps in prudence I ought to have done with a single Ship.

The ship remained at anchor all the next day, if only to allow the captain and crew to regroup. The break allowed Banks and Solander to collect specimens on the shoals. Banks wrote:

> The shoal we went upon was the very reef we had so near been lost upon yesterday, now no longer terrible to us; it afforded little provision for the ship, no turtle, only 300lb of Great cockles, some were however of an immense size. We had in the way of curiosity much better success, meeting with many curious fish and mollusca besides Corals of many species, all alive, among which was the *Tubipora musica* [Organ pipe coral, now endangered]. I have often lamented that we had not time to make proper observations upon this curious tribe of animals but we were so intirely taken up with the more conspicuous links of the chain of creation as fish, Plants, Birds &c &c that it was impossible.

In the ensuing days, Cook stayed close in with the land. At all times he kept a boat ahead of the ship sounding, a man at the masthead, and crew ready to drop anchor. He gave up trying to sail anywhere after dark. Cook's confidence in this approach is clear in his remarks of the 18 August (calendar 19 August) that:

> to the Northward and Eastward lay several other Islands and Shoals, so that we were now incompassed on every side by one or the other, but so much does a great danger Swallow up lesser ones, that these once so much dreaded spots were now looked at with less concern.

That afternoon he was at the Bird Isles, well inside the maze of shoals he simply labelled 'Labyrinth'. On 21 August 1770, he anchored just south of Adolphus Island, in the eastern approach to Torres Strait. He got under way at daylight on 22 August, and passed up the Adolphus Channel in latitude 10 degrees 36 minutes 30 seconds south (he managed to miss Quetta Rock and Mid Rock, the former undiscovered until it tore the bottom out of the steamship *Quetta* in 1890, killing 134). Cook soon realised he was at the northern tip of the mainland and wrote in his journal of 21 August (calendar 22 August):

> The nearest part of the Main, and which we soon after found to be the Northermost, bore West southerly, distant 3 or 4 Miles [4.8 or 6.4 kilometres]; the Islands which form'd the passage before mentioned extending from North to North 75 degrees East, distant 2 or 3 Miles [3.2 or 4.8 kilometres] … The point of the Main, which forms one side of the Passage

before mentioned, and which is the Northern Promontory of this Country, I have named York Cape, in honour of his late Royal Highness, the Duke of York. It lies in the Longitude of 218 degrees 24 minutes West [here he's out by one degree], the North point in the Latitude of 10 degrees 37 minutes South, and the East point in 10 degrees 41 minutes [which it is].

Cook had now sailed the entire length of the east coast of mainland Australia, from Bass Strait to Torres Strait. In the afternoon of 22 August he continued steering west for a group of islands off the mainland, the boats ahead instructed to explore the channels closest to the continent. The nearest proved rocky and strewn with shoals, as the *Buijs* had found when blocked from coming from the opposite direction in 1756 (see Chapter 9). The next channel north was deep enough for navigation. Passing between the two islands that flanked it, the ship then anchored just inside the entrance of what was to become Endeavour Strait.

Out to the west Cook could see no land, and was starting to suspect he was gazing upon the Arafura Sea. To be sure, he landed on one of the islands (Possession Island), with Banks and Solander, where he came across a group of local inhabitants, including one with a bow and arrow, the first seen by the *Endeavour's* crew while on the coasts of Australia. Unmolested, Cook climbed a small hill and from a height 'twice or thrice the height of the Ship's Mastheads' the view to the west left him in little doubt about the existence of Torres Strait.

Having satisfied myself of the great Probability of a passage, thro' which I intend going with the Ship, and therefore may land no more upon this Eastern coast of New Holland, and on the Western side I can make no new discovery, the honour of which belongs to the Dutch Navigators, but the Eastern Coast from the Latitude of 38 degrees South down to this place, I am confident, was never seen or Visited by any European before us; and notwithstanding I had in the Name of his Majesty taken possession of several places upon this Coast, I now once More hoisted English Colours, and in the Name of His Majesty King George the Third took possession of the whole Eastern coast from the above Latitude down to this place by the Name of New Wales [later amended to New South Wales on his charts] together with all the Bays, Harbours, Rivers, and Islands, situated upon the said Coast; after which we fired 3 Volleys of small Arms, which were answer'd by the like number from the Ship.

At ten the following morning, at low water, the *Endeavour* sailed south-west.

In the afternoon Cook turned to the north-west and came across a bank with just 5.5 metres of water over it. He anchored once more, sent the boats ahead and they found depths of 12.5 metres. This was what Luis Vaéz de Torres had found when he wrote: 'At the end of the eleventh degree the bank became shoaler. Here were very large islands, and there appeared more to the southward.' The difference was that Cook knew that he had a mainland to his south.

Towards afternoon, Cook and Banks landed on what they named Booby Island. Wrote Cook:

> I made but very short stay at this Island before I return'd to the Ship; in the meantime the wind had got to the South-West, and although it blow'd but very faint, yet it was accompanied with a Swell from the same quarter. This, together with other concuring Circumstances, left me no room to doubt but we had got to the Westward of Carpentaria, or the Northern extremity of New Holland, and had now an open Sea to the Westward; which gave me no small satisfaction, not only because the danger and fatigues of the Voyage was drawing near to an end, but by being able to prove that New Holland and New Guinea are 2 separate Lands or Islands, which until this day hath been a doubtful point with Geographers.

Once again, Cook's interpretation of the signs of the sea was entirely correct. And he knew that from that point on he was in charted waters. A neat bookend to the voyage comes from Banks' journal of 27 August (calendar 28 August). While Cook had used the work of Tasman to guide him to New Holland for the start of the voyage up the east coast, Banks connected the end of the voyage with the discoveries that extended around to Cape York (see Chapter 7). He wrote:

> In the Evening a small bird of the Noddy *(sterna)* kind hoverd much about the ship and at night settled on the rigging where he was taken, and provd exactly the same bird as Dampier has describd and given a rude figure of under the Name of a Noddy From New Holland.

Cook reached England on 13 July 1771 after a voyage of just under three years. Through his initiative much had been discovered and carefully charted that was entirely new. Most significant of all, he'd found several places in New South Wales where ships could water, fuel and anchor. And for the first time in New Holland's history, he and the botanist Banks had described it using words like 'green' and 'fertile'.

The discoveries couldn't be more timely. For while Cook had been voyaging in the South Seas, more trouble was brewing in Britain's American colonies. In Boston, a protest had ended in the massacre of angry colonists by British troops. To placate the outraged Americans the English government lifted all duties, except the one on tea. But the American cause now had martyrs, and the pressure for freedom was growing.

Not that this concerned Lieutenant James Cook on 14 August 1771. On that day he was presented to King George III, and promoted to captain. In Cook, the King and the Admiralty realised they had more than a competent navigator; they had a great one. Soon he was sent on a second voyage to the South Seas, but his was by no means the only expedition bound for New Holland and New South Wales.

11

THE RACE FOR BOTANY BAY

FRENCH CLAIMS TO NEW HOLLAND •
COOK'S SECOND VOYAGE •AMERICA'S WAR
OF INDEPENDENCE •A NAVAL SOLUTION TO
THE CONVICT PROBLEM • LA PÉROUSE •
THE FRENCH REVOLUTION • BLIGH IN
TORRES STRAIT •*PANDORA* IN TORRES
STRAIT • VANCOUVER ON THE SOUTH COAST •
D'ENTRECASTEAUX'S SEARCH FOR LA
PÉROUSE • WAR BETWEEN ENGLAND AND
FRANCE • THE FATE OF LA PÉROUSE •
MALASPINA IN SYDNEY COVE •

Within a year of James Cook's return to England, Australia was claimed by
the French, twice. For just as Alexander Dalrymple had pressed for an
English search for the South Land, supported by the strategic possibilities it
presented for the navy, so the French had their advocates for maritime exploration. Charles de Brosses had put forward the case in 1756 in his *Histoire
des Navigations aux Terres Australes*. Glory and love of country were among
his arguments for searching for what he termed Australasia. However, colonial expansion may have provided an additional and less noble motivation.

De Brosses' book had prompted the voyage of Louis Antoine de
Bougainville (see Chapter 9), but in 1772, two more expeditions reached the
South Seas. The first was led by Marc-Joseph Marion du Fresne, who was
so enthusiastic for exploration that he offered to sail with his own ship
Le Mascurin, escorted by the French navy's *Le Marquis De Castries*,
commanded by Nicholas Thomas.

The ships followed Abel Janszoon Tasman's course and, on 3 March 1772, became the second European expedition to reach Van Diemen's Land. There du Fresne had more luck than Tasman in his contacts with the indigenous population, but events soon turned. On 4 March du Fresne anchored in Frederik Hendrik's Bay. On shore a group of 30 tribesmen assembled. The next morning he sent boats ashore and the natives approached. They were noted as being of ordinary size, rather than the giants Tasman evoked in his journals. They were all naked, the women carrying their children in rope baskets. All the men were armed with spears and stone axes.

The local people piled some wood on the shore, and gave the French a lighted stick. Unsure what the ceremony implied, the sailors used the stick to light the pile. There was no noticeable reaction, but when du Fresne came ashore an hour later and repeated the ceremony, the locals retreated to a nearby knoll and starting throwing stones. Du Fresne and his captain were both wounded. After a volley of shots, the French got in their boats and rowed along the shore. The warriors followed, thwarting attempts at landing with showers of spears. The French fired back, wounding several people and killing one.

Later, du Fresne sent two parties of armed men to search for water, trees suitable for masts and to shoot game. However, nothing suitable was found during the six days the ships were anchored in the bay. While there, they spotted a Tasmanian tiger, observed plentiful birdlife, and caught numerous stingrays, fish and shellfish. Du Fresne was generally disappointed with the prospects at Van Diemen's Land, despite claiming it for France, and on 10 March he set sail for New Zealand. There he became yet another European to run foul of the fierce Maori. Du Fresne and more than 20 of his crew were eventually killed.

Later in 1772 a second French expedition of two ships sailed for the west coast of New Holland. Separated in the Indian Ocean by a storm, only Louis Francois de St Allouarn pressed on in the *Gros Venture*. He's believed to have sighted the mainland in the vicinity of Cape Leeuwin, before turning north and following the coast to Shark Bay, and perhaps as far as Melville Island. It's claimed that he landed on Dirk Hartog Island and buried an Act of Possession claiming the land for the French king.

While the French were claiming the Dutch territories for themselves, the English were bound for New Holland as well. Cook's second expedition, comprising the frigates HMS *Adventure* and HMS *Resolution*, left England in 1772. They, too, became separated in the Indian Ocean, but with a plan to rendezvous at Queen Charlotte Sound, in New Zealand. Thus alone, Captain Tobias Furneaux visited Van Diemen's Land in 1773.

He reached the South-West Cape on 9 March, where he named a collection of rocks that reminded him of 'the Mewstone, particularly one which we so named, about four or five leagues ESE ½ E off the above cape, which Tasman has not mentioned, or laid down in his draughts'. In fact, the Mewstone was the lion-shaped island Tasman referred to in his journal, but didn't chart (see Chapter 5).

While the ship coasted offshore, Furneaux sent boats to reconnoitre. The land they saw appeared fertile, and they noted cascades of fresh water pouring off the cliffs that fronted the sea, but they were unable to find anywhere to land or anchor. Continuing along the shore the ship found an anchorage in a bay within the wider expanse of Storm Bay, now called Adventure Bay.

Here Furneaux found good supplies of water and fuel. The hills were well wooded, bird and fish were plentiful, and while there was no close contact with the local population, Furneaux observed that they were,

> from what we could judge, a very ignorant and wretched set of people; though natives of a country capable of producing every necessary of life, and a climate the finest in the world. We found not the least sign of any minerals or metals.

After nearly a week at Adventure Bay Furneaux sailed up the east coast of Van Diemen's Land. At latitude 40 degrees 50 minutes south, the coast turned to the west, but Furneaux didn't follow it. With numerous islands and shoals to his west (the Furneaux Group), he continued north until he was in latitude 39 degrees, where he believed he could see land due north of him. At best it was a cloudbank.

Furneaux was now in the same waters that led Cook to suspect the existence of a strait between Van Diemen's Land and New South Wales. Furneaux thought otherwise. He wrote that 'that there is no strait between New Holland and Van Diemen's Land, but a very deep bay'. Thus in error, but creating an uncertainty that wouldn't be resolved for more than 20 years, he altered course for his rendezvous with Cook.

During this voyage Cook didn't revisit the southern continent, but he did discover Norfolk Island, in 1774. He believed it had great promise as a naval base, claiming it had good anchorage, water and pines that looked like they could be used for masts and spars; he actually used one for that purpose.

On this voyage Cook was sailing with a copy of the Harrison 4 chronometer, Kendall 1, which made finding longitude at sea so easy that he referred to it as 'our trusty friend the Watch' and 'our never failing guide, the Watch'. Its main drawback was that it cost some £450, while the tables used in computing lunars only cost £20. Cook had several other inferior chronometers aboard, as he was conducting field tests for the Board of Longitude. Given that his voyage ranged from the equator to the Antarctic Circle, the chronometers were exposed to every climatic extreme, as were Cook and his crew.

On his third voyage to the far side of the world, James Cook (by 1777 promoted to the rank of post-captain) again touched on the shore of Van Diemen's Land. He sighted land on 24 January, and anchored at Furneaux's Adventure Bay on 26 January. He was the third European to visit Van

Diemen's Land in five years, compared with one in the preceding 130 years. This, his third major voyage, was to end in disaster. During a dispute with the inhabitants of Tahiti on 13 February 1779, the great navigator was clubbed, stabbed and, unable to reach the safety of a boat that was trying to get to him, he was set upon and drowned.

Not to be outdone by their explorers, English politicians were finding new ways to antagonise the American colonies. In 1773 they removed the duty on tea, but only in England. The colonists were so outraged that a group boarded ships in Boston harbour and threw their cargos of tea overboard. The cry 'No taxation without representation' was followed by action as the first American congress met the following year. In 1775, the American revolutionary war broke out. The colonists were ill-prepared to confront the might of England head on, but they managed to harry their enemy and avoid pitched battles until they could build their forces. In 1776, they issued their Declaration of Independence, but years of struggle lay ahead.

Unable to resist an opportunity to get at the English, the French took the American side in their fight for independence. The Anglo–French struggle soon eclipsed that between the English and the Americans.

The British dominated at sea, in part thanks to the increasing use of chronometers. Horologists were turning them out in increasing numbers, and prices were falling quickly. It was soon found that the chronometer, used in concert with lunar observations, could make finding longitude at sea far more accurate than ever before. In 1779 Dalrymple published *Some Notes Useful to those who have Chronometers at Sea*. The expression was first used in 1714, but Dalrymple wrote: 'The machine used for measuring time at sea is here named chronometer; so valuable a machine deserves to be known by a name instead of a definition.'

Unfortunately, superior navigation couldn't compensate for the blow Britain suffered when the Dutch joined the war against England on the side of the French and the Americans. Suddenly, the sea route to India was threatened by the Dutch base at the Cape of Good Hope. In 1782 Admiral Edward Hughes realised that 'the fate of the national possessions [in India] greatly if not wholly depended' on the exertions of his squadron in the Indian Ocean. In a series of battles his ships were badly damaged, yet he managed to gain the upper hand. Then, due to his lack of bases, he was forced to yield the initiative. Among the line of battle ships there was 'not a servicable Lower Mast on board any of them, nor a Fish for a Mast, or a Spar for a Topmast to be found but at Bombay'.

Fortunately, the combatants exhausted themselves in the same year, and a preliminary peace was signed; one that acknowledged the existence of the fledgling United States. The peace, however, presented its own problems. In particular, there was the question of what the English were to do with the convicts they'd been transporting to America.

The government considered establishing a new colony, but not just for penal purposes. When the new prime minister, Pitt the Younger, contemplated a colony in New South Wales, he found it recommended by a number of government advisors, including Sir Joseph Banks. Cook's opinion of Botany Bay as a safe anchorage and its narrow entrance that could easily be fortified made this an ideal location for a colony. Banks noted its fertile soils. It had a healthy climate; a settlement would exclude the French and Dutch; and it was reasonably close to other English possessions, as James Matra (an English diplomat, correspondent with Banks and former midshipman on the *Endeavour*) put it 'about a months run to the Cape of Good Hope; five weeks from Madras and the same from Canton; very near the Moluccas and less than a Months run to Batavia'. Cook's discovery of Norfolk Island even offered a supply of naval materials that would support English squadrons, such as that commanded by Hughes.

In 1785 the Beauchamp Commission convened to examine the possibility of transporting convicts to New South Wales, and in August 1786 the decision was made to colonise Botany Bay. The proposed settlement was to be the first European colony on the shores of New Holland/New South Wales in the 180 years since the continent's first discovery by white man. The Dutch had only considered the possibility on economic grounds, but the world in which the English made their decision was one where the strategic value of the colony was just as potent. According to John Blankett, a naval captain in the Pitt government's confidence, Pitt made the disposal of the convicts 'a naval question'.

In the ensuing nine months, the First Fleet was assembled – comprising the frigate *Sirius*, brig *Supply*, and nine other vessels commanded by a retired naval captain, Arthur Phillip – and set sail for Botany Bay on 13 May 1787.

However, the plan to settle Botany Bay wasn't the only outcome of the latest Anglo–French struggle. It had also sent the French broke. Despite this the king, Louis XVI, lived lavishly but the country's finances degenerated to crisis point in 1787, and while the fleet sailed for Australia, a rising anger seized the population of France.

Oblivious to the gathering storm, the First Fleet started arriving at Botany Bay from 18 January 1788. Their first impression was completely unlike that of Cook and Banks. The bay was too shallow, too exposed to south-easterlies and while there was water, it wasn't sufficient for a settlement. The harshest evaluation coming from Watkin Tench, a captain of the marines, writing in his journal the following year:

> We were unanimously of the opinion that had not the nautical part of Mr Cook's description been so accurately laid down, in which we include the latitude and longitude of the bay, there would exist the utmost reason to believe that those who have described the contiguous country had never seen it. On the side of the harbour, a line of sea coast more than thirty miles [48 kilometres] long, we did not find two hundred acres [80 hectares] which could be cultivated.

So no sooner had the fleet arrived than the pressing need for immediate maritime exploration became clear. Phillip took a boat north to examine Port Jackson, less than 20 kilometres up the coast, and was relieved to find one of the finest harbours on the face of the planet. In his often-quoted words 'a thousand sail of the line [might] ride in the most perfect security'.

However, before the ships could weigh anchor for the short trip to the new settlement, the colonists got the shock of their lives. A sail was sighted on the horizon, then another. Tench recorded in his journal:

> By this time the alarm had become general, and everyone appeared in conjecture. Now they were Dutchmen sent to dispossess us, and the moment after storeships from England with supplies for the settlement. The improbabilities which attended both these conclusions were sunk in the agitation of the moment. It was by Governor Phillip that this mystery was at length unravelled, and the cause of the alarm pronounced to be two French ships, which, it was recollected, were on a voyage of discovery in the Southern Hemisphere. Thus were our doubts cleared up, and our apprehensions banished.

The vessels were *La Boussole* and *L'Astrolabe*, commanded by Jean-François de Galaup, Compte de La Pérouse. They may well have been on a voyage of discovery, but it was remarkable that they happened on the site of the fledgling colony at the very moment it was being established, especially since La Pérouse was to remark to Lieutenant (later Governor) Philip Gidley King of the supply, 'Mr Cook has done so much that he has left me nothing to do but admire his work.'

Yet the affable La Pérouse was remarkably open in his dealings, and after spending two weeks examining Botany Bay and the reaches of what is now the Georges River, he provided copies of his charts to the English and took advantage of their returning transports to send messages back to France. Lieutenant King, who spoke fluent French, visited the sociable French several times and was always well received.

To their north, the settlement at Sydney Cove was established on 26 January, and shortly after a contingent was sent to Cook's potential naval base at Norfolk Island 'to secure the same to us and prevent its occupation by any other European power'.

La Pérouse set sail soon after, making for New Caledonia, but was never heard of again. Many ships kept a lookout or searched for him among the reefs and shoals on the north-eastern coast of New Holland, but his fate remained a mystery for more than three decades.

The settlers of the First Fleet had more than enough to keep them busy at Sydney Cove, but the poor soils they found gave a new emphasis to maritime exploration. They had to find good farmland quickly, and since the waterways of Port Jackson were more easily navigated than the scrub on its shores, they took to their boats to search for greener pastures. Soon they were on what became known as the Parramatta River (the local aboriginal term for 'place where eels lie down'), and not long after they found the rich soils of Rose Hill.

Phillip (who was now the governor) also ventured north of Port Jackson, finding yet another harbour, which he named Pittwater, after the English prime minister. Compared to the rest of New South Wales and New Holland, the coast adjacent to Port Jackson had an embarrassment of sheltered waterways.

Well to the south, however, Adventure Bay was proving increasingly popular. In 1788 Captain William Bligh put in to resupply his ship, the *Bounty*. Bligh was on his way to Tahiti to secure breadfruit plants that it was hoped could be transplanted in the West Indies. While in Adventure Bay, Bligh planted plants and trees that might prove useful to any ships that might follow, and in encountering the indigenous population he gave them presents. He noted that 'they took the articles out, and placed them on their heads'. It was later noticed (by Matthew Flinders) that this reaction had also been recorded by the Dutchman Nicolaas Corneliszoon Witsen in his references to Dutch expeditions on the west coast of Cape York.

Back in Europe, 1789 was exploding into a year of revolution. In July the French could endure their hardships and Louis XVI's excesses no more. The Bastille in Paris was attacked and taken, and the mob next made for the King's palace at Versailles. The leaders of the revolt issued a declaration of the rights of man, which included the right to liberty, property, security and resistance to oppression.

Revolt was also taking place on a smaller scale at Tahiti. Aboard Bligh's *Bounty*, the crew mutinied. Bligh and those who remained loyal to him were cast adrift in a small open boat, whereupon Bligh proposed to face the open sea and make for Coepang, on East Timor. It was a voyage of some 4000 kilometres that would make Bligh only the third navigator to negotiate Torres Strait.

From his journal, one gets a sense of the kind of man who would attempt such a voyage. Having found a passage through the outer shoals of the Barrier Reef, he touched at Restoration Island and sent his crew to gather birds' eggs. Bligh noticed one crewman concealing some and wrote:

> I thereupon gave him a good beating. On another occasion one of the men went so far as to tell me, with a mutinous look, that he was as good a man as myself. It was not possible for me to judge where this would end if not stopped in time; therefore, to prevent such disputes in future, I determined either to preserve my command or die in the attempt, and seizing a cutlass, I ordered him to take hold of another and defend himself. On this he called out that I was going to kill him, and made concessions.

In Torres Strait, Bligh sailed not by Endeavour Strait but by a passage to the north of Prince of Wales Island, now known as Bligh Strait. As Cook had suspected, there might be better passages than his, and Bligh Strait was deeper and more easily navigable, although still treacherous.

The same year, another expedition (from Sweden) called at the de facto supply depot that Van Diemen's Land was rapidly becoming. Commanded by John Henry Cox, the *Mercury* was using an extended version of the Brouwer Route to sail from Europe to north-west America. Touching at the west coast of Van Diemen's Land in July, Cox found a bay with fresh water, and close to it a basic shelter. He then proceeded east, missing Adventure Bay, which he'd intended to visit, but finding Oyster Bay, on the inside of Maria Island. The bay was well sheltered, and it had abundant wood and water.

Two years later, in 1791, the Barrier Reef snared its second victim (after Cook's near disaster). On 28 August the *Pandora*, Edward Edwards master, was trying to negotiate a passage through what is now known as Pandora Reef when the current swept the ship onto the coral, as had almost happened to Cook 21 years before. *Pandora* was battered until the following morning, when she sank leaving 39 survivors to take to the ship's boats (35 having been lost). Aboard were some of the mutineers from the *Bounty* who'd been captured in Tahiti and were being taken for trial in England. They were kept in a cage on deck and would have drowned if not for the compassion of the boatswain's mate James Moulter, who threw the keys to the prisoners (against Edwards' orders) as the ship went down. Yet again the survivors faced an epic voyage of 1600 kilometres through scarcely charted reefs and Torres Strait to reach Coepang, on the island of Timor.

The same year, another expedition sailing for north-west America visited the mainland. Captain George Vancouver with the ships *Discovery* and *Chatham* sighted the south coast of Western Australia on 26 September at Cape Chatham. Vancouver (who had sailed with Cook on his second and third voyages) was the first European to visit this coast since Pieter Nuyts in 1627 (see Chapter 3). Sailing east, he anchored in a large bay he named King George Sound. The site of present-day Albany, it's one of the few sheltered, deep-water anchorages on that section of coast. Vancouver found no major rivers in the Sound, but water and game were plentiful, and he found the climate 'agreeable'. Albany is now one of the most popular tourist destinations in Western Australia.

Leaving King George Sound on 11 October, Vancouver continued along the coast to Termination Island, where contrary winds forced him away from the coast. Before leaving it, though, Vancouver noted how accurate Nuyts had been in laying down the coast he'd passed so many years before.

The accuracy of the Dutch on the northern coastline was also confirmed in 1791. John McCluer, commanding an English East India Company ship, sailed along the coast of Arnhem Land while returning from a voyage to the west coast of New Guinea. Although often out of sight of land, he sailed from 135 degrees 15 minutes east of Greenwich (just west of the Wessel

Islands) to 129 degrees 55 minutes (just east of what is still known as Cape Van Diemen, on the north-west tip of Melville Island).

The following year, 1792, marked the beginning of 23 years of the most violent convulsions Europe has ever experienced. After three years of French revolutionary government, during which the King had been held under house arrest, the French republic was declared. By then, The Terror had gripped the nation. Members of the French nobility and people suspected of supporting the monarchy, were arrested and executed. Other Europeans were often shocked by the notion of commoners running one of the most powerful nations on the continent, and fearful that their own people might get the same idea. The declaration prompted Austria and Prussia to attack.

Oblivious to these developments, Rear Admiral Joseph-Antoine Raymond Bruny d'Entrecasteaux, with the 500-tonne frigates *La Recherche* and *L'Espérance*, Huon de Kermadec master, were searching for La Pérouse. On 20 April they sighted Van Diemen's Land and on 21 April entered what they thought was Storm Bay, hoping to resupply at Adventure Bay. However, they mistook a smaller bay just to the west for Storm Bay. Nevertheless they soon discovered a sheltered anchorage at what is now Recherche Bay.

The ships spent a couple of weeks in the bay, and while there the French established small kitchen gardens. It was hoped they'd be considered a 'gift from the French people to the natives of the new land' and would provide them with a first experience of the arts of cultivation. Remarkably, the low stone walls of the gardens were rediscovered on private land on the Huon Peninsula in 2003, and found to have contained chicory, cabbages, sorrel, radishes, cress and potatoes.

The crews of the ships also explored a channel leading to the north-east, and after some 50 kilometres found that it entered the real Storm Bay. It was named D'Entrecasteaux Channel and the island it separated from Van Diemen's Land was named Bruny Island. When the ships moved on, they sailed up the channel to Storm Bay, where they noted another inlet entering it from the north. However, they were unable to investigate due to the pressing need to search for La Pérouse. The ships sailed on to New Caledonia, the Solomon Islands, Bougainville and skirted the northern side of New Guinea to the Moluccas without gathering any information on the missing expedition.

Meanwhile, in September, the British navy frigates *Providence* and *Assistant*, under Captain Bligh and Captain Portlock, were passing through Torres Strait, via Bligh Channel, this time successfully conveying breadfruit from Tahiti to the West Indies. Sailing with Bligh was a young midshipman who was seeing the Strait for the first time. Matthew Flinders' initial impression was that: 'Perhaps no space of $3\frac{1}{2}°$ [of longitude] in length, presents more dangers than Torres' Strait; but, with caution and perseverance, the captains Bligh and Portlock proved them to be surmountable; and within a reasonable time [19 days].'

Flinders later noted a reference in Bligh's *Voyage to the South Seas in HM Ship Bounty*, in which the captain wrote: 'I cannot with certainty reconcile the situation of some parts of the coast [near Cape York] that I have seen, to his [Captain Cook's] survey.' Flinders added, in his book *A Voyage to Terra Australis*, that

> from the situation of the high islands on the west side of the Strait, which had been seen from the *Bounty's* launch, and were now subjected to the correction of the *Providence's* time-keepers; he [Bligh] was confirmed in the opinion, that some material differences existed in the positions of the lands near Cape York.

The timekeepers referred to were, of course, chronometers. And it was the improved accuracy they provided when calculating longitude at sea that explained the differences. Now that navigators had such instruments, they found that very little was exactly where it was said to be. This they sometimes learned at their peril; at other times it gave them cause to go back and replot everything.

This was not to say that the navigators of the 1790s considered their predecessors beneath their respect. Indeed, when d'Entrecasteaux returned to the southern coasts of New Holland (still searching for La Pérouse), he was as impressed by the charts made by Nuyts as had been Vancouver. D'Entrecasteaux sighted land on 5 December, coasting from Cape Leeuwin to what is now the extensive Archipelago of the Recherche. Here the ships were forced to shelter from a south-westerly gale, and during the ensuing week the ships' naturalists and officers examined those islands they could reach, finding seals, penguins and kangaroos. However, they could not find sufficient water. Continuing to the east from 17 December to 24 December, outside the chain of islands but within sight of the mainland, d'Entrecasteaux noted that 'the latitude of Point Leeuwin, and of the coast of Nuyts' Land, were laid down with an exactness, surprising for the remote period in which they had been discovered'.

Beyond the archipelago, the coast turned east-north-east and gave way to the extensive cliffs of the Great Australian Bight. As mentioned in Chapter 3, there is no record of Nuyts' reaction to the prospect he viewed. However, d'Entrecasteaux was moved to comment that: 'It is not surprising that Nuyts has given no details of this barren coast; for its aspect is so uniform, that the most fruitful imagination could find nothing to say of it.'

A shortage of water that showed no signs of being remedied anywhere along this coast caused him to abandon his survey on 3 January 1793, and to sail directly for Van Diemen's Land. He was just short of the furthest extent of Nuyts' discoveries, around latitude 134 degrees east of Greenwich. In turning away when he did, d'Entrecasteaux missed the opportunity of making new discoveries on the southern coasts of Australia, the only significant section that remained to be mapped. However, while making for Van Diemen's Land d'Entrecasteaux noted currents flowing to the east, which led him to suspect, as Cook had done, that there may have been a passage between Van Diemen's Land and New South Wales. His thirsty situation, however, prevented further investigation.

D'Entrecasteaux returned to Recherche Bay on 21 January, where he carried out repairs on *L'Espérance*. He was now the second person after Tasman to circumnavigate Australia, in fact he had done so one-and-a-half times. When the repairs were complete, the expedition moved up D'Entrecasteaux Channel to Green Island, and from there explored both the channel and the northern side of Storm Bay. A party sailed up what is now the Derwent (they named it La Rivière du Nord) for 30 kilometres to one of its tributaries, the Glenorchy Rivulet.

Flinders was to note later that:

The charts of the bays, ports, and arms of the sea at the south-east end of Van Diemen's Land, constructed in this expedition by Mons Beautemps-Beaupré [d'Entrecasteaux's cartographer] appear to combine scientific accuracy and minuteness of detail, with an uncommon degree of neatness in the execution: they contain some of the finest specimens of marine surveying, perhaps ever made in a new country.

After leaving Van Diemen's Land disaster befell d'Entrecasteaux's expedition. Both the rear admiral and the master died on the way to Java, from what was described as '*une colique bilieuse*'. The officer who took command, Alexandre d'Hesmity-d'Auribeau, got the ships to Java, where the news was waiting that Louis XVI had been executed on the guillotine in January 1793. The information split the crews. The officers were all Royalists, the sailors mostly Republicans. Fearful that his officers would be murdered if he set sail, d'Auribeau handed both his ships to the Dutch. D'Auribeau died not long after, while the remaining crew were conveyed to England as prisoners of war, for the execution of Louis XVI had propelled the Dutch and English into war against France as well.

As for La Pérouse, the King is said to have asked as he mounted the scaffold, 'At least is there any news of Monsieur de La Pérouse?' It was only in 1826 that an English East India Company ship, the *St Patrick* under Captain Peter Dillon, learned of his fate. Dillon discovered that La Pérouse had been wrecked near Vanikoro in the Solomon Islands, finding evidence there in 1827 that supported the story. La Pérouse's ships had driven onto a reef on a stormy night. Most of the crews were drowned, some were massacred by the locals. The survivors tried to make the perilous voyage to civilisation but all were lost at sea.

In 1793 two more vessels braved Torres Strait; the ships *Hormuzeer* and *Chesterfield*, commanded by William Bampton and Matthew Alt. Their passage was extremely difficult, both in encountering reefs and having to backtrack, as Luis Vaéz de Torres had done (see Chapter 2) at Turnagain Island, and being attacked by natives (resulting in some of the crew being killed, and others separated and forced to sail for Timor in a whale boat). It was increasingly apparent that Torres Strait might afford a shortcut, but not without considerable risk.

The year 1793 didn't pass without an odd historical footnote as well. On 13 March Sydney was visited by an Italian, Alejandro Malaspina, commanding two Spanish vessels, the *Descubierta* and *Atrevida*. Malaspina had been exploring New Guinea and New Caledonia when he decided to call in at Sydney. He was well received, and spent nearly a month at the fledgling colony before leaving for Tonga on 11 April. It was the first time Spanish vessels had visited Australia since Torres in 1606. As far as the search for the South Land and the Isles of Gold went, it was far too little and definitely too late.

The next year, yet another expedition visited Storm Bay. Captain John Hayes, from the Bombay Marine, sailed up D'Entrecasteaux Channel with the ships *Duke* and *Duchess*. It appears Hayes knew of the French expedition's discoveries, but not the names they'd given the features they charted. Hayes didn't hesitate to give his own names to the features he saw. He explored further up La Rivière du Nord than d'Entrecasteaux's men, giving the river the name it still bears, the Derwent. However, with the exception of that further exploration, Hayes' sketch of Storm Bay added nothing new, and the French cartographers had done a better job.

By this time, however, the rivalry between the French and English was enough to overcome the etiquette of naming rights. In 1795, the French marched into the Netherlands. In response, the English occupied Cape Town on behalf of their conquered allies the Dutch. That year also saw two events that at first glance appear to have widely differing significance. In Paris the fast-rising young general, Napoleon Bonaparte, put down an insurrection by the mob that was dissatisfied with the quality of life under the Republic, thereby saving the government and winning its gratitude. In Sydney a ship arrived carrying the young midshipman Matthew Flinders. The link between the two men is the final chapter in the maritime exploration of the southern continent.

12
AUSTRALIA

In 1795, 189 years after its coasts had been glimpsed by Europeans (and seven after it was colonised), the charting of the southern continent was still incomplete. Van Diemen's Land to Nuyts Archipelago in the Great Australian Bight remained blank. To the north, someone had to do better than James Cook's 'Labyrinth'. Even on the north-west coast Trial Rocks remained elusive. Fortunately, in 1795 a man who was more than willing to fill in the gaps stepped ashore at Sydney Cove.

Midshipman Matthew Flinders was only 21 when his ship, the *Reliance*, brought the colony a new governor: Captain John Hunter. Flinders was born at Donnington in Lincolnshire on 16 March 1774, into a family of surgeons. However Flinders was, 'induced to go to sea against the wishes of my friends from reading Robinson Crusoe' (based in part on the experiences of Alexander Selkirk related in Chapter 7). He was just 15 when he joined the

navy aboard the *Alert*, becoming a midshipman on the line-of-battle ship *Bellerophon* in 1790. He voyaged with William Bligh on the *Providence*, before rejoining the *Bellerophon* in time for her engagement in the naval battle of 1 June 1794, which became known as the Glorious First of June.

Flinders' passion was for exploration rather than battle, and during the voyage to New South Wales he found a fellow enthusiast in the ship's surgeon, George Bass. Bass was almost as young as Flinders, born only a year earlier at Aswarby, also in Lincolnshire. His father, a farmer, had died when he was young, but his mother ensured he got a good education leading to training as a surgeon. She got him a job as an apothecary, but his heart wasn't in it. When he got an appointment as surgeon on the *Reliance*, he was off.

The young men were birds of a feather – seabirds, without doubt – and no sooner had they landed than they started exploring. As Flinders wrote later in *A Voyage to Terra Australis*:

> It appeared that the investigation of the coast had not been greatly extended
> beyond the three harbours [Sydney, Botany Bay and Pittwater]; and even in
> these, some of the rivers were not altogether explored. Jervis Bay, indicated
> but not named by captain Cook, had been entered by lieutenant Richard
> Bowen; and to the north, Port Stephens had lately been examined by Mr C
> Grimes, land surveyor of the colony, and by captain WR Broughton of HM
> ship *Providence*; but the intermediate portions of coast, both to the north
> and south, were little further known than from captain Cook's general
> chart; and none of the more distant openings, marked but not explored by
> that celebrated navigator, had been seen.

Flinders also described Bass as 'a man whose ardour for discovery was not to
be repressed by any obstacles, nor deterred by danger'. Better still, Bass had a
boat. He'd managed to get a small sailing skiff aboard the *Reliance*, the *Tom
Thumb*, measuring just 2.4 metres long by 1.6 metres wide. That's small, even

Matthew Flinders, engraving published by Joyce Gold, Naval Chronicle Office, 1814.
nla.pic-an9455829-1, National Library of Australia

for a skiff, but it's even smaller when it's taken to sea. The pair headed down the coast to Botany Bay in October 1795 with Bass' serving boy, Martin, along for the adventure. They set about exploring the George's River, one of two that enter Botany Bay (the other being the Cooks River), managing to survey some 30 kilometres further than any previous expedition.

Wrote Flinders:

> The sketch made of this river and presented to the governor, with the favourable report of the land on its borders, induced His Excellency to examine them himself shortly afterward; and was followed by establishing there a new branch of the colony, under the name of Bank's Town.

Duty next took the pair to Norfolk Island aboard the *Reliance* in January, 1796, but on her return in March they made a second voyage down the coast. This time they took a slightly larger boat, the *Tom Thumb II*, and sailed beyond Botany Bay aiming to explore the next bay down the coast. They again had Martin with them, but this time the risks of a sea voyage in a minute boat were realised. Wrote Flinders:

> We sailed out of Port Jackson early in the morning of March 25, and stood a little off to sea to be ready for the sea breeze. On coming in with the land in the evening, instead of being near Cape Solander, we found ourselves under the cliffs near Hat Hill, six or seven leagues [30–35 kilometres] to the southward, whither the boat had been drifted by a strong current. Not being able to land, and the sea breeze coming in early next morning from the northward, we steered for two small islets [off present-day Wollongong], six or seven miles [10 or 12 kilometres] further on, in order to get shelter; but being in want of water, and seeing a place on the way where, though the boat could not land, a cask might be obtained by swimming, the attempt was made, and Mr Bass went on shore. Whilst getting off the cask, a surf arose further out than usual, carried the boat before it to the beach, and left us there with our arms, ammunition, clothes and provisions thoroughly drenched and partly spoiled.

They bailed the boat out and set off again as darkness approached. They headed for the islands, hoping to spend the night safe from the indigenous population, but found they couldn't land. So they anchored until the next day, when the north-easterly still prevented their return. After talking to some 'Indians' who told them where they could find water, they explored the area around Lake Illawarra. They eventually found themselves in company with the local people, fearful for their safety as their gunpowder was still wet.

While it dried, they introduced the novelty of barbering the men, which kept them occupied until they could escape.

On 28 March, they were finally able to head north, but not without more difficulty. Rowing when they could, anchoring when forced to, they were finally overtaken by a southerly buster, a fast moving storm, on 29 March. Flinders described their peril:

> March 29. By rowing hard we got four leagues [19 kilometres] nearer home; and at night dropped our stone [a rudimentary anchor] under another range of cliffs, more regular but less high than those near Hat Hill. At ten o'clock, the wind, which had been unsettled and driving electric clouds in all directions, burst out in a gale at south, and obliged us to get up the anchor immediately, and run before it. In a few minutes the waves began to break; and the extreme danger to which this exposed our little bark, was increased by the darkness of the night, and the uncertainty of finding any place of shelter. The shade of the cliffs over our heads, and the noise of the surfs breaking at their feet, were the directions by which our course was steered parallel to the coast. Mr Bass kept the sheet of the sail in his hand, drawing in a few inches occasionally, when he saw a particularly heavy sea following. I was steering with an oar, and it required the utmost exertion and care to prevent broaching to; a single wrong movement, or a moment's inattention, would have sent us to the bottom. The task of the boy was to bale out the water which, in spite of every care, the sea threw in upon us. After running near an hour in this critical manner, some high breakers were distinguished ahead; and behind them there appeared no shade of cliffs. It was necessary to determine, on the instant, what was to be done, for our bark could not live ten minutes longer. On coming to what appeared to be the extremity of the breakers, the boat's head was brought to the wind in a favourable moment, the mast and sail taken down, and the oars got out. Pulling then towards the reef during the intervals of the heaviest seas, we found it to terminate in a point; and in three minutes were in smooth water under its lee. A white appearance, further back, kept us a short time in suspense; but a nearer approach showed it to be the beach of a well-sheltered cove, in which we anchored for the rest of the night. So sudden a change, from extreme danger to comparatively perfect safety, excited reflections which kept us some time awake.

The three were lucky. Wattamolla, in what is now the Royal National Park, is the only place on that section of coast that affords any shelter from a southerly. Heading north the next day, ten kilometres on they entered and explored Port Hacking, finding poor anchorage. They noted that two local people they met spoke a different dialect to those around the colonial settlement. Leaving the bay they returned to Sydney the same day, 2 April.

Flinders spent the rest of the year voyaging aboard the *Reliance* getting stock for the colony from the Cape of Good Hope, but Bass got leave and turned his attention inland. With a small party of men he pushed west for two weeks, hoping to find a way through the Blue Mountains, but without success. When the *Reliance* returned, with Flinders now a lieutenant, she was found so strained by her long voyage that Flinders was compelled to stay aboard to assist with her repair. The *Reliance*, however, wasn't the only vessel to succumb to the long ocean voyage to Sydney Cove.

In February 1797, the merchant ship *Sydney Cove*, Guy Hamilton master, en route to the colony from India with a cargo of trade goods, started leaking so badly she was forced to beach on the islands of the Furneaux Group, on the eastern side of Bass Strait. While some of the crew salvaged the cargo, 18 others sailed for Sydney in the ship's longboat. It was wrecked on the northern side of Bass Strait, upon which the 18 set out for Sydney on foot. Only three made it.

George Bass, Matthew Flinders and William Martin battling a storm in the Tom Thumb, *1796.* From the Collections of the Wollongong City Library and the Illawarra Historical Society

Nevertheless, the wreck and her survivors contributed to the further exploration of the coasts south of the colony. In *The Naval Pioneers of Australia*, Louis Becke and Walter Jeffery wrote:

> At Wattamolla [the survivors] had halted to cook a scanty meal of shell-fish, and the smoke of their fire revealed their presence to a fishing boat from the settlement at Port Jackson. The fire by which this cooking was done was made from coal found on the beach there; so reported brave Clarke, the supercargo of the *Sydney Cove*, who found it.

Governor John Hunter reported to England that:

> I have lately [June 1797] sent a boat to that part of the coast, in which went Mr Bass, surgeon of the *Reliance*. He was fortunate in discovering the place, and informed me he found a stratum six feet deep in the face of a steep cliff, which was traced for eight miles [12.8 kilometres] in length; but this was not the only coal they discovered, for it was seen in various places.

The place is actually south of Wattamolla, and still known as Coalcliff.

Rescue vessels were also sent to the wreck, and in December 1797, while Flinders was busy with the repairs to the *Reliance*, Bass was sent south again to examine the coast as far as he could go with safety. He left in a whaleboat on 3 December, visiting Jervis Bay on 10 December, Twofold Bay on 19 December and Cape Howe just after that.

As Governor Hunter reported:

> His perseverance against adverse winds and almost incessant bad weather led him as far south as the latitude of 40°00 S, or a distance from this port, taking the bendings of the coast, of more than 600 miles [1000 kilometres] … He explored every accessible place until he came as far as the souther-most parts of this coast seen by Captain Cook, and from thence until he reached the northernmost land seen by Captain Furneaux, beyond which he went westward about 60 miles [100 kilometres], where the coast falls away in a west-northwest direction. Here he found an open ocean westward, and by the mountainous sea which rolled in from that quarter, and no land discoverable in that direction, we have much reason to conclude that there is an open strait through, between the latitude of 39 and 40°12′ S, a circum-stance which, from many observations made upon tides and currents there-abouts, I had long conjectured …

Short of provisions, Bass was forced to turn back, but not before finding a good anchorage at present-day Western Port. On the return voyage he was astounded to discover a group of seven convicts on a small island. With seven others they'd been trying to escape the penal settlement at Sydney Cove in a boat, and had been abandoned. Bass, whose whaleboat was too small to return them all to Sydney, conveyed them to the mainland and gave them directions for reaching the colony, over 800 kilometres away. He took the two sickest with him, but the others were never seen again.

The whaleboat returned to Sydney on 25 February, with Bass dismissing the dangers and hardships with only passing mention of the boat being leaky, having to weather heavy seas and that 'we collected and salted for food on our homeward voyage stormy petrels'.

While Bass was voyaging, Hunter also found a use for Lieutenant Flinders. The schooner *Francis* had made a trip to the *Sydney Cove* wreck at what were now named Preservation Island and Rum Island (the former where the crew were saved, the latter where the grog was kept from them) in December. He sent Flinders with it again in February. As he reported:

> I sent in the schooner Lieutenant Flinders, of the *Reliance* (a young man well qualified), in order to give him an opportunity of making what observations he could amongst those islands; and the discoverys which was made there by him and Mr Hamilton, the master of the wrecked ship, shall be annexed to those of Mr Bass in one chart and forwarded to your Grace herewith, by which I presume it will appear that the land called Van Diemen's, and generally supposed to be the southern promontory of this country, is a group of islands separated from its southern coast by a strait, which it is probable may not be of narrow limits, but may perhaps be divided into two or more channels by the islands near that on which the ship *Sydney Cove* was wrecked.

Who better than the intrepid Bass and Flinders to confirm the situation? In September 1798 (incidentally, the year Nelson defeated a French fleet in a bold flanking manoeuvre at the Battle of the Nile) Hunter wrote that he was sending the pair to settle the question, and if possible, sail around Van Diemen's Land. They were given the 25-tonne sloop *Norfolk* and set sail from Sydney Cove on 7 October 1798, commissioned 'to sail beyond Furneaux Islands, and, should a strait be found, pass through it, and return by the south end of Van Diemen's Land'.

They set about doing this, and, on 9 December, Flinders noted in his *Narrative of the Colonial Sloop Norfolk*:

The land which lays immediately to the Southward, and about Three miles distant from the larger of the two high steep Islands [in what he called Hunter Isles, but are now the Fleurieu Group], is what we now considered to be the NW point of Van Diemens land, for the direction of the coast, the set of the tides and the great swell from the SW did now completely satisfy us that a very wide strait did really exist betwixt Van Diemens Land and New South Wales, and also now that we had certainly passed it; This NW point [which he named Cape Grim] is terminated by steep black cliffs, and there are two lumps of rock laying off it, which are equally high and inaccessible.

He and Bass went on to become the first to circumnavigate Van Diemen's Land, returning to Sydney on 12 January 1799. They also discovered Port Dalrymple, site of the present day Launceston, charted more of the New South Wales and Victorian coasts, and the north and west coasts of Van Diemen's Land.

Upon their return, wrote Flinders:

To the strait which had now been the great object of research, and whose discovery was now completed, Governor Hunter, at my recommendation, gave the name of Bass' Straits. This was no more than a just tribute to my worthy friend and companion for the extensive dangers and fatigues he had undergone in first entering it in the whale-boat, and to the correct judgment he had formed from various indications of the existence of a wide opening between Van Dieman's Land and New South Wales.

The following year Bass and Flinders went their separate ways, Bass returning to England while Flinders explored to the north, hoping to find a river entering Glasshouse Bay or Hervey's Bay. He was thwarted by shoals and forced to conclude:

I must acknowledge myself to have been disappointed in not being able to penetrate into the interior of New South Wales, by either of the openings examined in this expedition; but, however mortifying the conviction might be, it was then an ascertained fact, that no river of importance intersected the East Coast between the 24th and 39th degrees of south latitude.

It was later found that there are in fact several rivers of appreciable size entering the sea along this stretch of coast, but Flinders missed them all.

After this voyage Flinders sailed for England in the *Reliance*, where he found a nation that had been defeated everywhere on land, but still ruled the waves. On the continent, Napoleon Bonaparte had appointed himself first consul. The Corsican would soon be in a position to indulge an interest in the southern continent that was nurtured by the works of Charles de Brossos, and by the exploits of James Cook, Marc-Joseph Marion du Fresne, Jean-François de Galaup Compte de La Pérouse and Joseph-Antoine Raymond Bruny d'Entrecasteaux.

In February 1800, the 60-tonne *Lady Nelson* set sail for Australia with instructions to sail through the newly-discovered Bass Strait. Commanded by Lieutenant James Grant the vessel became the first to pass through the Strait from west to east (coasting parts of the northern shore but not doing a detailed survey), arriving in Sydney on 16 December 1800.

Grant and the *Lady Nelson*, with a small colonial vessel, *The Bee*, then returned to Bass Strait on 8 March 1801, in order to survey the northern coast-line in detail. It was already considered an important strategic asset (ships using the Strait shaved a month off the duration of the voyage from England) and the ships returned on 2 May having, according to Grant, 'Now gained a complete survey of the coast from Western Point [actually Westernport] to Wilson's Promontory.' Thus, the only section of Australian coast that now remained uncharted was the section from Westernport to the Nuyts Archipelago. Not surprisingly, the emphasis of exploration soon focussed there.

Directing the French effort was Bonaparte. His fascination with the southern continent reached back to an application to join the voyage of La Pérouse on his ill-fated expedition 25 years earlier, but history's course was set when he wasn't selected. His interest continued, however. He collected and propagated many of the plants from the South Land, and he was known to speak knowledgeably of the platypus. In October 1800, the master of Europe sent *Le Géographe*, Nicolas Baudin commander and *Le Naturaliste*, Emmanuel Hamelin captain, to the South Seas. Their stated objective was exploration but there may have been other agendas.

In England, Flinders was writing *Observations on the Coasts of Van Diemen's Land, On Bass's Straits, etc* which was published in 1801. He dedicated it to Sir Joseph Banks and wrote to him offering to explore the whole coast of New Holland and New South Wales, providing the government gave him a proper ship. Banks wrote to the Secretary of the Admiralty who replied, 'Any proposal you may make will be approved; the whole is left entirely to your decision.'

Matters may have been helped by England and France once more exhausting themselves in war. In 1801, preliminary terms for a peace were agreed, thus the navy could spare the 334-tonne sloop-of-war *Investigator*, formerly the *Xenophon*, with 83 hands. Her complement was augmented with an artist, botanists, astronomers and other scientists.

Flinders was promoted to the rank of commander on 16 February, marrying Ann Chappell two months later. He sought permission for her to accompany him on his voyage, which the Admiralty refused, and he left her behind when he sailed three months later. What Flinders did obtain, however, was a passport from the French. It specified that the *Investigator* was to be assisted in her purely scientific voyage by any French representatives she encountered, just as similar passports provided for *Le Géographe* and *Le Naturaliste* in English territory.

Science, however, was only part of the story. As Flinders wrote:

> Many circumstances, indeed, united to render the south coast of Terra Australis one of the most interesting parts of the globe, to which discovery could be directed at the beginning of the nineteenth century. Its investigation had formed a part of the instructions to the unfortunate French navigator La Pérouse, and afterwards of those to his countryman D'Entrecasteaux; and it was, not without some reason, attributed to England as a reproach, that an imaginary line of more than two hundred and fifty leagues extent, in the vicinity of one of her colonies, should have been so long suffered to remain traced upon the charts, under the title Of UNKNOWN COAST. This comported ill with her reputation as the first of maritime powers; and to do it away was, accordingly, a leading point in the instructions given to the *Investigator*.

However, by the time Flinders sailed, *Le Naturaliste* and *Le Géographe* were already on the New Holland coast. They'd reached the west in May 1801. Soon after, the boatswain of *Le Naturaliste* found Willem de Vlamingh's plate on Dirk Hartog Island (see Chapter 8), half buried in the sand. As Ernest Favenc wrote: 'Captain Hamelin, with rare good taste, had a new post made, and the plate erected in the old spot.' He recorded his own voyage, but both plates were removed in 1818 by Louis de Freycinet (who was part of the Baudin voyage), who returned aboard the survey ship *L'Uranie* and took them to the Institute of Paris.

The *Investigator* made Cape Leeuwin on 6 December 1801, and immediately commenced surveying the southern coast. Flinders noted the swarm of islands and reefs of the Recherche Archipelago, which he considered beyond his ability to completely survey. On reaching the first cliffs of the Great Australian Bight on Monday 18 January 1802, he remarked:

> A surveyor finds almost no object here whose bearing can be set a second time. Each small projection presents the appearance of a steep cape as it opens out in sailing along; but before the ship arrives abreast of it, it is lost in the general uniformity of the coast.

After passing a break in the cliffs, he came to the main line of cliffs on 26 January. In *A Voyage to Terra Australis*, he conjectured:

> The bank may even be a narrow barrier between an interior and the exterior sea, and much do I regret the not having formed an idea of this probability at the time; for notwithstanding the great difficulty and risk, I should certainly have attempted a landing upon some part of the coast to ascertain a fact of so much importance.

At the end of January, Flinders reached the Nuyts Archipelago, which he surveyed for a week before moving on to the 'unknown coast'. As it turns out, by then four vessels were either there or converging on the scene. Flinders was sailing east, naming every feature he could after those who had supported the expedition. When he ran out of names, he resorted to the features of his homeland, Lincolnshire in particular. The two French ships had resupplied at Timor and were now exploring the east coast of Van Diemen's Land, intending to head west through Bass Strait and then commence their discoveries on the 'unknown coast'.

On 5 January, the *Lady Nelson*, commanded by Lieutenant John Murray, who had relieved Grant, was already there, sailing west. She lay off the mouth of what was to become Port Phillip Bay. Murray found the weather too rough to permit him to enter, so he sent Lieutenant Bowen to examine the bay. The ship wasn't able to enter until 15 February, whereupon the examination continued until Murray took possession of what he named Port King (it was later renamed in honour of the first governor). Incidentally, not far inland from Port Phillip lay reefs of gold the like of which the world had never seen. They weren't the Isles of Gold sought in Chapter 1 and Chapter 2; they were better.

Flinders spent February charting the coastline from Denial Bay to Smoky Bay (the former because it had denied him access to the interior) and on to Coffin Bay. He arrived off Port Lincoln (named after Lincolnshire), on the southern tip of the Eyre Peninsula, on 20 February. There, on 21 February, the *Investigator's* master, John Thistle, took the cutter to the mainland to look for a safe anchorage. On the way back, disaster struck, as Flinders records:

> At dusk in the evening the cutter was seen under sail, returning from the main land; but not arriving in half an hour, and the sight of it having been lost rather suddenly, a light was shown and lieutenant Fowler went in a boat, with a lanthorn, to see what might have happened. Two hours passed without receiving any tidings. A gun was then fired, and Mr Fowler returned soon afterward, but alone. Near the situation where the cutter had been last seen he met with so strong a rippling of tide that he himself narrowly escaped being upset; and there was reason to fear that it had actually happened to Mr Thistle. Had there been daylight, it is probable that some or all of the people might have been picked up; but it was too dark to see anything, and no answer could be heard to the hallooing or to the firing of muskets. The tide was setting to the southward and ran an hour and a half after the missing boat had been last seen, so that it would be carried to seaward in the first instance; and no more than two out of the eight people being at all expert in swimming, it was much to be feared that most of them would be lost.

After an extensive search, the boat was eventually found, badly battered after being swept onto rocks, along with oars and a keg belonging to Thistle. Of the men there was no sign. Hopes of at least finding their bodies were diminished by the numerous sharks in the area. Flinders named the scene of the loss Cape Catastrophe, and some adjacent islands after all the missing men.

Thistle had been with both Bass and Flinders for nearly a decade, as Flinders noted:

> Mr Thistle was truly a valuable man, as a seaman, an officer, and a good member of society. I had known him, and we had mostly served together, from the year 1794. He had been with Mr Bass in his perilous expedition in the whale-boat, and with me in the voyage round Van Diemen's Land, and in the succeeding expedition to Glass-house and Hervey's Bays. From his merit and prudent conduct he was promoted from before the mast to be a midshipman, and afterwards a master in his Majesty's service.

Despite the loss Flinders continued his exploration, sailing north into Spencer Gulf. Here he started to entertain the possibility that he'd at last found the hoped-for passage between New Holland and New South Wales. However, while following the low western shore, the line of ranges to the east (now known as the Flinders Ranges) drew ever nearer. Finally, on 9 March near the head of the gulf he was forced to concede:

> Our prospect of a channel or strait, cutting off some considerable portion of Terra Australis, was lost, for it now appeared that the ship was entered into a gulph; but the width of the opening round Point Lowly left us a consolatory hope that it would terminate in a river of some importance.

As it turned out, not even this proved the case. He'd penetrated as far north as the coasts of present-day South Australia allow, only to find out why it's the driest state in the most parched continent on earth. Nevertheless, his speculations, and those of William Dampier and before him the Dutch, reinforced the misconception that there might be a vast inland sea. They thought that if the rivers didn't drain to the coast, they had to drain inland. In fact they do, but they're swallowed by the deserts and the only sea is the vast artesian basin, deep underground. Unfortunately, this was only learned after several explorers had sought the inland sea, some of them dragging boats through arid landscapes, in some cases at the cost of their lives.

On 30 March, *Le Géographe* and *Le Naturaliste* also reached the southern coast of New South Wales. They claimed the discovery of the coast west of Bass' exploration to Westernport for themselves, although Baudin did later admit that Murray had visited Port Phillip, which he sailed past without noticing. West of Port Phillip, however, Baudin was also on the unknown coast, naming features as he went. Despite a storm separating his two ships, Baudin continued exploring.

The beginning of April saw Flinders exploring Gulf St Vincent (site of present-day Adelaide) and the coasts of Kangaroo Island, before turning east once more. It was late in the afternoon of 8 April, just east of Kangaroo Island, that the masthead lookout on the *Investigator* thought he saw a white rock on the horizon.

Flinders soon found otherwise:

> On approaching nearer it proved to be a ship standing towards us, and we cleared for action, in case of being attacked. The stranger was a heavy-looking ship, without any top-gallant masts up; and our colours being hoisted, she showed a French ensign, and afterwards an English jack forward, as we did a white flag. At half-past five, the land being then five

miles [8 kilometres] distant to the north-eastward, I hove to, and learned, as the stranger passed to leeward with a free wind, that it was the French national ship *Le Géographe*, under the command of captain Nicolas Baudin. We veered round as *Le Géographe* was passing, so as to keep our broadside to her, lest the flag of truce should be a deception.

Taking the naturalist, Robert Brown, as an interpreter, Flinders boarded *Le Géographe* and was introduced to Baudin. Both men proffered their respective passports. Baudin then offered Flinders a detailed explanation of his maritime explorations, while obtaining very little from Flinders. As Flinders noted in *A Voyage to Terra Australis*:

> It somewhat surprised me that captain Baudin made no enquiries concerning my business upon the unknown coast, but as he seemed more desirous of communicating information, I was happy to receive it.

Baudin told a different version in his *Journal of Post-Captain Nicolas Baudin*:

> The English captain, Mr Flinders ... came aboard, expressed great satisfaction at this agreeable meeting, but was extremely reserved on all other matters.

In a letter to Banks of 20 May, Flinders wrote:

> [Baudin] expressed some surprise at meeting me, whom he knew by name, and observed that it was unnecessary for him to presecute his survey as the coast was now already done; and therefore he should come to Port Jackson when the winter weather set in.

The following morning, in what Flinders was to name Encounter Bay, the two captains breakfasted aboard *Le Géographe*. They exchanged further details of their respective discoveries, Flinders explaining to Baudin (whose men were in poor health) where water and food could be found, especially on Kangaroo Island.

Soon after, they parted. Flinders was convinced that he'd discovered all the most interesting things that had remained on the southern coast of New Holland and New South Wales (in particular Spencer Gulf). Baudin found little of interest between Encounter Bay and Western Port.

One irony of the two ships meeting in (or more probably off) Encounter Bay is that neither noticed an opening on the shore near present-day Goolwa. It was the mouth of the Murray River, the most substantial river in the continent, navigable for thousands of kilometres inland, and just the thing such maritime explorers were hoping to find. It would have been a feather in either commander's cap, but each may have been too distracted by the other to notice the not-particularly prominent opening, and the adjacent 90-kilometre-long sheet of fresh water known as The Coorong.

Nevertheless, 8 April 1802, marks the completion of the overall exploration of the southern continent. It had taken 196 years, and there were still plenty of small gaps, but the story should conclude at Encounter Bay. However the rivalry between the French and English means there are still a few twists before the end of this tale.

After his encounter with the French, Flinders sailed on until he reached Port Phillip on 26 April 1802. He thought he'd made another discovery (one the French had missed), but learned otherwise when he arrived at Sydney on 9 May and heard about the *Lady Nelson's* prior visit. A month

Nicolas Baudin by Francois Bonneville, 1800. The commander of the French ships Le Géographe *and* Le Naturaliste *sent by Napoleon Bonaparte to explore Australia for 'scientific purposes'.* nla.pic-an9288315, National Library of Australia

later, Baudin (who'd briefly investigated Kangaroo Island and Spencer Gulf) arrived in Sydney as well, with both his ships. There the French were treated well.

However, as Flinders noted:

> The first lieutenant, Mons Freycinet, even made use of the following odd expression, addressing himself to me in the house of governor King, and in the presence of one of his companions, I think Mons Bonnefoy: 'Captain, if we had not been kept so long picking up shells and catching butterflies at Van Diemen's Land, you would not have discovered the South Coast before us.'

The French, many of them suffering scurvy, spent five months in Sydney before leaving (*Le Géographe* to continue surveying, *Le Naturaliste* to return to France). Despite being open about their purely scientific activities there were suspicions that they were going to claim parts of Van Diemen's Land for France. King sent the schooner *Cumberland* after Baudin, which in December found the French on King Island, on the western side of Bass Strait. The English planted their colours near the French tents, under guard, and King maintains that Baudin took the move amicably. Baudin actually wrote to him that Abel Janszoon Tasman hadn't discovered Van Diemen's Land solely for the English, and added:

> I was well convinced that the arrival of the Cumberland had another motive than merely to bring your letter, but I did not think it was for the purpose of hoisting the British flag precisely on the spot where our tents had been pitched a long time previous to her arrival. I frankly confess that I am displeased that such has taken place. That childish ceremony was ridiculous, and has become more so from the manner in which the flag was placed, the head being downwards, and the attitude not very majestic. Having occasion to go on shore that day, I saw for myself what I am telling you. I thought at first it might have been a flag which had served to strain water and then hung out to dry; but seeing an armed man walking about, I was informed of the ceremony which had taken place that morning. I took great care in mentioning it to your captain, but your scientists, with whom he dined, joked about it, and Mr Petit, of whose cleverness you are aware, made a complete caricature on the event. It is true that the flag sentry was sketched. I tore up the caricature as soon as I saw it, and gave instructions that such was not to be repeated in future.

By then Flinders had resumed what was now a maritime survey, rather than exploration. In Cook's Labyrinth he added to the knowledge of passages among the countless reefs and islands, although he too was forced offshore. He was also taken by the sheer beauty of what he saw, writing:

> We had wheat sheaves, mushrooms, stags horns, cabbage leaves, and a variety of other forms, glowing under water with vivid tints of every shade betwixt green, purple, brown, and white; equalling in beauty and excelling in grandeur the most favourite *parterre* of the curious florist.

He next coasted the Gulf of Carpentaria, despite experiencing increasing difficulty with the leaky *Investigator*. In March 1803 he headed for Timor for repairs, after which he sailed to the supposed position of Trial Rocks, over 1000 kilometres from the west coast of New Holland. There he found nothing but unfathomable ocean. The *Investigator* was now barely seaworthy, so Flinders sailed for Cape Leeuwin then directly for Sydney, which he reached on 9 June 1803, becoming the third mariner to circumnavigate New Holland. The same month Baudin and *Le Géographe* visited Timor, while *Le Naturaliste* with her precious cargo of charts and natural specimens reached France.

By now the *Investigator* was a virtual wreck. Louis Becke and Walter Jeffery quote a report of the naval captains in Sydney at the time:

> On the port side out of ninety-eight timbers, eleven were sound, and sixty-three were uncertain if strained a little; on the starboard five out of eighty-nine timbers were good, fifty-six were uncertain, and twenty-eight rotten; the planking about the bows and amidships was so soft that a stick could be poked through it.

In July Baudin also abandoned hopes of any further exploration and sailed for Mauritius. In August, Flinders took passage for England aboard a small ship, the *Porpoise*, Robert Fowler master, in company with the convict transports *Cato* and *Bridgewater*. On deck a greenhouse was built to protect the plants his naturalists had collected for the King's garden at Kew. Alas, the Great Barrier Reef intervened. Four days from Sydney, 1200 kilometres north, there came the cry, 'Breakers ahead'. Swept by the current, the *Porpoise* and *Cato* piled onto a reef. The *Bridgewater*, which must have witnessed the disaster, left the other two vessels to their fate and continued on her voyage. Her skipper escaped censure as she disappeared without trace after calling at India.

Much of the *Porpoise* and *Cato's* cargoes were saved, with 94 survivors (three boys drowned while getting ashore), but they were left on little more than a sandbank. On 25 August, Flinders took a small boat, christened the *Hope,* and sailed for Sydney. He arrived on 8 September, a shadow of his former self, and immediately reported to Governor King. Wrote Flinders of his reception:

> As soon as he was convinced of the truth of the vision, and learned the
> melancholy cause, a tear started from the eye of friendship and compassion,
> and we were received in the most affectionate manner.

That month, too, the unfortunate French suffered yet another calamity. En route to Mauritius, Baudin fell ill. Reaching the island, he died, probably from tuberculosis.

Flinders, meanwhile, took command of the schooner *Cumberland* and set out with several other vessels to rescue the survivors of the *Porpoise* and *Cato* wrecks. They arrived on 11 October to find the survivors thriving on eggs collected from a nearby island and ample rainfall. They'd even built another boat. After relieving the survivors, Flinders sailed for England aboard the tiny *Cumberland,* heading through Torres Strait once more. However, by December he realised the little vessel was leaking so badly, and was so short of supplies, that he needed to call at Mauritius. On 6 December 1803, he made landfall.

He soon discovered that hostilities between England and France had been renewed. Worse, his passport only applied to the *Investigator,* a ship of over 300 tonnes, rather than a tiny schooner of only 29. All of this struck General Charles Decaen, commander of the island, as highly suspicious. Then, in Flinders' documents, Decaen found a note written by Flinders stating his intention to make an examination of the disposition of Mauritius, particularly as a potential port of call for ships voyaging to and from the colony in New South Wales.

Flinders, accustomed to the civility of men of science and navigation, was unprepared for the uncompromising stance of the commander of a pivotal island on the enemy's sea route to India. Decaen, aware that his island's defences were highly vulnerable, informed Flinders that he was a prisoner of war. He was to remain so for the next six-and-a-half years.

The obvious consequence of Flinders' imprisonment was that the French were able to publish their accounts and charts from the voyages of

Le Naturaliste and *Le Géographe* first. Before that, in 1804, the French Empire was declared, with Napoleon Bonaparte its emperor. Eventually, the imprisoned Flinders was to learn that:

> Mons Peron, naturalist in the French expedition, has laid a claim for his nation [in volume one of his *Voyage aux Decouvertes aux Terres Australes*, published in 1807] to the discovery of all the parts between Western Port in Bass Strait, and Nuyts' Archipelago; and this part of New South Wales is called Terre Napoléon. My Kangaroo Island, a name which they openly adopted in the expedition, has been converted at Paris into L'Isle Decrés; Spencer's Gulph is named Golfe Bonaparte; the Gulph of St Vincent, Golfe Josephine; and so on along the whole coast to Cape Nuyts, not even the smallest island being left without some similar stamp of French discovery ...
>
> How then came M Peron to advance what was so contrary to truth? Was he a man destitute of all principle? My answer is, that I believe his candour to have been equal to his acknowledged abilities; and that what he wrote was from over-ruling authority, and smote him to the heart; he did not live to finish the second volume [he died in 1810, the second volume was published a year later]. The motive for this aggression I do not pretend to explain. It may have originated in the desire to rival the British nation in the honour of completing the discovery of the globe; or be intended as the forerunner of a claim to the possession of the countries so said to have been first discovered by French navigators.

Flinders, however, was to have the last word. Despite his release having been ordered in 1806, Decaen continued to hold him captive. Not until four years later, as a British naval blockade was about to force Decaen's surrender, was Flinders finally released, in June 1810. He arrived in England on 24 October 1810, where he had 'an affecting reunion' with his wife, Ann, who had only seen her husband for the first three months of their nine-year marriage.

Flinders lost no time in getting to work. Despite dinners in his honour and an audience with the future king, William IV, and failing health, he spent the next four years preparing his *Voyage to Terra Australis* and his maps for publication.

Finally, in 1814, as Flinders sank under the effects of a chronically infected bladder (that a post mortem revealed had almost disintegrated), his book was finished. The first copy was delivered to his home on 18 July 1814, but by then, Flinders was unconscious. He died the following day, 19 July, without seeing his life's work in print.

Yet had he opened the accompanying charts, he'd have seen the outline of the continent he'd circumnavigated. His map was like that already published by the French, but it differed in one important respect. Flinders' map included the melodic name that he preferred for the continent. It wasn't the first time the word had been used, but it was the first time it was applied to the combined landmass of New Holland and New South Wales. Flinders first employed it on a chart he'd sent Banks in 1804 (via a fellow English prisoner at Mauritius who was being exchanged with a captured Frenchman), but after the map's publication in 1814, the name was soon in common use throughout the colony itself. By the 1830s, the name had stuck. The shadowy land that had been thought of as part of New Guinea in 1606 was clearly outlined in every atlas and known to the world as Australia.

EPILOGUE

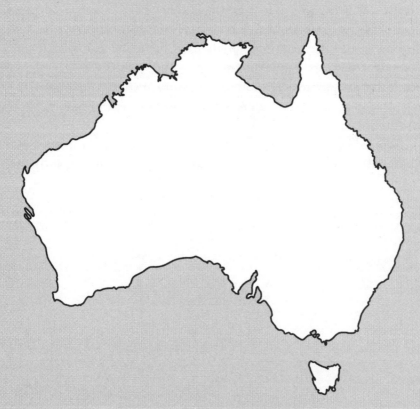

When Flinders and Baudin met at Encounter Bay in 1802, the general outline of the continent of Australia was completed. It had taken 196 years since the mainland had first been sighted by Willem Janszoon and the *Duyfken* in 1606. Now all that remained was to fill in the details. The question of the Trial Rocks, for example, would only be solved in part in 1818, when a ship came upon the Trials, a few kilometres off the coast of Western Australia in the Monte Bello group. Major contributions to maritime surveying were carried out by the tenacious Phillip Parker King, John Lort Stokes and many others over the ensuing decades. Indeed, it continues to the present day, especially as navigational technologies improve beyond the wildest imaginings of the mariners described in this volume.

George Bass gave up exploration after his return to England, and his subsequent marriage, but he continued to voyage to Australia aboard trading vessels. He disappeared on a voyage to South America in 1804 while trying to obtain guanacos (herd animals like a llama) for the colony. His fate remains unknown.

Napoleon Bonaparte's fate is, of course, well known. Finally defeated at the Battle of Waterloo in 1815, he was exiled to St Helena, in the mid-Atlantic. The disgraced emperor's Terre Napoleon soon became a historical footnote. On St Helena, Bonaparte consoled himself by growing Australian paper daisies. They flourish on the island to this day.

REFERENCES

1 > The Little Dove

Boat Safe, horizon calculator <http://www.boatsafe.com> (cited 31 October 2005).
Cook, James, *Journal Daily Entries*, 23 August 1770.
Gilbert, Kevin, *Living Black: Blacks Talk to Kevin Gilbert*, Penguin, Ringwood, 1978.
Heeres, Jan Ernst, *The Part Borne by the Dutch in the Discovery of Australia*, Luzac and Co, London, 1899.
Henderson, James, *Sent Forth A Dove: Discovery of the Duyfken*, UWA Press, Perth 1999.
Hercus, Luise and Sutton, Peter (eds), *This Is What Happened*, Australian Institute of Aboriginal Studies, Canberra, 1986.
O'Neill, Richard (ed), *Patrick O'Brian's Navy*, Running Press Philadelphia/Salamander, London, 2003.
Scott, Ernest (ed), *Australian Discovery*, Dent, London, 1929.

2 > Torres

Heeres, Jan Ernst, *The Part Borne by the Dutch in the Discovery of Australia*, Luzac and Co, London, 1899.
Hilder, Brett, *The Voyage of Torres*, UQP, Brisbane, 1980.
Scott, Ernest, *A Short History of Australia*, Oxford University Press, Melbourne, 6th edition, 1936.
Scott, Ernest (ed), *Australian Discovery*, Dent, London, 1929.
Stevens, Henry (ed) and Barwick, George (translation), *New Light on the Discovery of Australia: As Revealed by the Journal of Captain Don Diego de Prado y Tovar*, Hakluyt Society, London, 1930.

3 > The Brouwer Route

Green, Jeremy, 'Australia's Oldest Wreck, The Loss of the Trial, 1622', *British Archaeological Reports*, Supplementary Series 27, 1977.
Heeres, Jan Ernst, *The Part Borne by the Dutch in the Discovery of Australia*, Luzac and Co, London, 1899.
Henderson, James, *Phantoms of the Tryall*, St George, Perth, 1993, p 19.
Lee, Ida, 'The First Sighting of Australia by the English', *Geographical Journal*, London, 1934.
Milton, John, *The Prose Works of John Milton: Volume II: Letters of State*, J Johnson, London, 1807.

4 > Desert Island

Dash, Mike, *Batavia's Graveyard*, Wiedenfeld & Nicolson, London, 2002.
Drake-Brockman, Henrietta, *Voyage to Disaster*, University of WA Press, Nedlands WA, 1995.
Green, Jeremy, 'Australia's Oldest Wreck, The Loss of the Trial, 1622', *British Archaeological Reports*, Supplementary Series 27, 1977.
Heeres, Jan Ernst, *The Part Borne by the Dutch in the Discovery of Australia*, Luzac and Co, London, 1899.
Siebenhaar, Willem, *The Abrolhos Tragedy*, a translation of *Ongeluckie Voyagie* by Jan Jansz, *The Western Mail*, Perth, 1897.

5 > Tasman

Heeres, Jan Ernst, *The Part Borne by the Dutch in the Discovery of Australia*, Luzac and Co, London, 1899.
Journal of Abel Janszoon Tasman 1642; Instructions to Tasman for his Voyage of 1644; extract from the *Book of Despatches* from Batavia (commencing 15 January 1644 to the 29 following) are reproduced in Heeres' book, as are details of all the other voyages mentioned.
Mitchel Virtual Tour <http://www.virtualtour.com.au/melocco/mitchel/peter.o.melocco-mitchel-history.htm> (cited 18 November 2005).
Flinders, Matthew, *Voyage to Terra Australis*, G and W Nicol, London, 1814.

6 > Wreck and Rescue Revisited

Churchill, Winston, *A History of the English Speaking-Peoples*, Volume 2, The New World, Cassell, London, 1974.
Heeres, Jan Ernst, *The Part Borne by the Dutch in the Discovery of Australia*, Luzac and Co, London, 1899.
Lee, Ida, *Early Explorers in Australia*, Methuen, London, 1925.
Playford, Phillip, *Carpet of Silver: The Wreck of the Zuytdorp*, UWA Press, Perth, 1996.

7 > The Buccaneer's Hideout

Dampier, William, *A New Voyage Around the World*, Black, London, 1937.
Dampier, William, *A Voyage to New Holland*, Knapton, London, 3rd edition, 1729.
Lee, Ida, *Early Explorers in Australia*, Methuen, London, 1925.
Scott, Ernest (ed), *Australian Discovery*, Dent, London, 1929.

8 > The Miserable South Land

Churchill, Winston, *A History of the English-Speaking Peoples*, Volume 3, The Age Of Revolution, Cassell, London, 1974.
Gerritsen, Rupert, *And Their Ghosts May Be Heard*, Fremantle Arts Centre, Press, Fremantle, 1994.
Heeres Jan Ernst, *The Part Borne by the Dutch in the Discovery of Australia*, Luzac and Co, London, 1899.
Lee, Ida, *Early Explorers in Australia*, Methuen, London, 1925.
Major, Richard Henry, *Early Voyages to Terra Australis*, Hakluyt Society, London, 1859.
Mulvaney Derek John and J Peter White (eds), *Australians to 1788*, Fairfax, Syme and Weldon, Sydney, 1987, p 385.
Playford, Phillip, *Voyage of Discovery to Terra Australis*, WA Museum, Perth, 1998.

9 > The British are Coming

Byron's Journal and *Carteret's Journal*, in Kerr, Robert, *A General History and Collection of Voyages and Travels*, Volume 12, Blackwood, Edinburgh and Cadell, London, 1824.
Kerr, Robert, *A General History and Collection of Voyages and Travels*, Volume 13, Blackwood, Edinburgh and Cadell, London, 1824.
Dalrymple, Alexander, *An Historical Collection of the Several Voyages and Discoveries in the South Pacific Ocean*, London, 1770–71, pp xxiv–xxix.

10 > Cook

Becke, Louis and Jeffery, Walter, *The Naval Pioneers of Australia*, John Murray, London, 1899.
Cook, James, *Captain Cook's Journal During his Voyage Round the World Made in HM Bark Endeavour 1768–71*, transcription by Captain WJL Wharton RN, London, Elliot Stock, 1893.
Favenc, Ernest, *The History of Australian Exploration From 1788 to 1888*, Turner and Henderson, Sydney, 1888.
Serle, Percival, *Dictionary of Australian Biography*, Angus and Robertson, Sydney, 1949.
Sobel, Dava, *Longitude*, Fourth Estate, London, 1998.
South Seas, *Voyaging and Cross Cultural Encounters in the Pacific 1760–1800* <http://southseas.nla.gov.au> (cited 18 November 2005).

11 > The Race for Botany Bay

Becke, Louis and Jeffery, Walter, *The Naval Pioneers of Australia*, John Murray, London, 1899.
Flinders, Matthew, *A Voyage to Terra Australis*, G and W Nicol, London, 1814.
La Billardière, JH, *Relation du Voyage a La Recherche de La Pérouse*, HJ Hansen, Paris, 1800.
Mulvaney Derek John and J Peter White (eds), *Australians to 1788*, Fairfax, Syme and Weldon, Sydney, 1987, p 385.
Scott, Ernest (ed), *Australian Discovery*, Dent, London, 1929.
Serle, Percival, *Dictionary of Australian Biography*, Angus and Robertson, Sydney, 1949.
Sobel, Dava, *Longitude*, Fourth Estate, London, 1998.
Tasmania's Historic French Gardens <http://www.justpacific.com/tasmania/huon/gardens.html> (cited 18 November 2005).
Tench, Watkin, *1788*, Text Publishing, 1996.
Vancouver, George, *A Voyage of Discovery to the North Pacific Ocean, And Round The World ...*, GG and J Robinson, London, 1798.

12 > Australia

Baudin, Nicolas, *Journal of Post-Captain Nicolas Baudin* (translated by Christine Connell), Libraries Board of South Australia, Adelaide, 1974.
Becke, Louis and Jeffery, Walter, *The Naval Pioneers of Australia*, John Murray, London, 1899.
Favenc, Ernest, *The History of Australian Exploration From 1788 to 1888*, Turner and Henderson, Sydney, 1888.
Flinders, Matthew, *A Voyage to Terra Australis*, G and W Nicol, London, 1814.
Flinders, Matthew, *Narrative of the Colonial Sloop Norfolk*, Historical Records of New South Wales, Government Printer, Sydney, 1901.
Flinders , Matthew, Electronic Archive, *Narrative of the Expedition of the Colonial Sloop Norfolk, 7 October 1798–12 January 1799, 9 December* <http://www.sl.nsw.gov.au/flinders/manuscripts/1.html> (cited 23 November 2005).
Flinders, Matthew, Electronic Archive, *Matthew Flinders – Private Letter Books, November 1801–July 1806 (Vol 1) To Sir Joseph Banks, 20 May 1802*, search <http://www.sl.nsw.gov.au/flinders> (cited 23 November 2005).
Ingleton, Geoffrey C, *Matthew Flinders: Navigator and Chartmaker*, Genesis, Guildford, Surrey, 1986.
Radio National, *Australian Plant Heritage*, 14 November 1999 <http://www.abc.net.au/rn/science/ockham/stories/s65943.htm> (cited 23 November 2005).

INDEX